ETHER

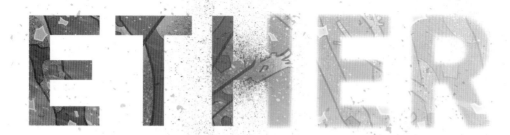

ETI

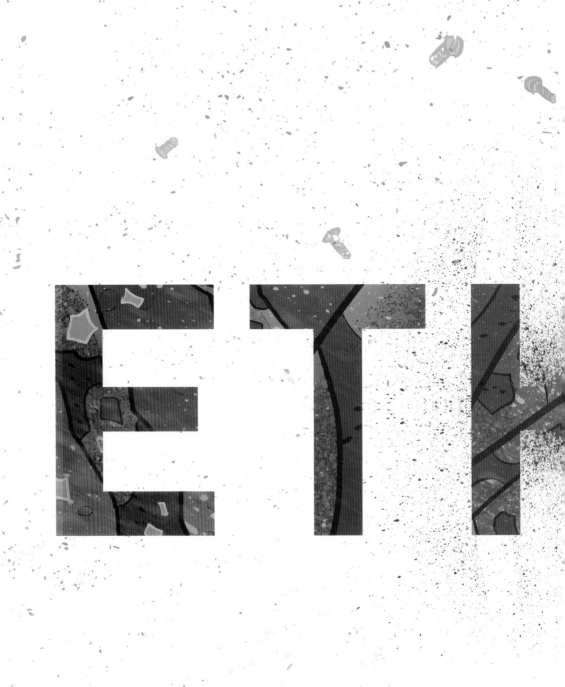

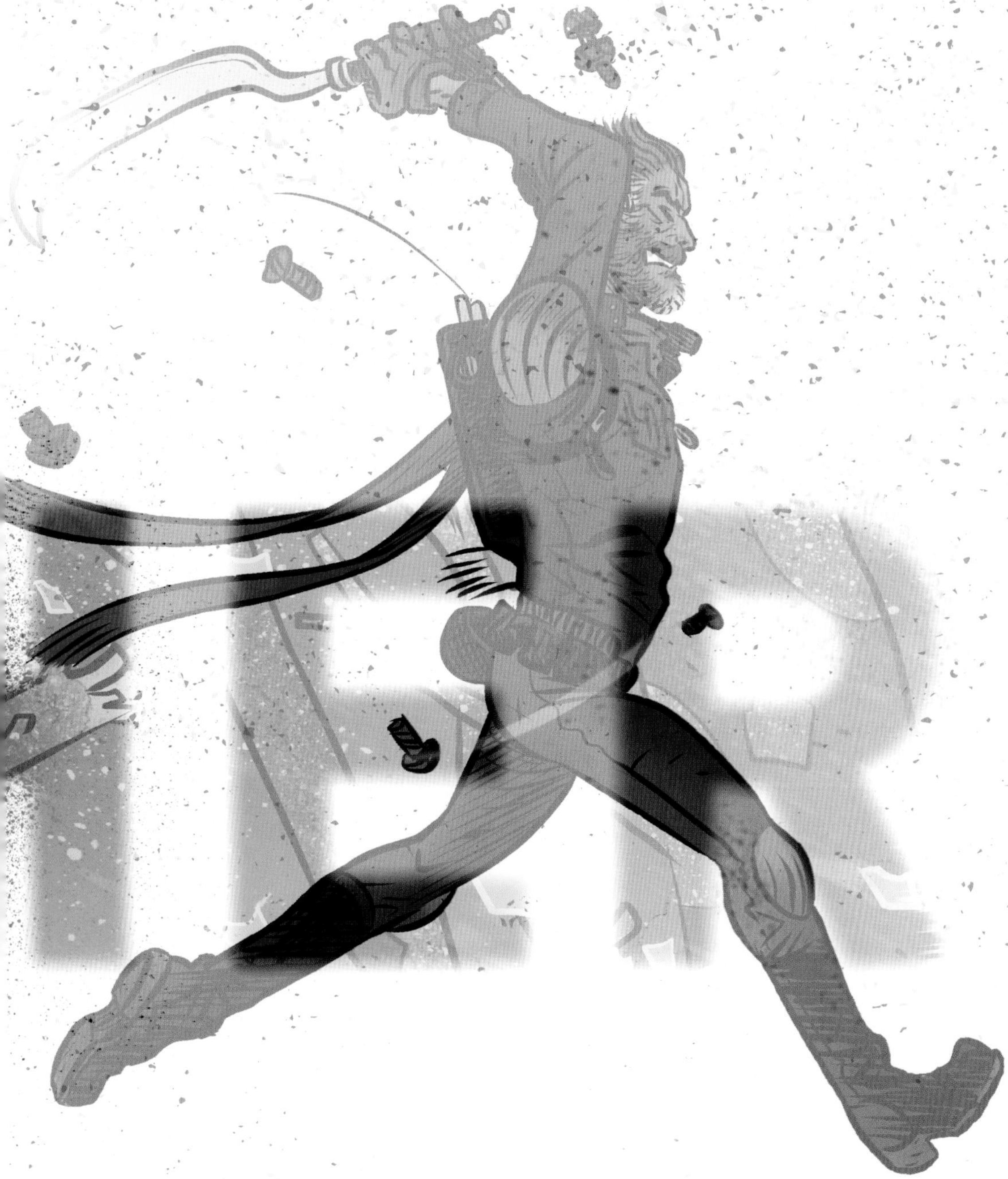

THE COPPER GOLEMS

written by **MATT KINDT**
art, colors, letters, and cover by **DAVID RUBÍN**
flats by **KIKE J. DÍAZ**
chapter breaks by **DAVID RUBÍN**

DARK HORSE BOOKS

president and publisher **MIKE RICHARDSON**

editor **DANIEL CHABON**

assistant editor **BRETT ISRAEL**

designers **ANITA MAGAÑA** & **PATRICK SATTERFIELD**

digital art technician **JOSIE CHRISTENSEN**

This volume collects issues #1–#5 of the Dark Horse Comics series *Ether: The Copper Golems*

Names: Kindt, Matt, writer. | Rubín, David, 1977- artist. | Diaz, Kike J.,
  artist.
Title: The copper golems / written by Matt Kindt ; art and cover by David
  Rubín ; flats by Kike Diaz ; chapter breaks by David Rubín.
Description: First edition. | Milwaukie, OR : Dark Horse Books, February
  2019. | Series: Ether ; 2 | "Collects issues #1-#5 of the Dark Horse
  Comics series Ether: The Copper Golems."
Identifiers: LCCN 2018038377 | ISBN 9781506705071
Classification: LCC PN6728.E85 K55 2019 | DDC 741.5/973--dc23
LC record available at https://lccn.loc.gov/2018038377

Published by
Dark Horse Books
A division of Dark Horse Comics, Inc.
10956 SE Main Street
Milwaukie, OR 97222

DarkHorse.com

To find a comics shop in your area, visit comicshoplocator.com.

First edition: February 2019
ISBN 978-1-50670-507-1

1 3 5 7 9 10 8 6 4 2
Printed in China

Neil Hankerson, Executive Vice President • Tom Weddle, Chief Financial Officer • Randy Stradley, Vice President of Publishing • Nick McWhorter, Chief Business Development Officer • Matt Parkinson, Vice President of Marketing • Dale LaFountain, Vice President of Information Technology • Cara Niece, Vice President of Production and Scheduling • Mark Bernardi, Vice President of Book Trade and Digital Sales Ken Lizzi, General Counsel • Dave Marshall, Editor in Chief • Davey Estrada, Editorial Director • Chris Warner, Senior Books Editor • Cary Grazzini, Director of Specialty Projects • Lia Ribacchi, Art Director Vanessa Todd-Holmes, Director of Print Purchasing • Matt Dryer, Director of Digital Art and Prepress Michael Gombos, Director of International Publishing and Licensing • Kari Yadro, Director of Custom Programs Kari Torson, Director of International Licensing

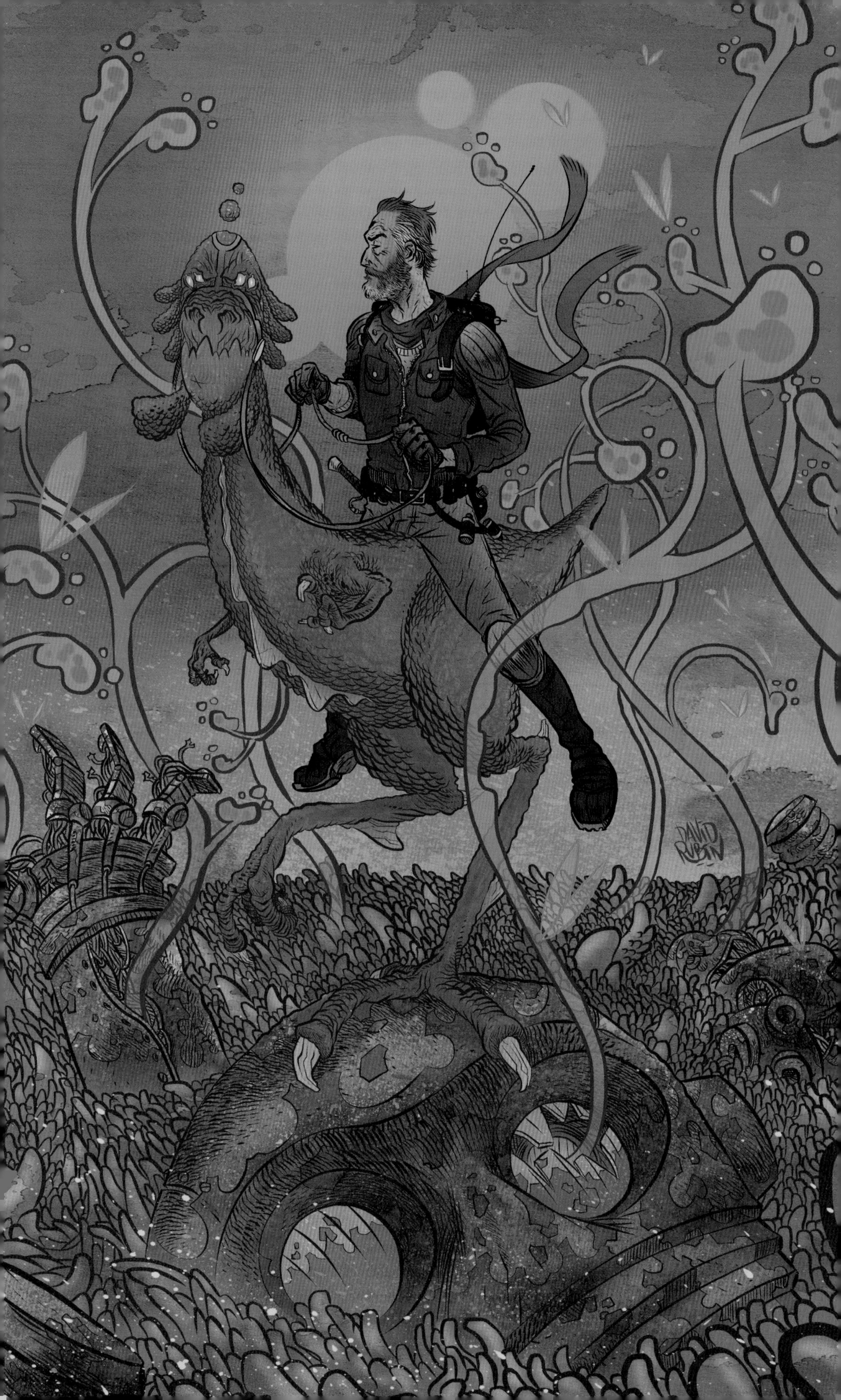
DAVID RUBIN

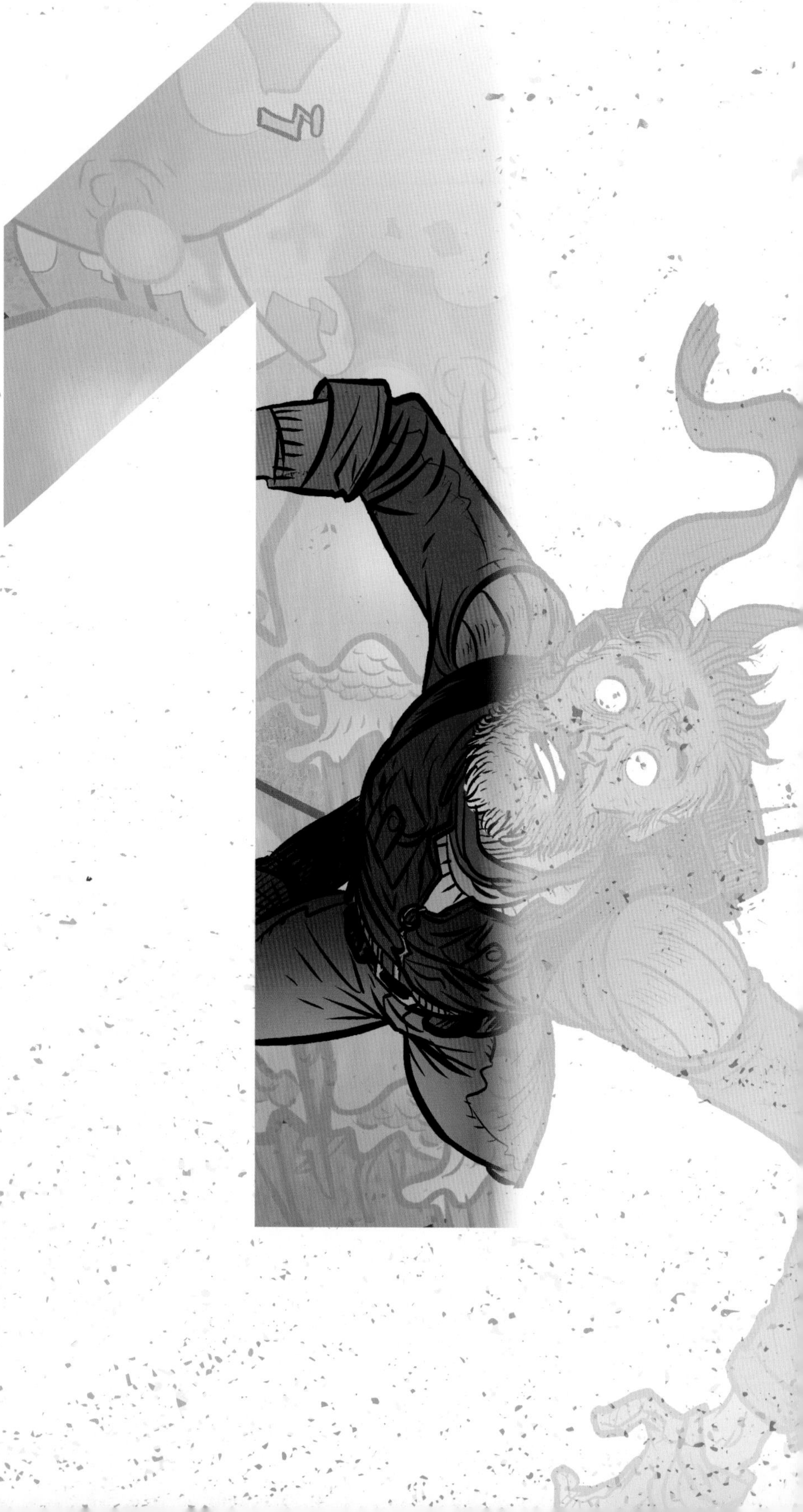

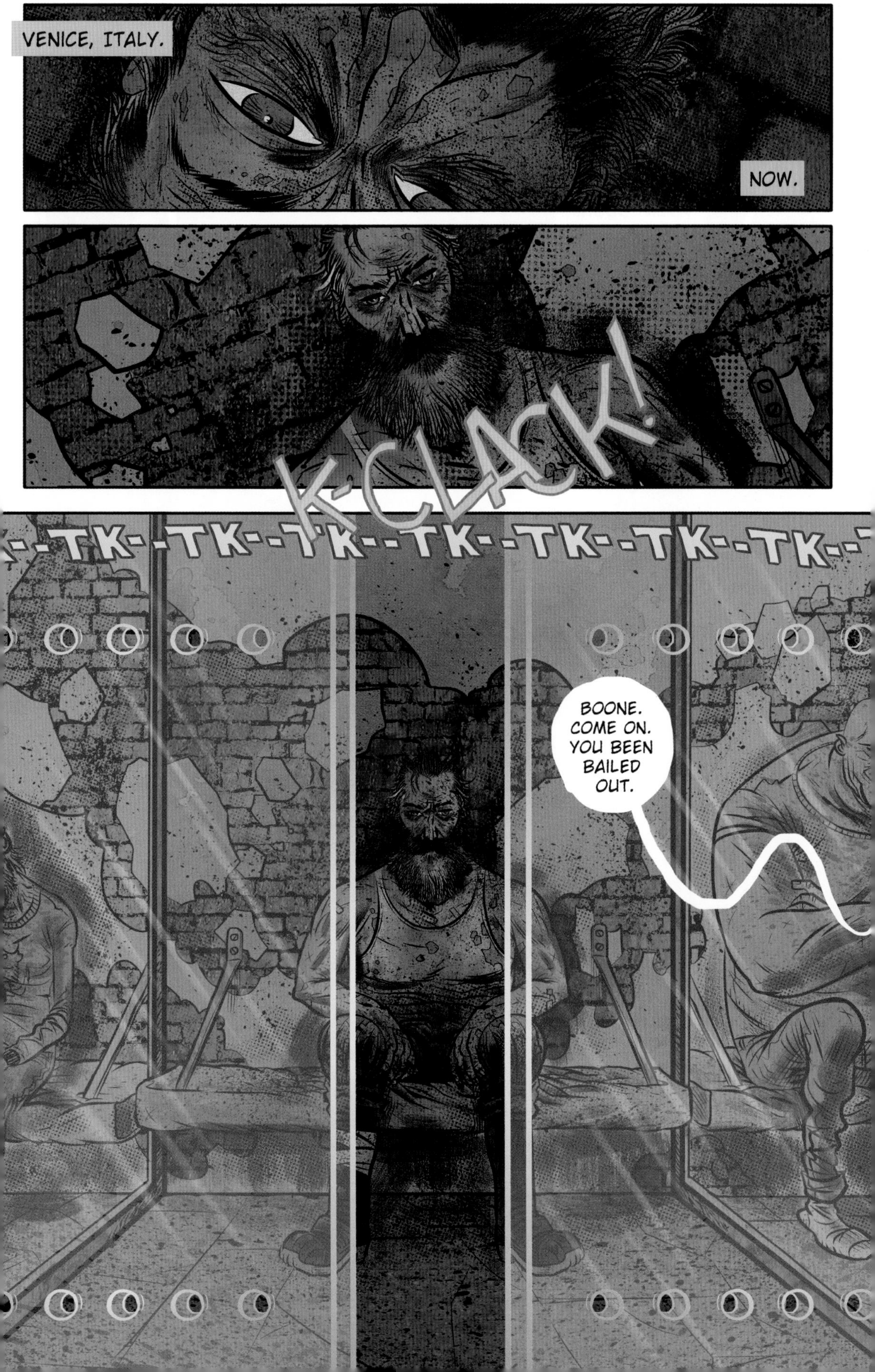
VENICE, ITALY.
NOW.
K-CLACK!
-TK--TK--TK--TK--TK--TK--TK--
BOONE. COME ON. YOU BEEN BAILED OUT.

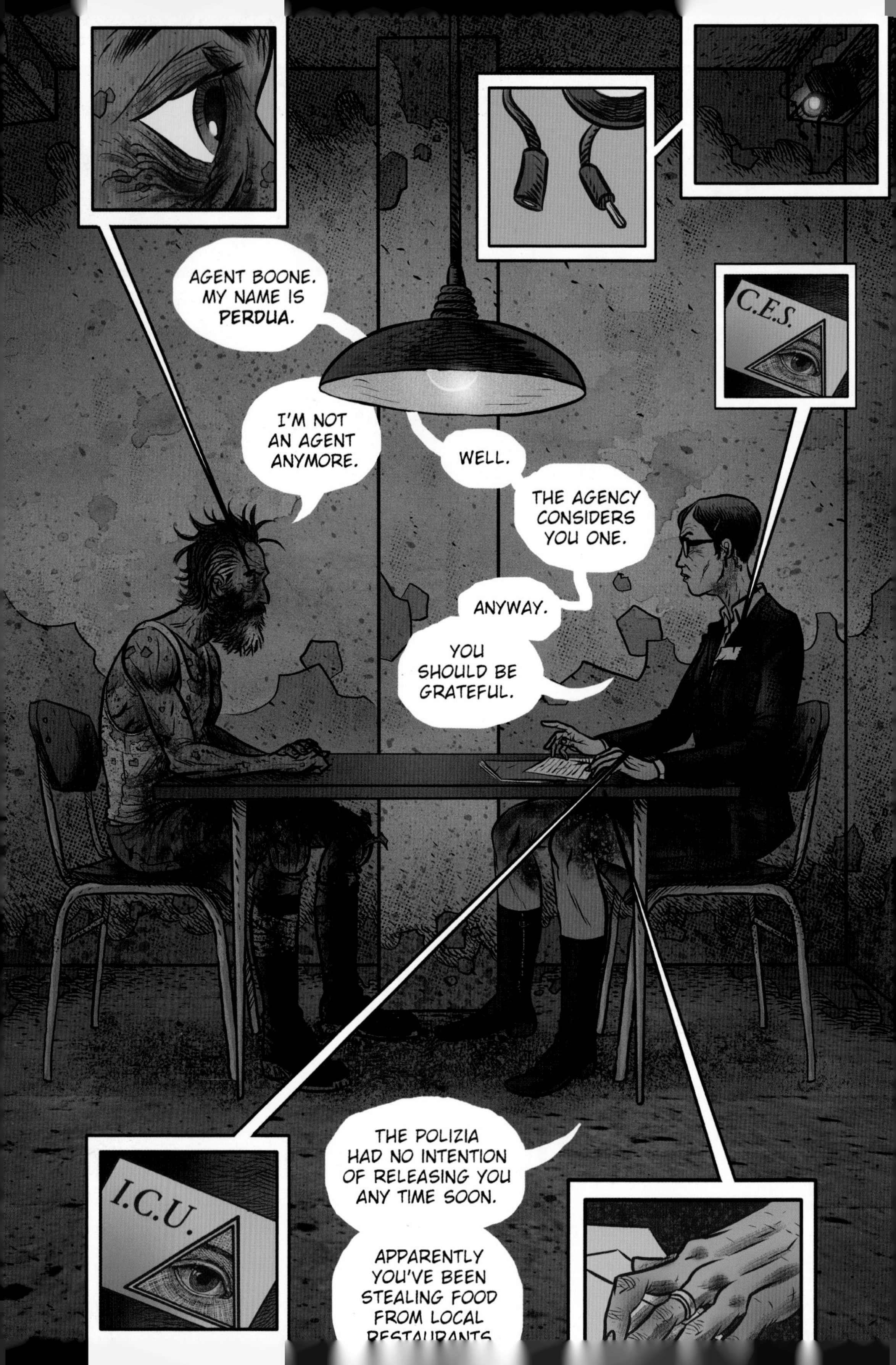
AGENT BOONE. MY NAME IS PERDUA.
I'M NOT AN AGENT ANYMORE.
WELL.
THE AGENCY CONSIDERS YOU ONE.
ANYWAY.
YOU SHOULD BE GRATEFUL.
C.E.S.
THE POLIZIA HAD NO INTENTION OF RELEASING YOU ANY TIME SOON.
APPARENTLY YOU'VE BEEN STEALING FOOD FROM LOCAL
I.C.U.

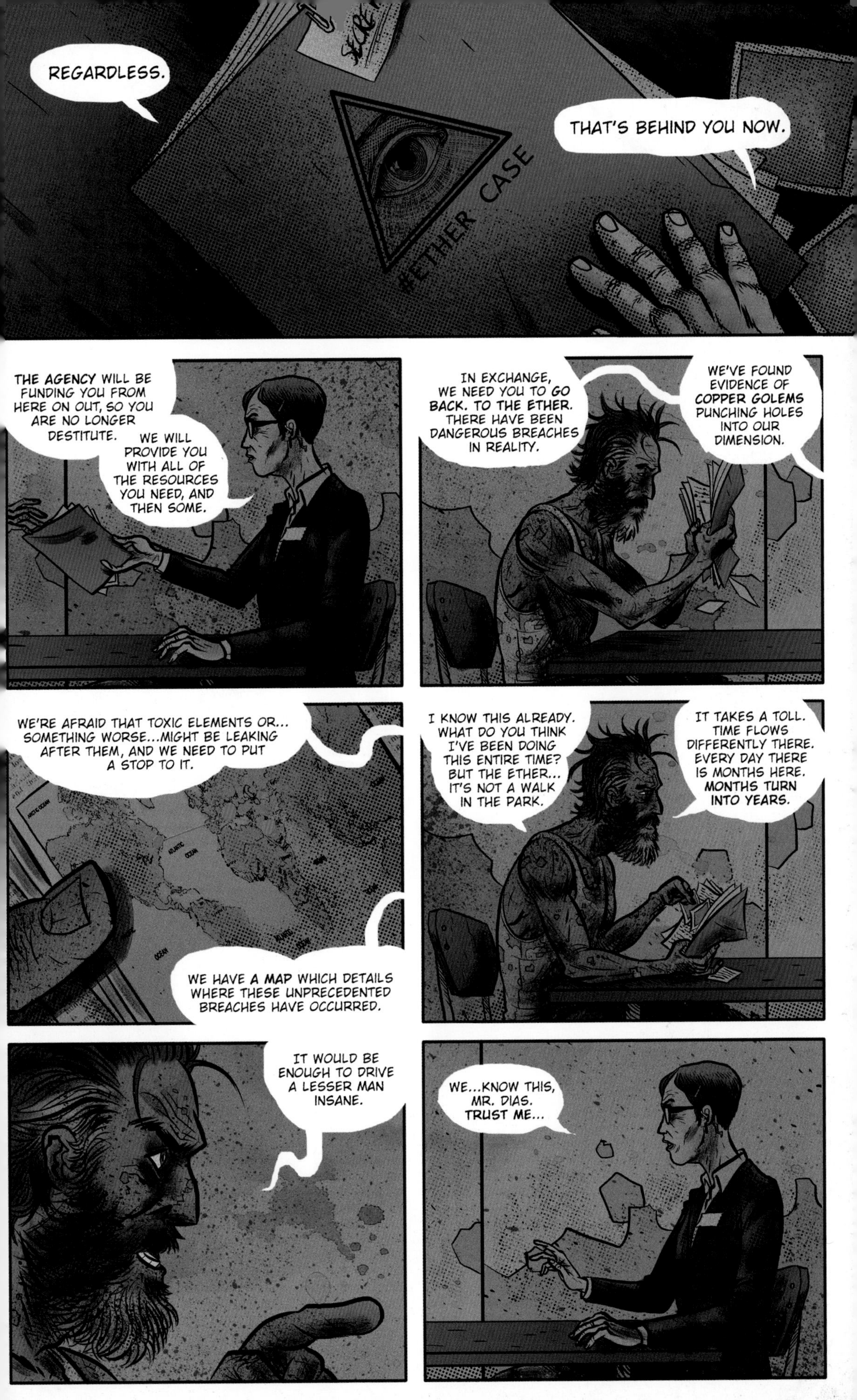

REGARDLESS.
#ETHER CASE
THAT'S BEHIND YOU NOW.
THE AGENCY WILL BE FUNDING YOU FROM HERE ON OUT, SO YOU ARE NO LONGER DESTITUTE.
WE WILL PROVIDE YOU WITH ALL OF THE RESOURCES YOU NEED, AND THEN SOME.
IN EXCHANGE, WE NEED YOU TO GO BACK. TO THE ETHER. THERE HAVE BEEN DANGEROUS BREACHES IN REALITY.
WE'VE FOUND EVIDENCE OF COPPER GOLEMS PUNCHING HOLES INTO OUR DIMENSION.
WE'RE AFRAID THAT TOXIC ELEMENTS OR... SOMETHING WORSE...MIGHT BE LEAKING AFTER THEM, AND WE NEED TO PUT A STOP TO IT.
WE HAVE A MAP WHICH DETAILS WHERE THESE UNPRECEDENTED BREACHES HAVE OCCURRED.
I KNOW THIS ALREADY. WHAT DO YOU THINK I'VE BEEN DOING THIS ENTIRE TIME? BUT THE ETHER... IT'S NOT A WALK IN THE PARK.
IT TAKES A TOLL. TIME FLOWS DIFFERENTLY THERE. EVERY DAY THERE IS MONTHS HERE. MONTHS TURN INTO YEARS.
IT WOULD BE ENOUGH TO DRIVE A LESSER MAN INSANE.
WE...KNOW THIS, MR. DIAS. TRUST ME...

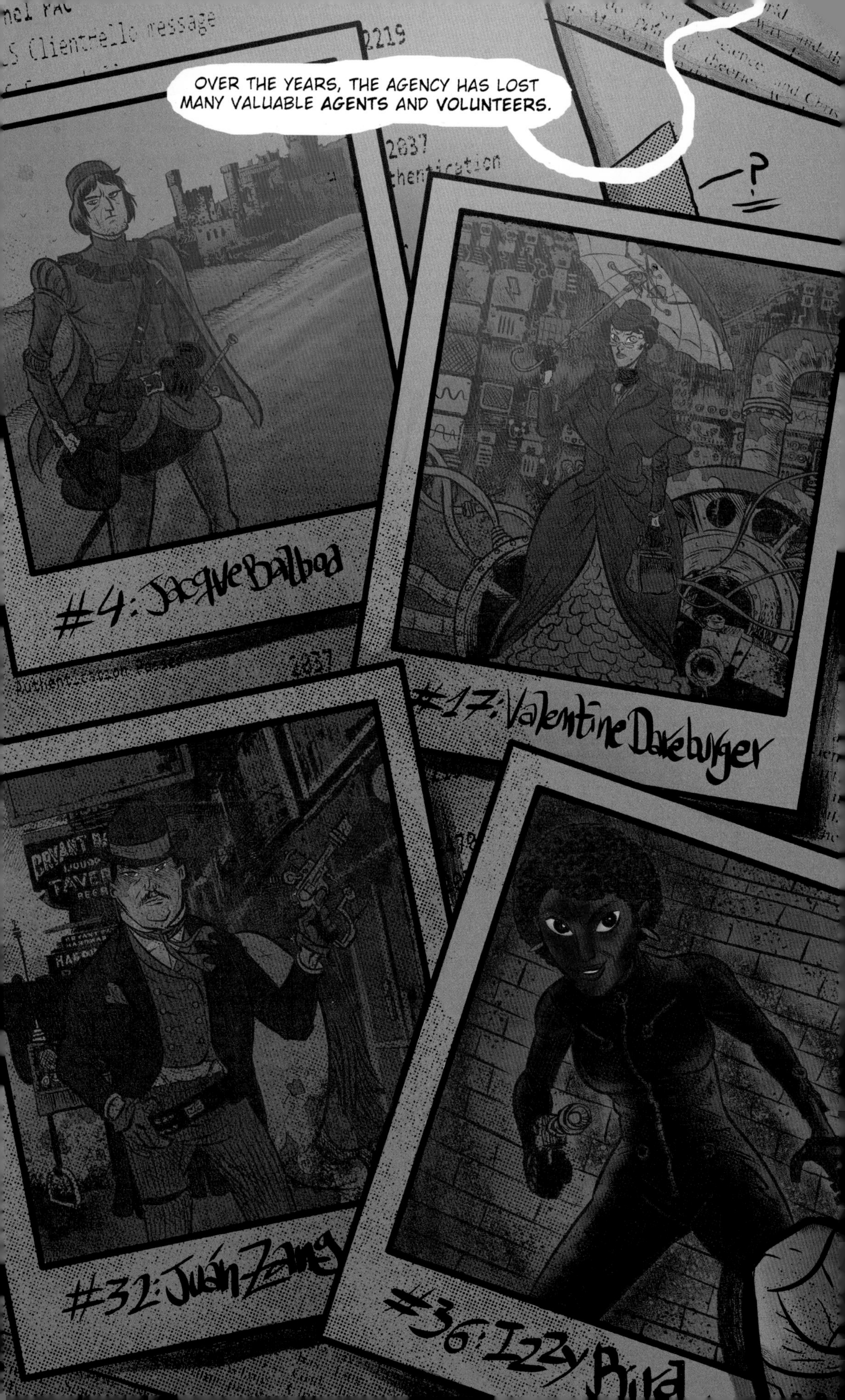
OVER THE YEARS, THE AGENCY HAS LOST MANY VALUABLE AGENTS AND VOLUNTEERS.
?
#4: Jacque Balboa
#17: Valentine Daveburger
#32: Juán Zang
#36: Izzy Bird

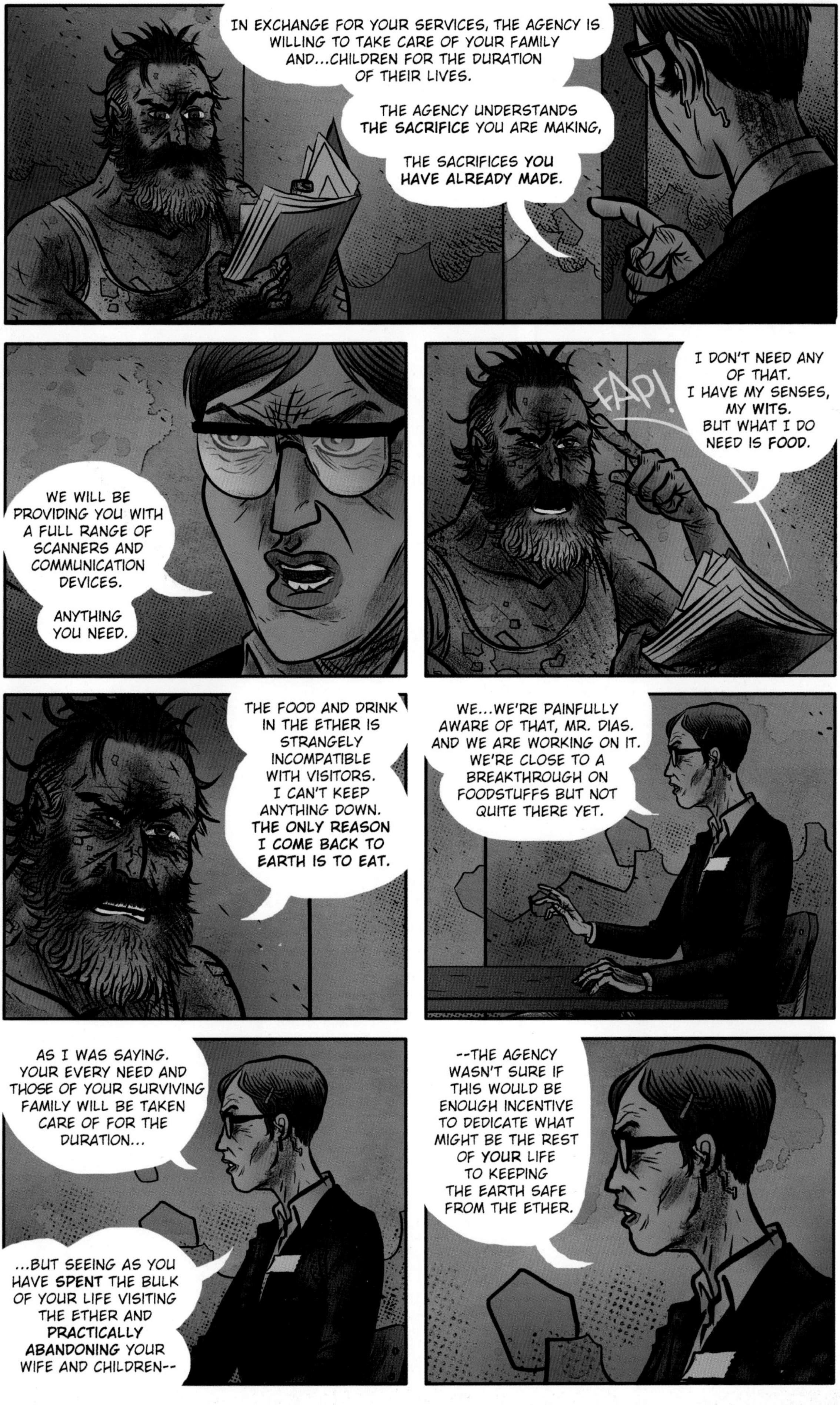
IN EXCHANGE FOR YOUR SERVICES, THE AGENCY IS WILLING TO TAKE CARE OF YOUR FAMILY AND...CHILDREN FOR THE DURATION OF THEIR LIVES.
THE AGENCY UNDERSTANDS **THE SACRIFICE** YOU ARE MAKING,
THE SACRIFICES **YOU HAVE ALREADY MADE.**
WE WILL BE PROVIDING YOU WITH A FULL RANGE OF SCANNERS AND COMMUNICATION DEVICES.
ANYTHING YOU NEED.
FAP!
I DON'T NEED ANY OF THAT. I HAVE MY SENSES, MY **WITS.** BUT WHAT I DO NEED IS **FOOD.**
THE FOOD AND DRINK IN THE ETHER IS STRANGELY INCOMPATIBLE WITH VISITORS. I CAN'T KEEP ANYTHING DOWN. **THE ONLY REASON I COME BACK TO EARTH IS TO EAT.**
WE...WE'RE PAINFULLY AWARE OF THAT, MR. DIAS. AND WE ARE WORKING ON IT. WE'RE CLOSE TO A BREAKTHROUGH ON FOODSTUFFS BUT NOT QUITE THERE YET.
AS I WAS SAYING. YOUR EVERY NEED AND THOSE OF YOUR SURVIVING FAMILY WILL BE TAKEN CARE OF FOR THE DURATION...
...BUT SEEING AS YOU HAVE **SPENT** THE BULK OF YOUR LIFE VISITING THE ETHER AND **PRACTICALLY ABANDONING** YOUR WIFE AND CHILDREN--
--THE AGENCY WASN'T SURE IF THIS WOULD BE ENOUGH INCENTIVE TO DEDICATE WHAT MIGHT BE THE REST OF **YOUR** LIFE TO KEEPING THE EARTH SAFE FROM THE ETHER.

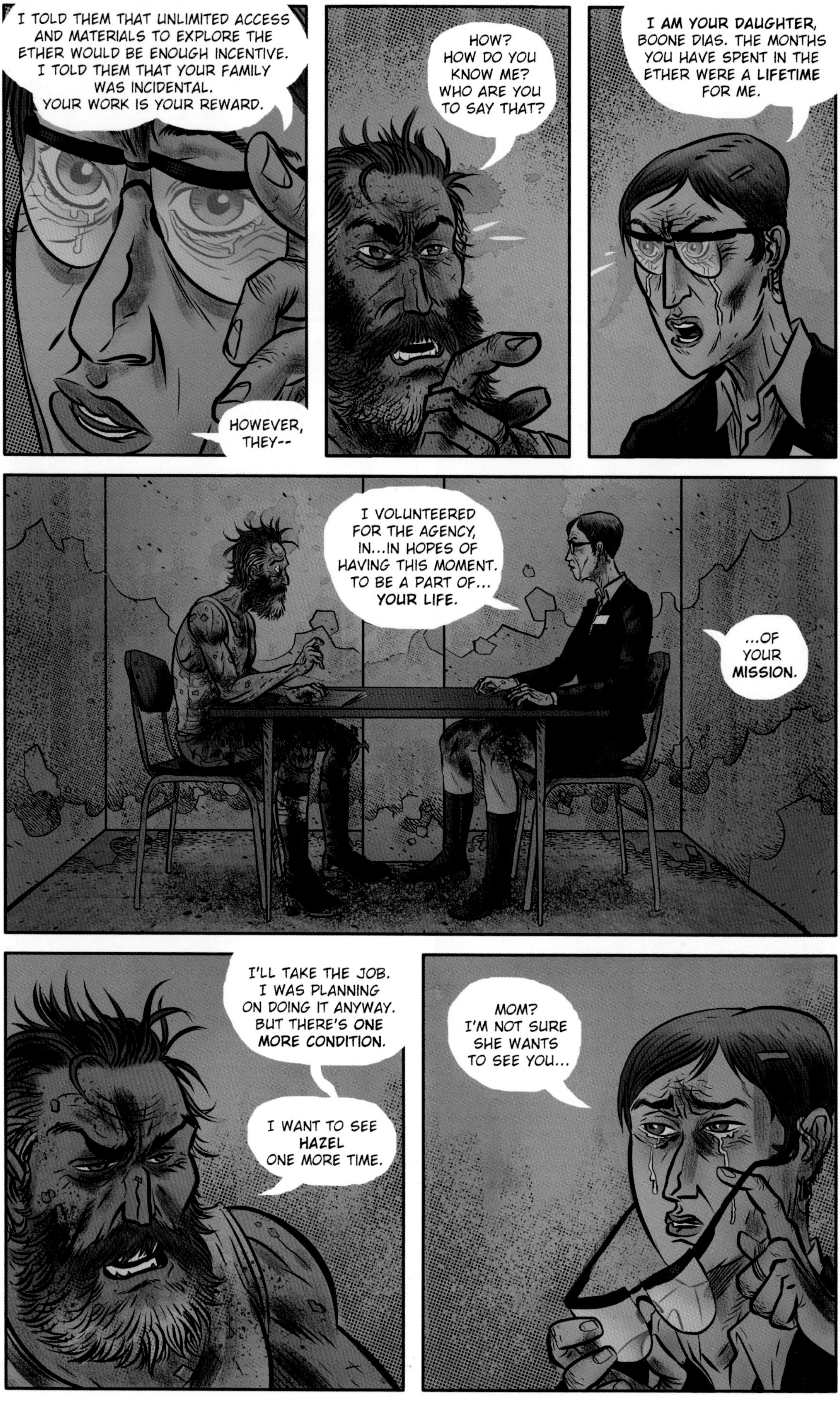
I TOLD THEM THAT UNLIMITED ACCESS AND MATERIALS TO EXPLORE THE ETHER WOULD BE ENOUGH INCENTIVE. I TOLD THEM THAT YOUR FAMILY WAS INCIDENTAL. YOUR WORK IS YOUR REWARD.
HOWEVER, THEY--
HOW? HOW DO YOU KNOW ME? WHO ARE YOU TO SAY THAT?
I AM YOUR DAUGHTER, BOONE DIAS. THE MONTHS YOU HAVE SPENT IN THE ETHER WERE A LIFETIME FOR ME.
I VOLUNTEERED FOR THE AGENCY, IN...IN HOPES OF HAVING THIS MOMENT. TO BE A PART OF... YOUR LIFE.
...OF YOUR MISSION.
I'LL TAKE THE JOB. I WAS PLANNING ON DOING IT ANYWAY. BUT THERE'S ONE MORE CONDITION.
I WANT TO SEE HAZEL ONE MORE TIME.
MOM? I'M NOT SURE SHE WANTS TO SEE YOU...

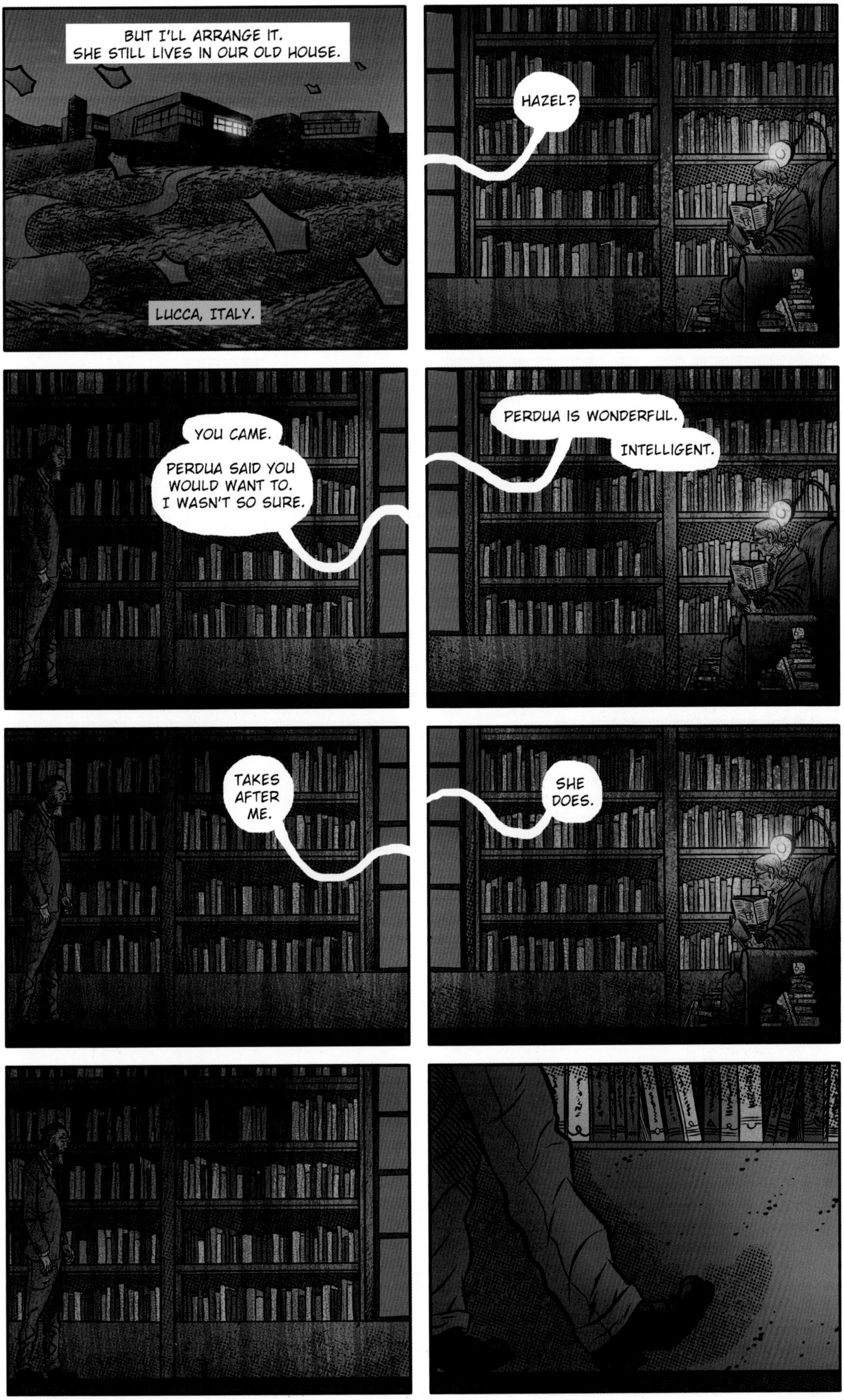
BUT I'LL ARRANGE IT. SHE STILL LIVES IN OUR OLD HOUSE.
LUCCA, ITALY.
HAZEL?
YOU CAME.
PERDUA SAID YOU WOULD WANT TO. I WASN'T SO SURE.
PERDUA IS WONDERFUL.
INTELLIGENT.
TAKES AFTER ME.
SHE DOES.

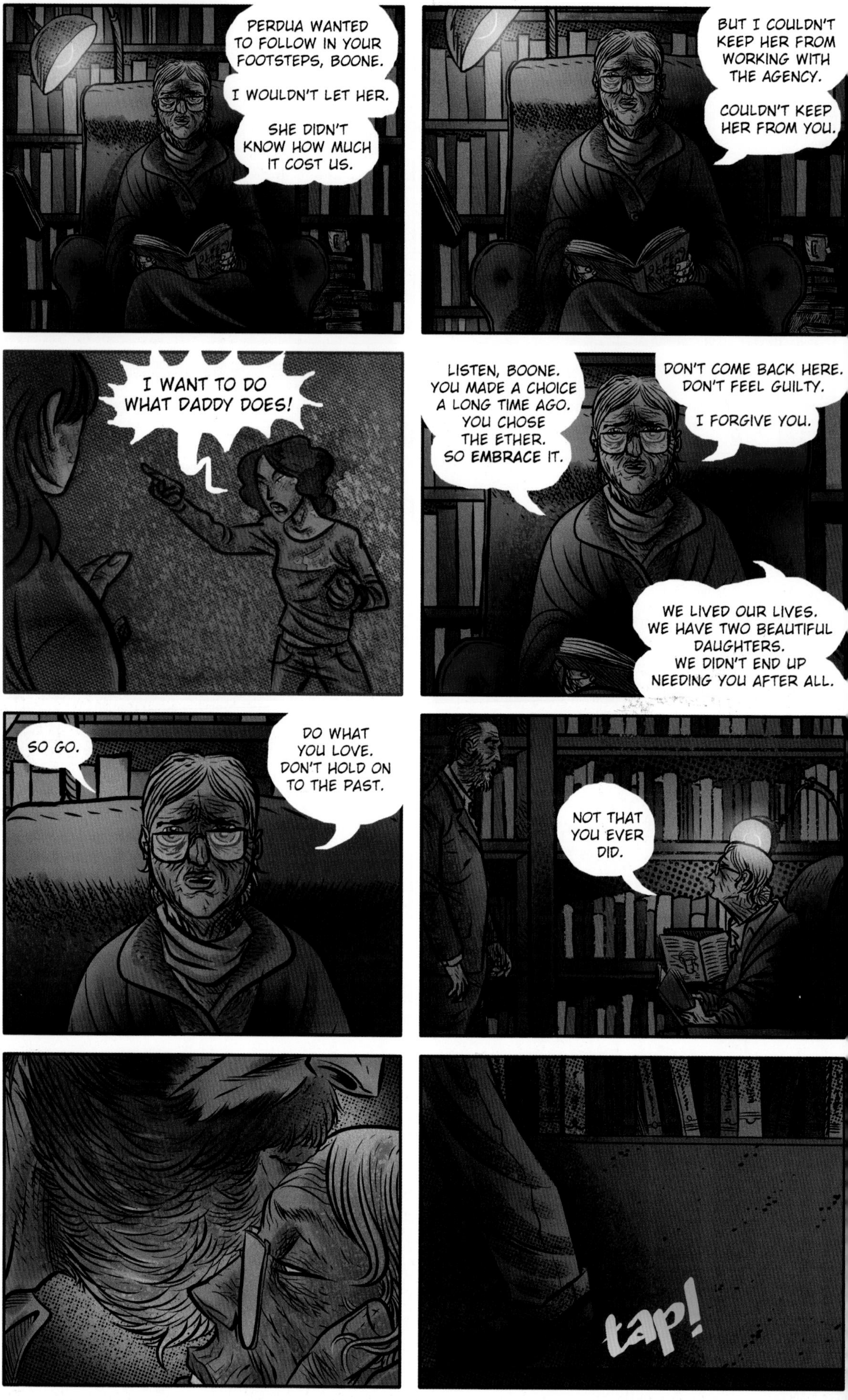
PERDUA WANTED TO FOLLOW IN YOUR FOOTSTEPS, BOONE.
I WOULDN'T LET HER.
SHE DIDN'T KNOW HOW MUCH IT COST US.
BUT I COULDN'T KEEP HER FROM WORKING WITH THE AGENCY.
COULDN'T KEEP HER FROM YOU.
I WANT TO DO WHAT DADDY DOES!
LISTEN, BOONE. YOU MADE A CHOICE A LONG TIME AGO. YOU CHOSE THE ETHER. SO **EMBRACE** IT.
DON'T COME BACK HERE. DON'T FEEL GUILTY.
I FORGIVE YOU.
WE LIVED OUR LIVES. WE HAVE TWO BEAUTIFUL DAUGHTERS. WE DIDN'T END UP NEEDING YOU AFTER ALL.
SO GO.
DO WHAT YOU LOVE. DON'T HOLD ON TO THE PAST.
NOT THAT YOU EVER DID.
tap!

VENICE, ITALY.

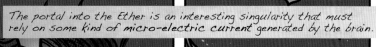

The portal into the Ether is an interesting singularity that must rely on some kind of micro-electric current generated by the brain.

FAPP!!

It's the only explanation for how one must enter the portal.

The only electrical impulse that will open the portal is generated when your mind prepares itself to die. When it accepts death...

That unique electrical pulse is like a key...

That unlocks...

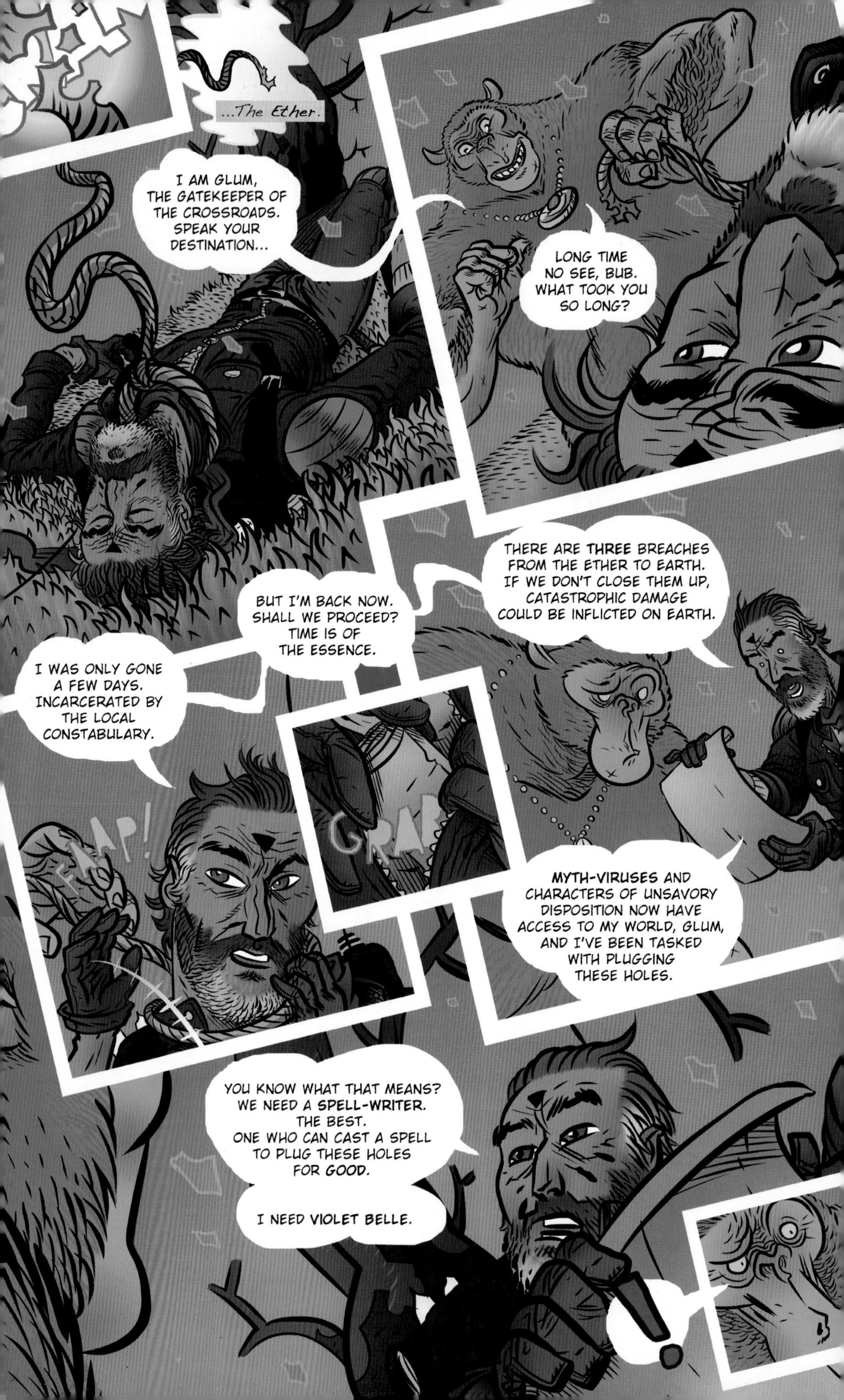

...The Ether.
I AM GLUM, THE GATEKEEPER OF THE CROSSROADS. SPEAK YOUR DESTINATION...
LONG TIME NO SEE, BUB. WHAT TOOK YOU SO LONG?
I WAS ONLY GONE A FEW DAYS. INCARCERATED BY THE LOCAL CONSTABULARY.
BUT I'M BACK NOW. SHALL WE PROCEED? TIME IS OF THE ESSENCE.
THERE ARE THREE BREACHES FROM THE ETHER TO EARTH. IF WE DON'T CLOSE THEM UP, CATASTROPHIC DAMAGE COULD BE INFLICTED ON EARTH.
FAAAP!
GRAB
MYTH-VIRUSES AND CHARACTERS OF UNSAVORY DISPOSITION NOW HAVE ACCESS TO MY WORLD, GLUM, AND I'VE BEEN TASKED WITH PLUGGING THESE HOLES.
YOU KNOW WHAT THAT MEANS? WE NEED A SPELL-WRITER. THE BEST. ONE WHO CAN CAST A SPELL TO PLUG THESE HOLES FOR GOOD.
I NEED VIOLET BELLE.
!

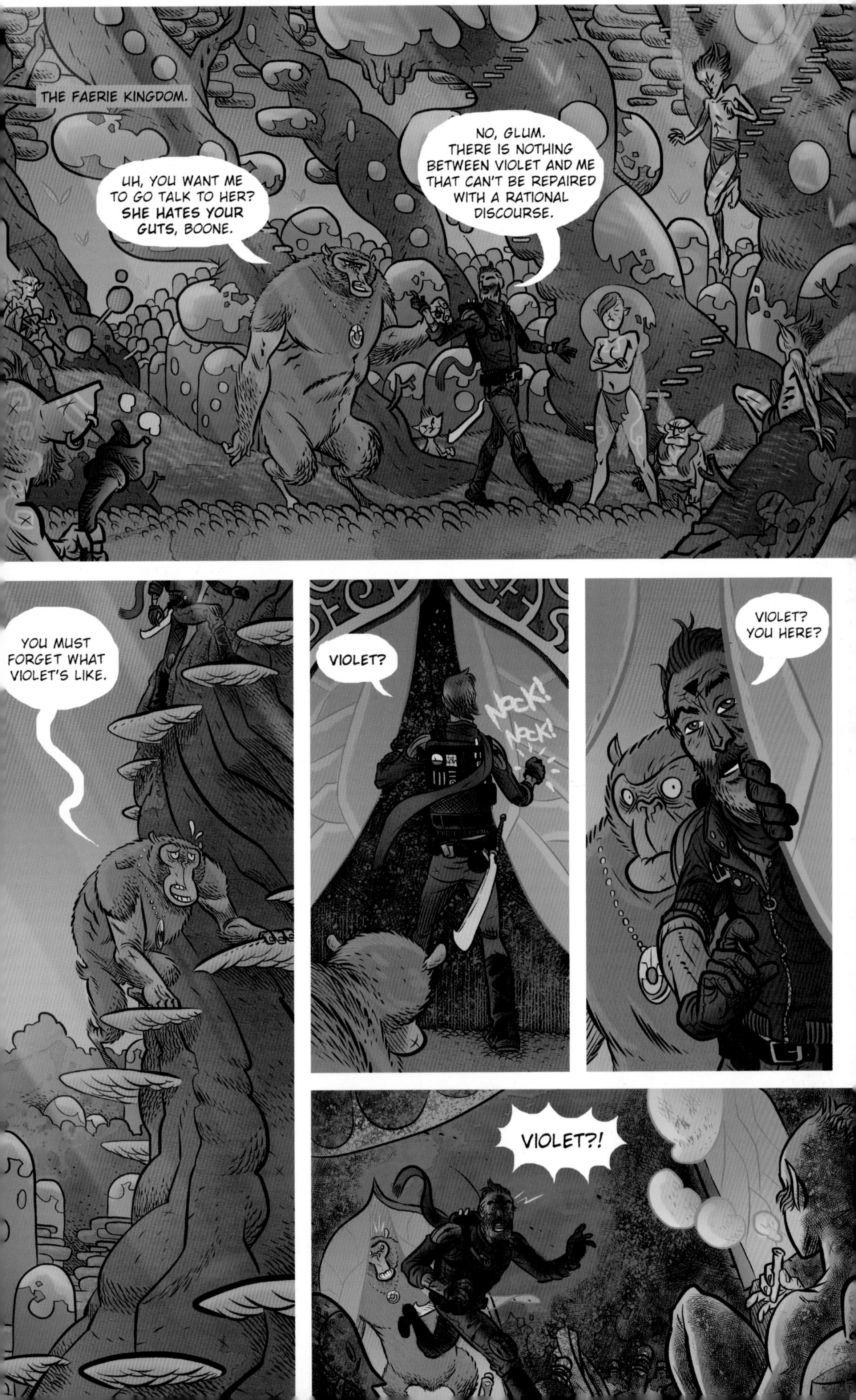
THE FAERIE KINGDOM.
UH, YOU WANT ME TO GO TALK TO HER? SHE HATES YOUR GUTS, BOONE.
NO, GLUM. THERE IS NOTHING BETWEEN VIOLET AND ME THAT CAN'T BE REPAIRED WITH A RATIONAL DISCOURSE.
YOU MUST FORGET WHAT VIOLET'S LIKE.
VIOLET?
NOCK! NOCK!
VIOLET? YOU HERE?
VIOLET?!

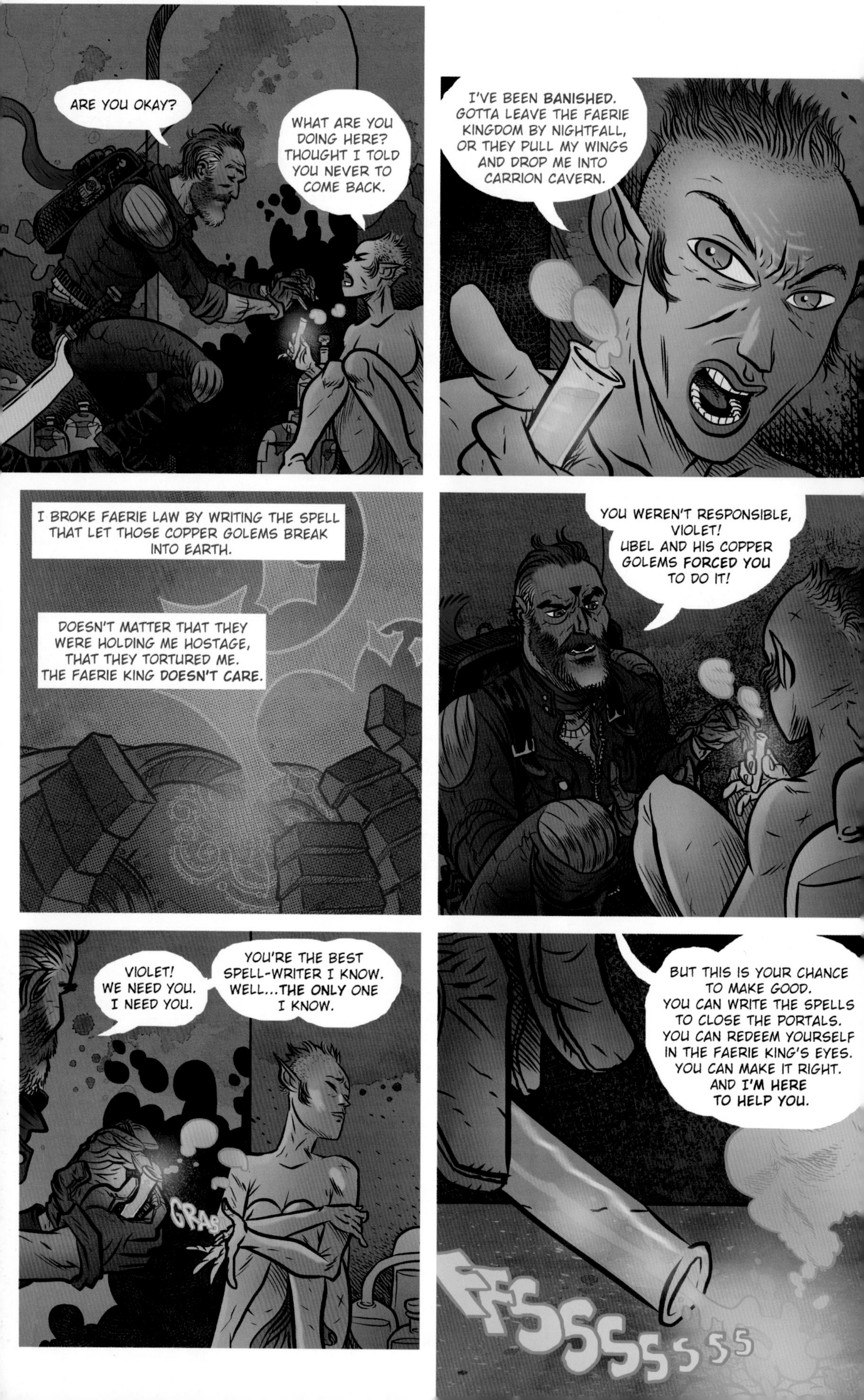
ARE YOU OKAY?
WHAT ARE YOU DOING HERE? THOUGHT I TOLD YOU NEVER TO COME BACK.
I'VE BEEN BANISHED. GOTTA LEAVE THE FAERIE KINGDOM BY NIGHTFALL, OR THEY PULL MY WINGS AND DROP ME INTO CARRION CAVERN.
I BROKE FAERIE LAW BY WRITING THE SPELL THAT LET THOSE COPPER GOLEMS BREAK INTO EARTH.
DOESN'T MATTER THAT THEY WERE HOLDING ME HOSTAGE, THAT THEY TORTURED ME. THE FAERIE KING DOESN'T CARE.
YOU WEREN'T RESPONSIBLE, VIOLET! UBEL AND HIS COPPER GOLEMS FORCED YOU TO DO IT!
VIOLET! WE NEED YOU. I NEED YOU.
YOU'RE THE BEST SPELL-WRITER I KNOW. WELL...THE ONLY ONE I KNOW.
GRAB
BUT THIS IS YOUR CHANCE TO MAKE GOOD. YOU CAN WRITE THE SPELLS TO CLOSE THE PORTALS. YOU CAN REDEEM YOURSELF IN THE FAERIE KING'S EYES. YOU CAN MAKE IT RIGHT. AND I'M HERE TO HELP YOU.
FFSSSSSSSS

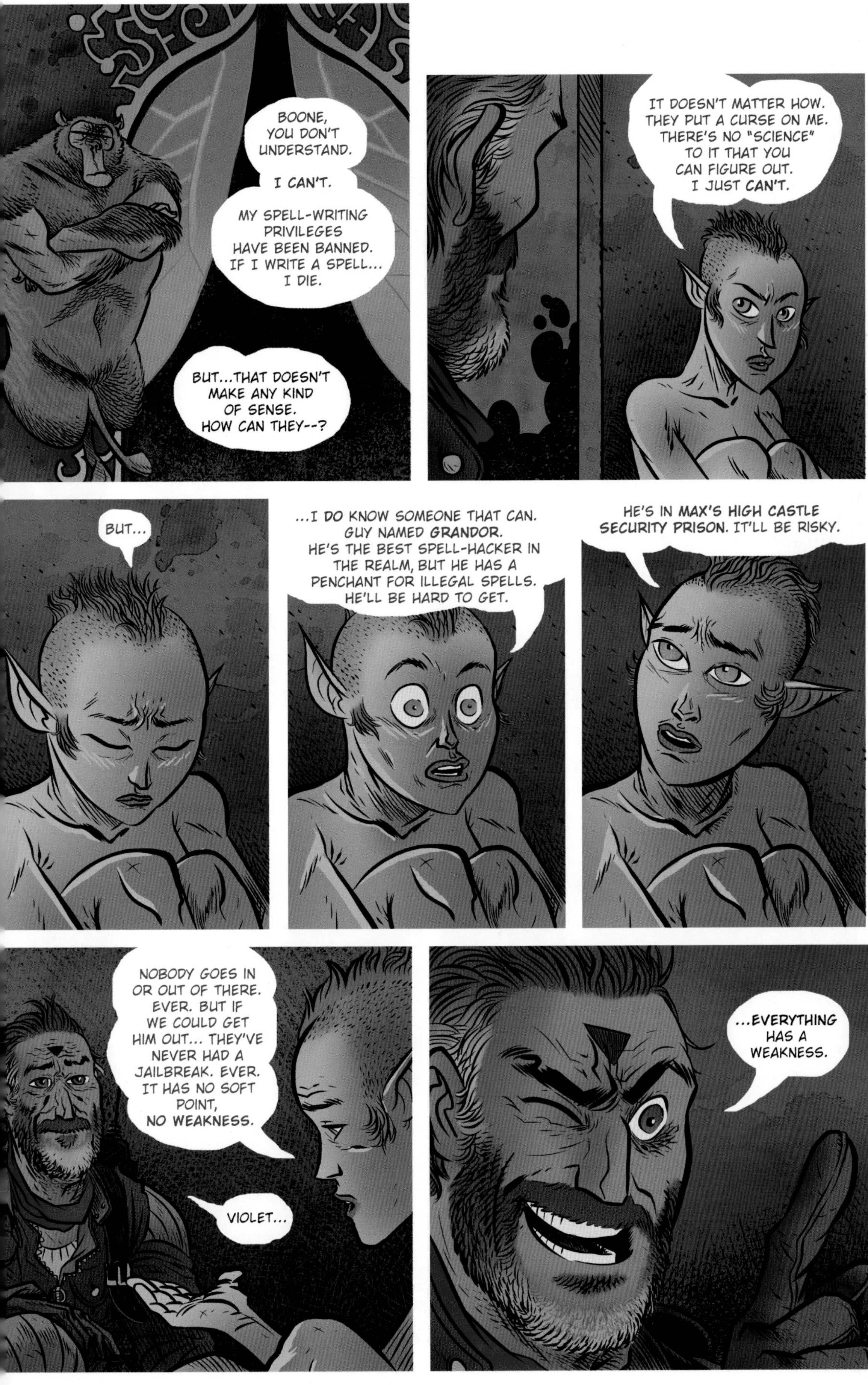
BOONE, YOU DON'T UNDERSTAND.
I CAN'T.
MY SPELL-WRITING PRIVILEGES HAVE BEEN BANNED. IF I WRITE A SPELL... I DIE.
BUT...THAT DOESN'T MAKE ANY KIND OF SENSE. HOW CAN THEY--?
IT DOESN'T MATTER HOW. THEY PUT A CURSE ON ME. THERE'S NO "SCIENCE" TO IT THAT YOU CAN FIGURE OUT. I JUST CAN'T.
BUT...
...I DO KNOW SOMEONE THAT CAN. GUY NAMED GRANDOR. HE'S THE BEST SPELL-HACKER IN THE REALM, BUT HE HAS A PENCHANT FOR ILLEGAL SPELLS. HE'LL BE HARD TO GET.
HE'S IN MAX'S HIGH CASTLE SECURITY PRISON. IT'LL BE RISKY.
NOBODY GOES IN OR OUT OF THERE. EVER. BUT IF WE COULD GET HIM OUT... THEY'VE NEVER HAD A JAILBREAK. EVER. IT HAS NO SOFT POINT, NO WEAKNESS.
VIOLET...
...EVERYTHING HAS A WEAKNESS.

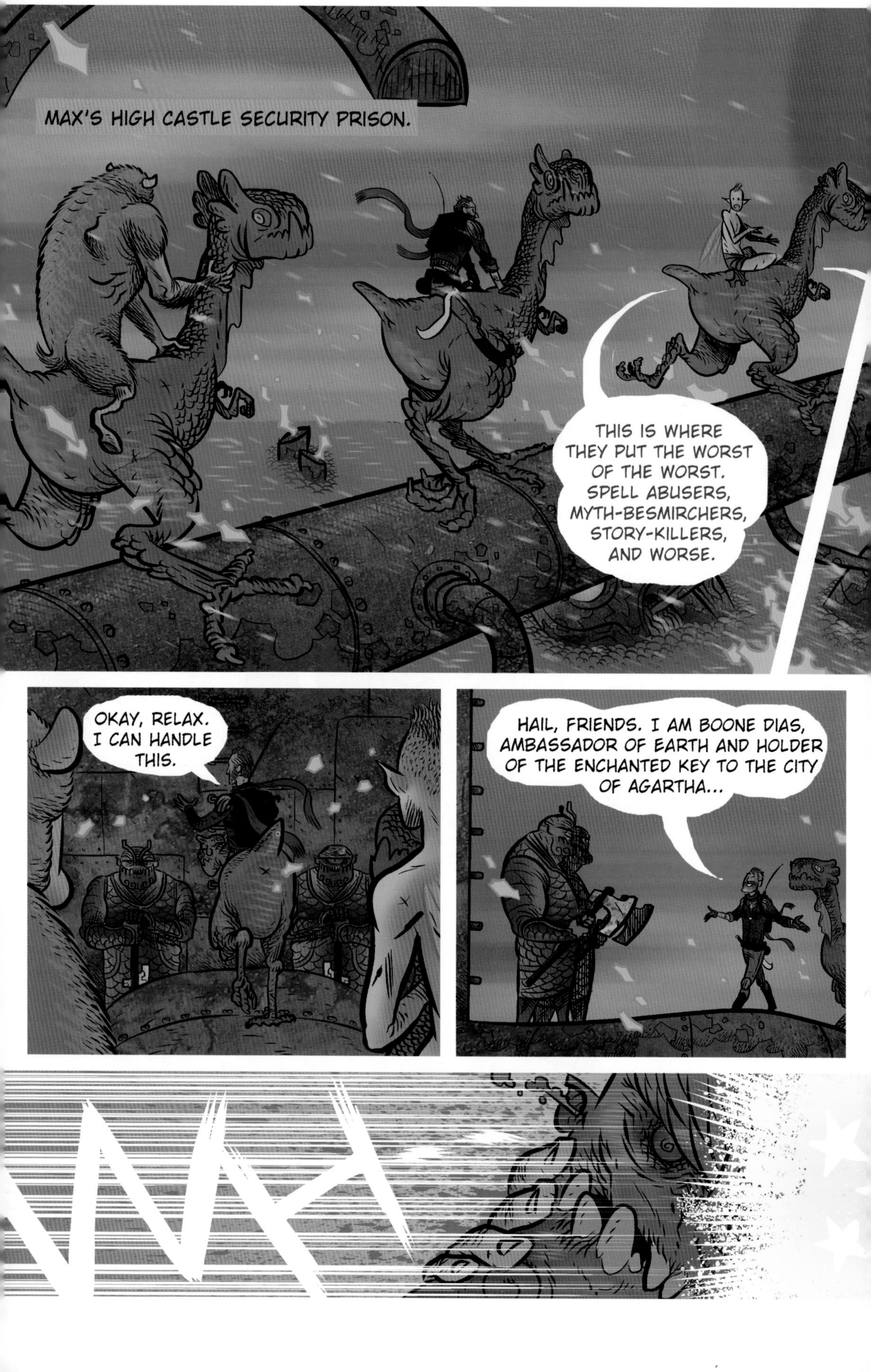
MAX'S HIGH CASTLE SECURITY PRISON.
THIS IS WHERE THEY PUT THE WORST OF THE WORST. SPELL ABUSERS, MYTH-BESMIRCHERS, STORY-KILLERS, AND WORSE.
OKAY, RELAX. I CAN HANDLE THIS.
HAIL, FRIENDS. I AM BOONE DIAS, AMBASSADOR OF EARTH AND HOLDER OF THE ENCHANTED KEY TO THE CITY OF AGARTHA...

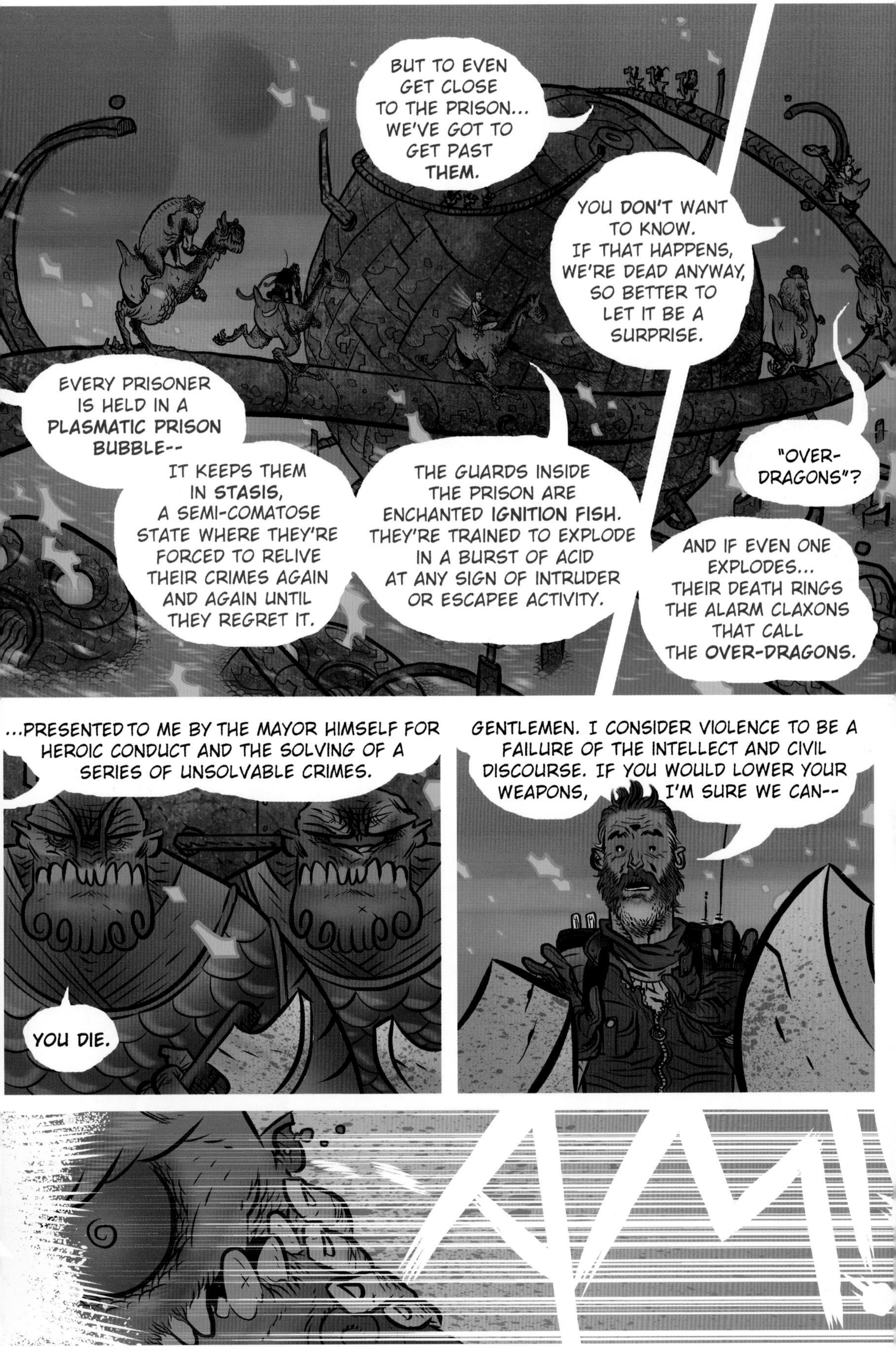

BUT TO EVEN GET CLOSE TO THE PRISON... WE'VE GOT TO GET PAST THEM.
EVERY PRISONER IS HELD IN A PLASMATIC PRISON BUBBLE--
IT KEEPS THEM IN STASIS, A SEMI-COMATOSE STATE WHERE THEY'RE FORCED TO RELIVE THEIR CRIMES AGAIN AND AGAIN UNTIL THEY REGRET IT.
THE GUARDS INSIDE THE PRISON ARE ENCHANTED IGNITION FISH. THEY'RE TRAINED TO EXPLODE IN A BURST OF ACID AT ANY SIGN OF INTRUDER OR ESCAPEE ACTIVITY.
AND IF EVEN ONE EXPLODES... THEIR DEATH RINGS THE ALARM CLAXONS THAT CALL THE OVER-DRAGONS.
"OVER-DRAGONS"?
YOU DON'T WANT TO KNOW. IF THAT HAPPENS, WE'RE DEAD ANYWAY, SO BETTER TO LET IT BE A SURPRISE.
...PRESENTED TO ME BY THE MAYOR HIMSELF FOR HEROIC CONDUCT AND THE SOLVING OF A SERIES OF UNSOLVABLE CRIMES.
YOU DIE.
GENTLEMEN. I CONSIDER VIOLENCE TO BE A FAILURE OF THE INTELLECT AND CIVIL DISCOURSE. IF YOU WOULD LOWER YOUR WEAPONS, I'M SURE WE CAN--

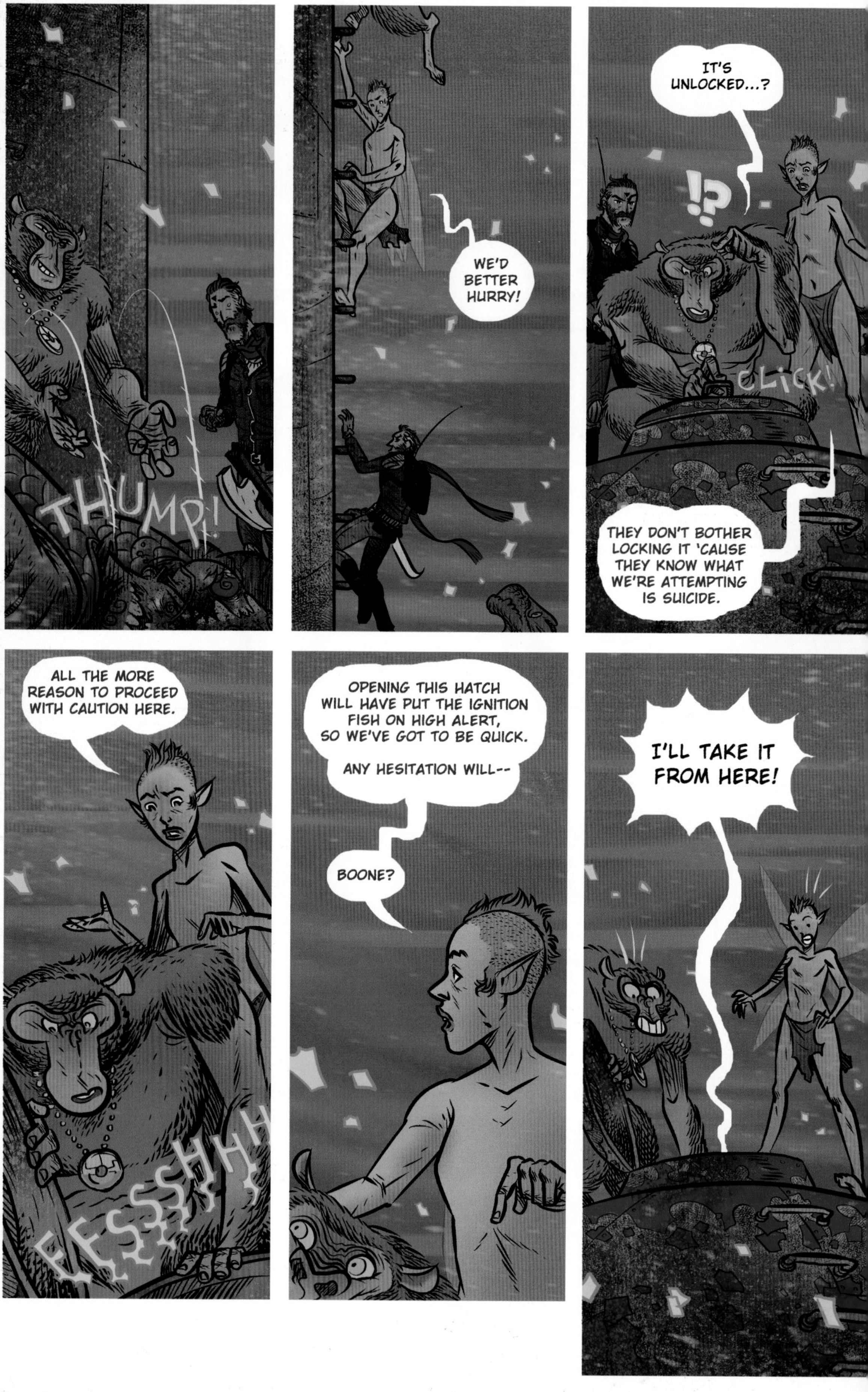
THUMP!
WE'D BETTER HURRY!
IT'S UNLOCKED...?
!?
CLICK!
THEY DON'T BOTHER LOCKING IT 'CAUSE THEY KNOW WHAT WE'RE ATTEMPTING IS SUICIDE.
ALL THE MORE REASON TO PROCEED WITH CAUTION HERE.
FFSSSHHH
OPENING THIS HATCH WILL HAVE PUT THE IGNITION FISH ON HIGH ALERT, SO WE'VE GOT TO BE QUICK.
ANY HESITATION WILL--
BOONE?
I'LL TAKE IT FROM HERE!

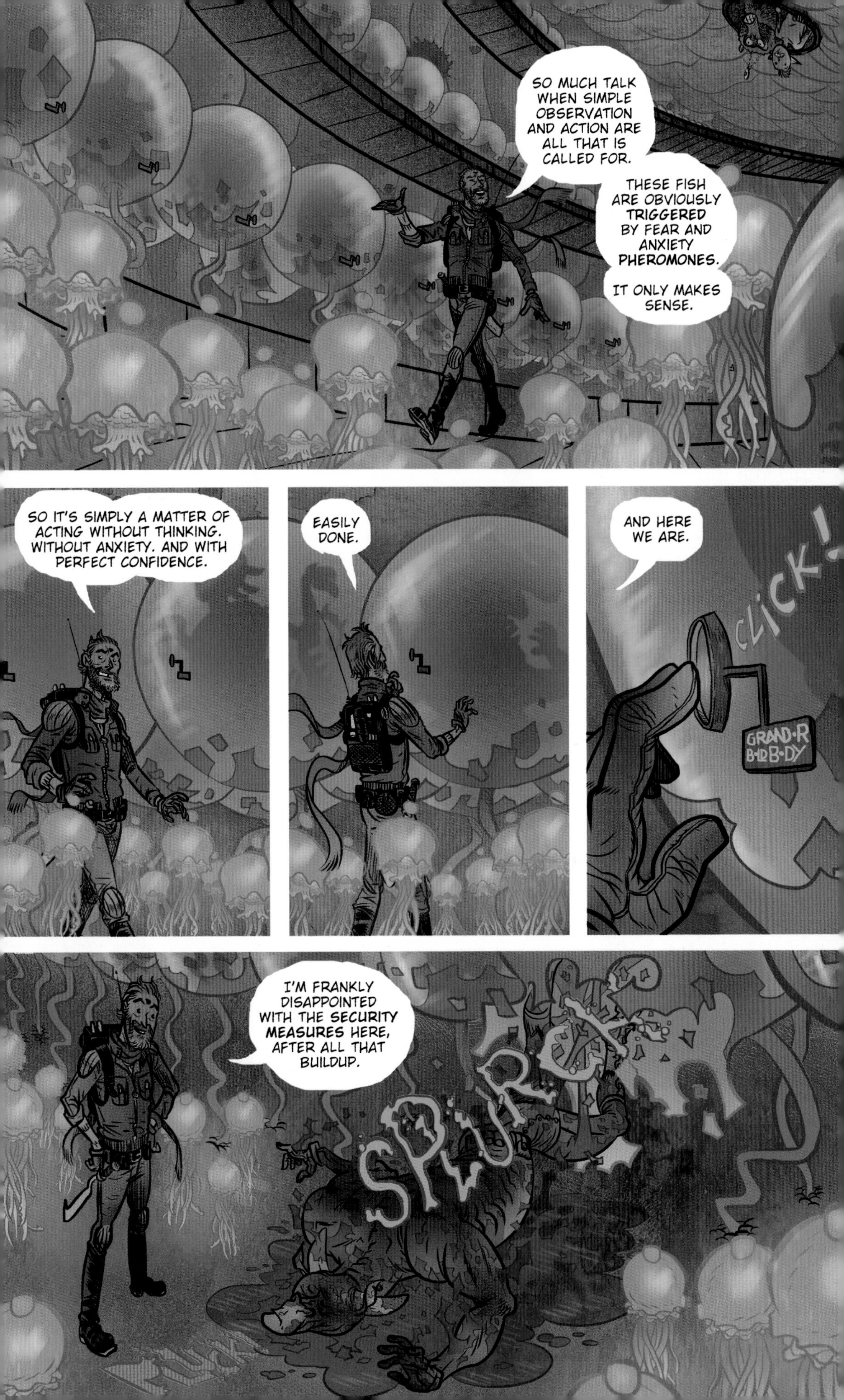
SO MUCH TALK WHEN SIMPLE OBSERVATION AND ACTION ARE ALL THAT IS CALLED FOR.
THESE FISH ARE OBVIOUSLY **TRIGGERED** BY FEAR AND ANXIETY **PHEROMONES.**
IT ONLY MAKES SENSE.
SO IT'S SIMPLY A MATTER OF ACTING WITHOUT THINKING. WITHOUT ANXIETY. AND WITH PERFECT CONFIDENCE.
EASILY DONE.
AND HERE WE ARE.
CLICK!
I'M FRANKLY DISAPPOINTED WITH THE **SECURITY MEASURES** HERE, AFTER ALL THAT BUILDUP.

GRANDOR BOLDBODY?
I'M BOONE DIAS AND I'M HERE TO RESCUE YOU.
IF YOU REMAIN CALM, WE SHOULD BE ABLE TO PROCEED TO THE EXIT WITHOUT AS MUCH AS--

HADES AND DAMNATION, THAT SUCKED!

NO, WAIT!
PLEASE! IT'S IMPERATIVE THAT YOU REMAIN CALM! YOUR PHEROMONES WILL SET THEM OFF--!

YOU COME HIGHLY RECOMMENDED BY MY COLLEAGUE. FEEL FREE TO TAKE A BRIEF RESPITE AND THEN WE CAN BE ON OUR--

WHAT ARE YOU TALKING ABOUT? WE GOTTA MOVE, SON, OR WE GONNA BE DRAGON FOOD!

IZZWEE-WEEOOWEEOOOWEEE

BOOM!!

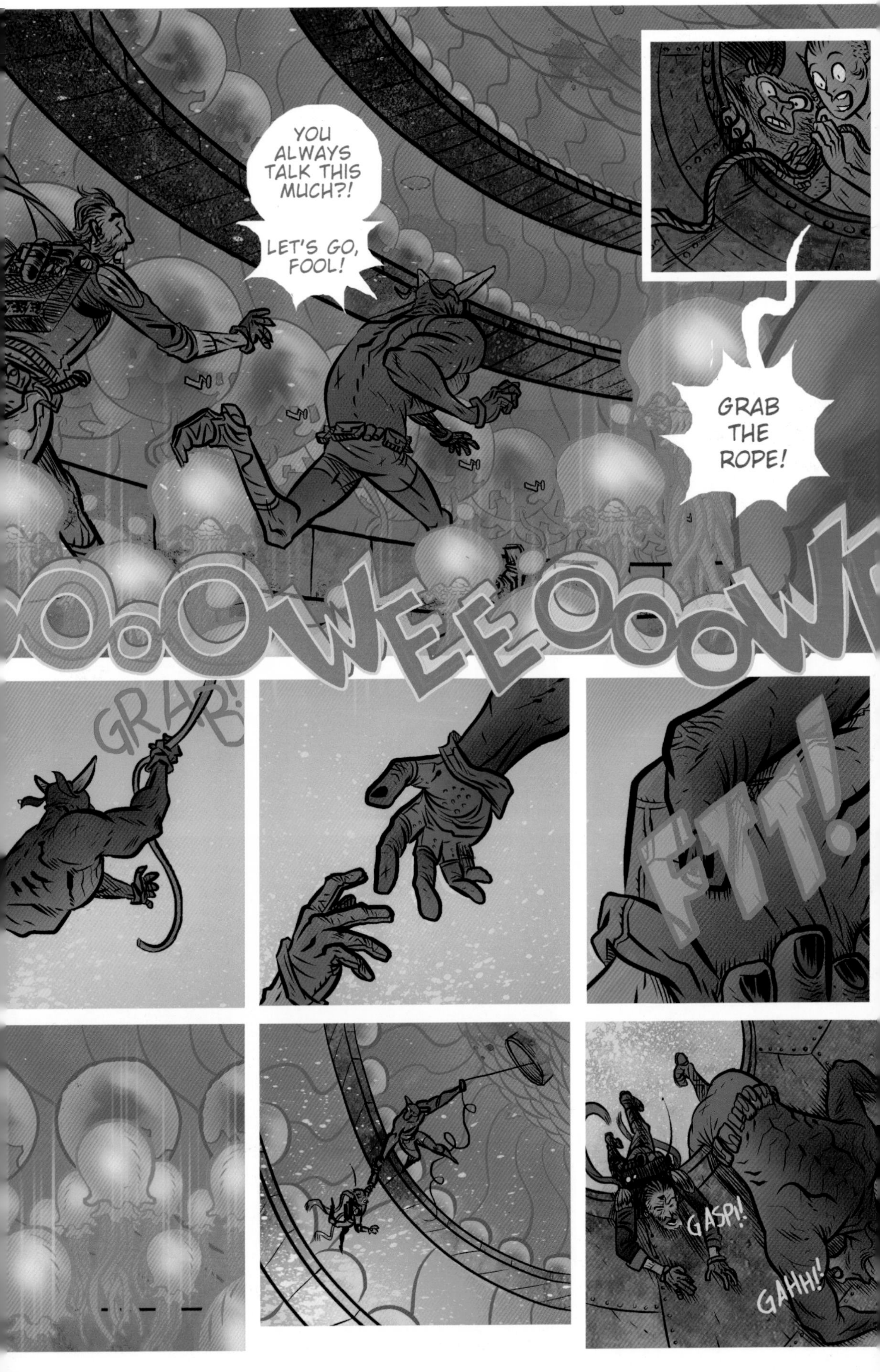
YOU ALWAYS TALK THIS MUCH?!
LET'S GO, FOOL!
GRAB THE ROPE!
OOOWEEOOOW
GRAB!
FTT!
GASP!
GAHH!

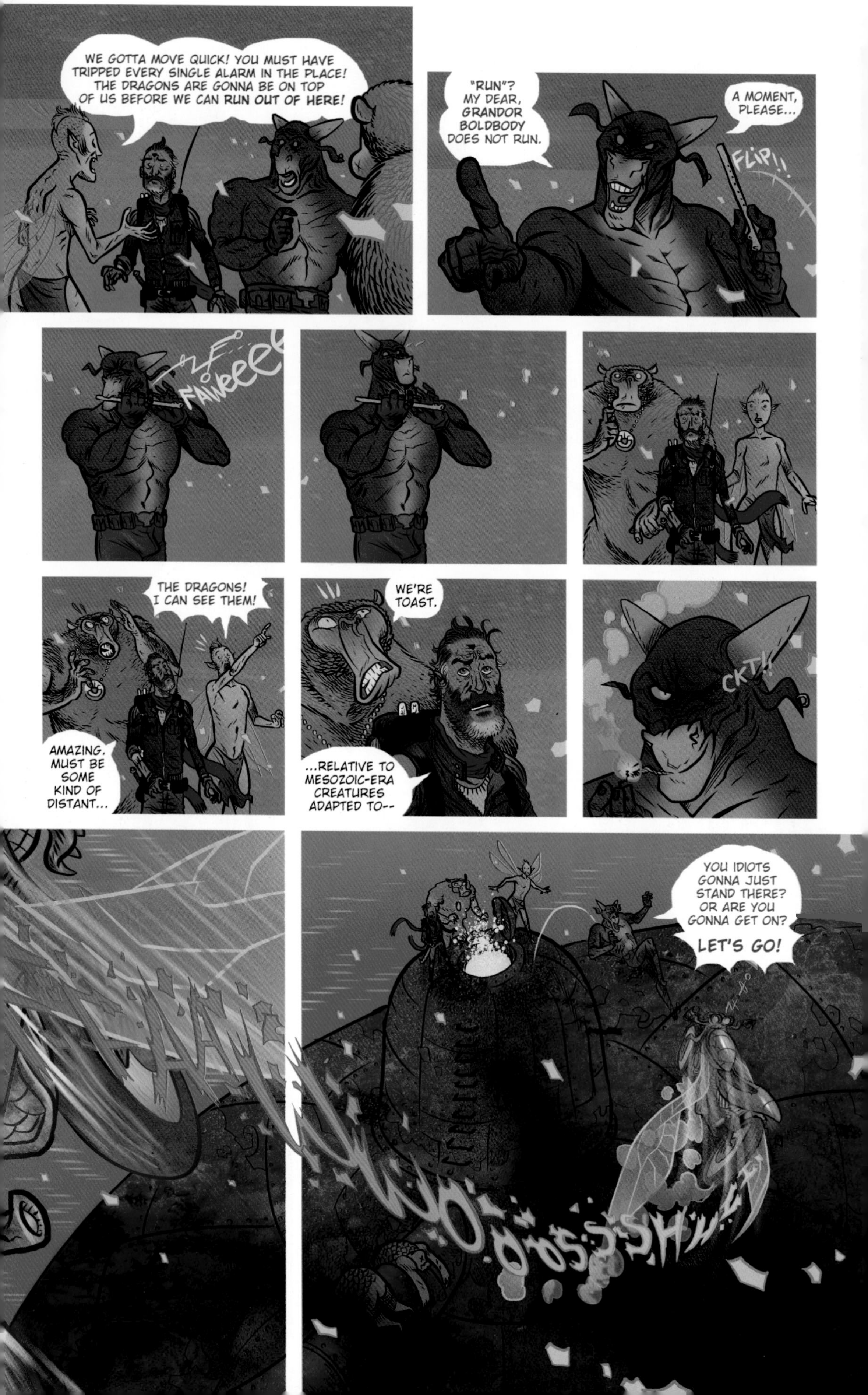
WE GOTTA MOVE QUICK! YOU MUST HAVE TRIPPED EVERY SINGLE ALARM IN THE PLACE! THE DRAGONS ARE GONNA BE ON TOP OF US BEFORE WE CAN RUN OUT OF HERE!
"RUN"? MY DEAR, GRANDOR BOLDBODY DOES NOT RUN.
A MOMENT, PLEASE...
FLIP!!
FAWEEEE
THE DRAGONS! I CAN SEE THEM!
AMAZING. MUST BE SOME KIND OF DISTANT...
WE'RE TOAST.
...RELATIVE TO MESOZOIC-ERA CREATURES ADAPTED TO--
CKT!!
YOU IDIOTS GONNA JUST STAND THERE? OR ARE YOU GONNA GET ON?
LET'S GO!

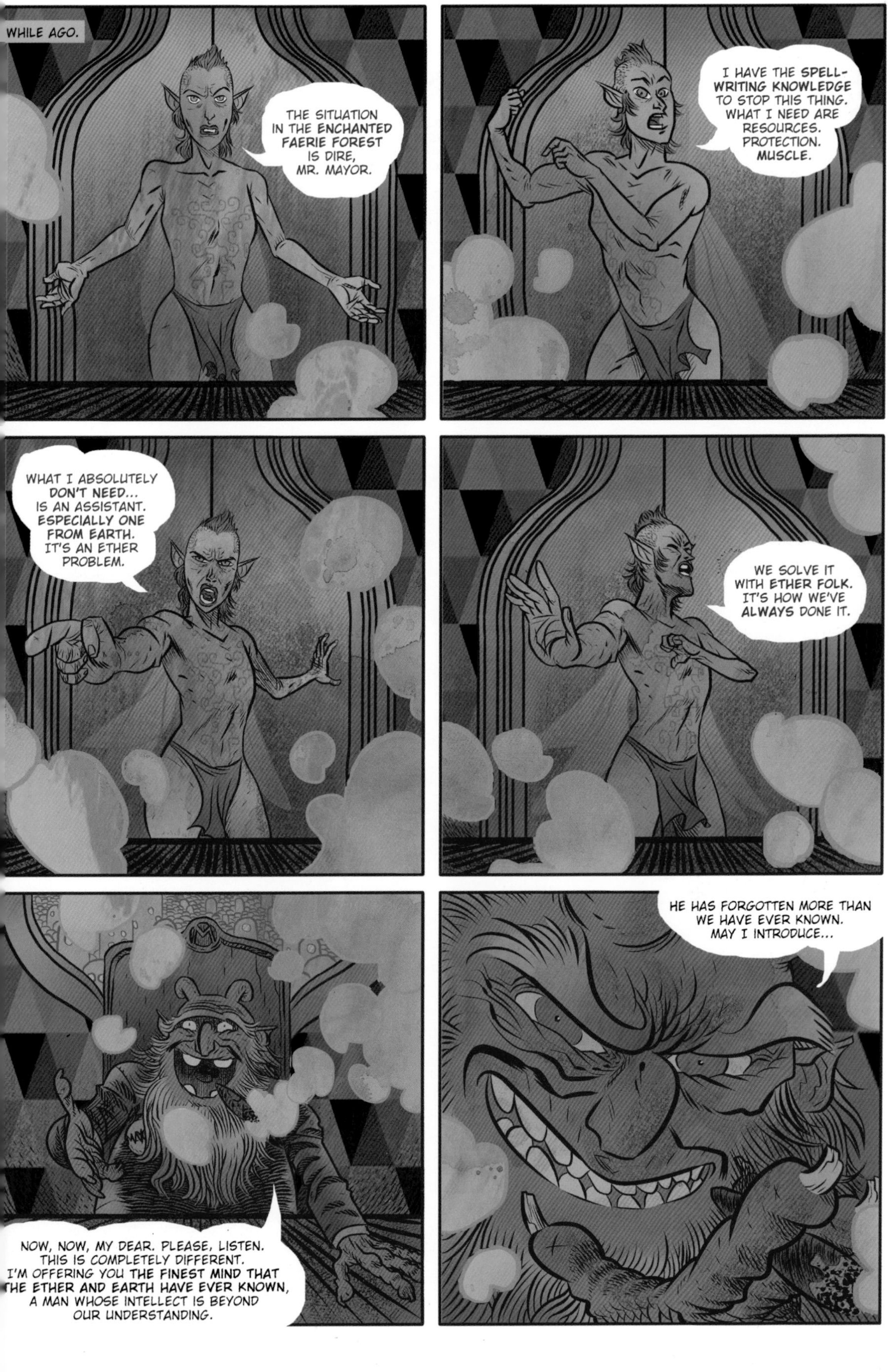
WHILE AGO.
THE SITUATION IN THE ENCHANTED FAERIE FOREST IS DIRE, MR. MAYOR.
I HAVE THE SPELL-WRITING KNOWLEDGE TO STOP THIS THING. WHAT I NEED ARE RESOURCES. PROTECTION. MUSCLE.
WHAT I ABSOLUTELY DON'T NEED... IS AN ASSISTANT. ESPECIALLY ONE FROM EARTH. IT'S AN ETHER PROBLEM.
WE SOLVE IT WITH ETHER FOLK. IT'S HOW WE'VE ALWAYS DONE IT.
NOW, NOW, MY DEAR. PLEASE, LISTEN. THIS IS COMPLETELY DIFFERENT. I'M OFFERING YOU THE FINEST MIND THAT THE ETHER AND EARTH HAVE EVER KNOWN, A MAN WHOSE INTELLECT IS BEYOND OUR UNDERSTANDING.
HE HAS FORGOTTEN MORE THAN WE HAVE EVER KNOWN. MAY I INTRODUCE...

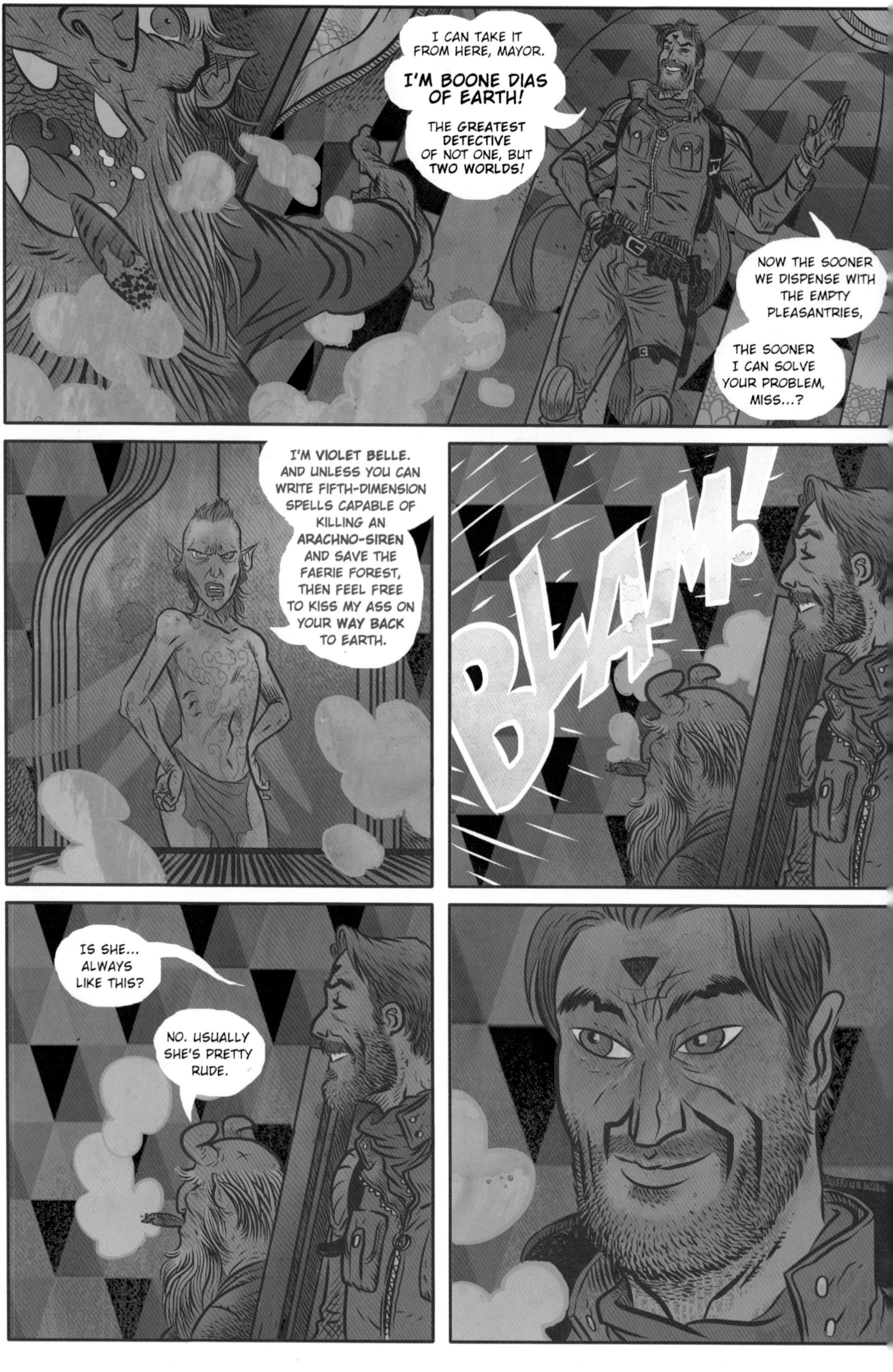
I CAN TAKE IT FROM HERE, MAYOR.
I'M BOONE DIAS OF EARTH!
THE GREATEST DETECTIVE OF NOT ONE, BUT TWO WORLDS!
NOW THE SOONER WE DISPENSE WITH THE EMPTY PLEASANTRIES,
THE SOONER I CAN SOLVE YOUR PROBLEM, MISS...?
I'M VIOLET BELLE. AND UNLESS YOU CAN WRITE FIFTH-DIMENSION SPELLS CAPABLE OF KILLING AN ARACHNO-SIREN AND SAVE THE FAERIE FOREST, THEN FEEL FREE TO KISS MY ASS ON YOUR WAY BACK TO EARTH.
BLAM!
IS SHE... ALWAYS LIKE THIS?
NO. USUALLY SHE'S PRETTY RUDE.

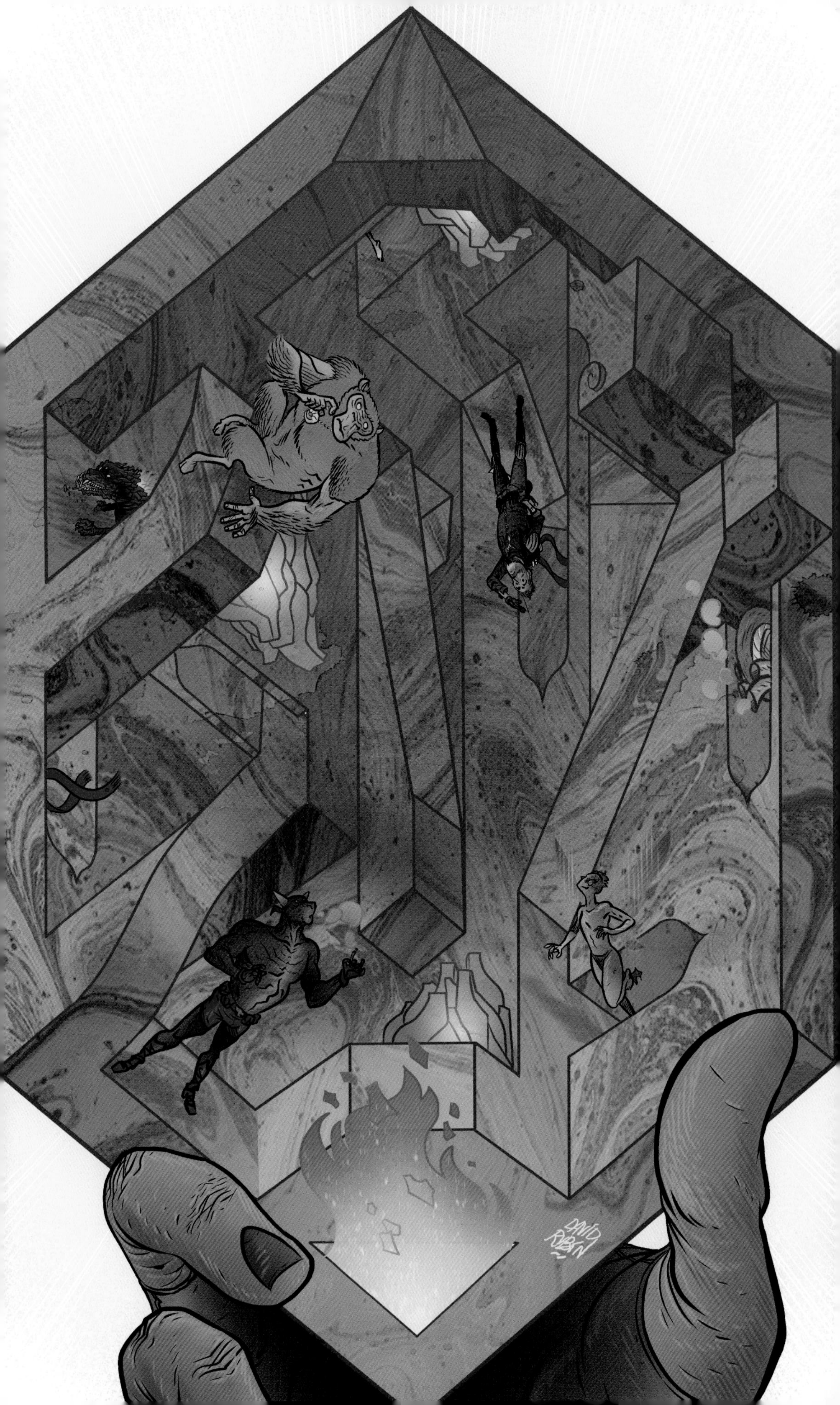
DAVID RUBÍN

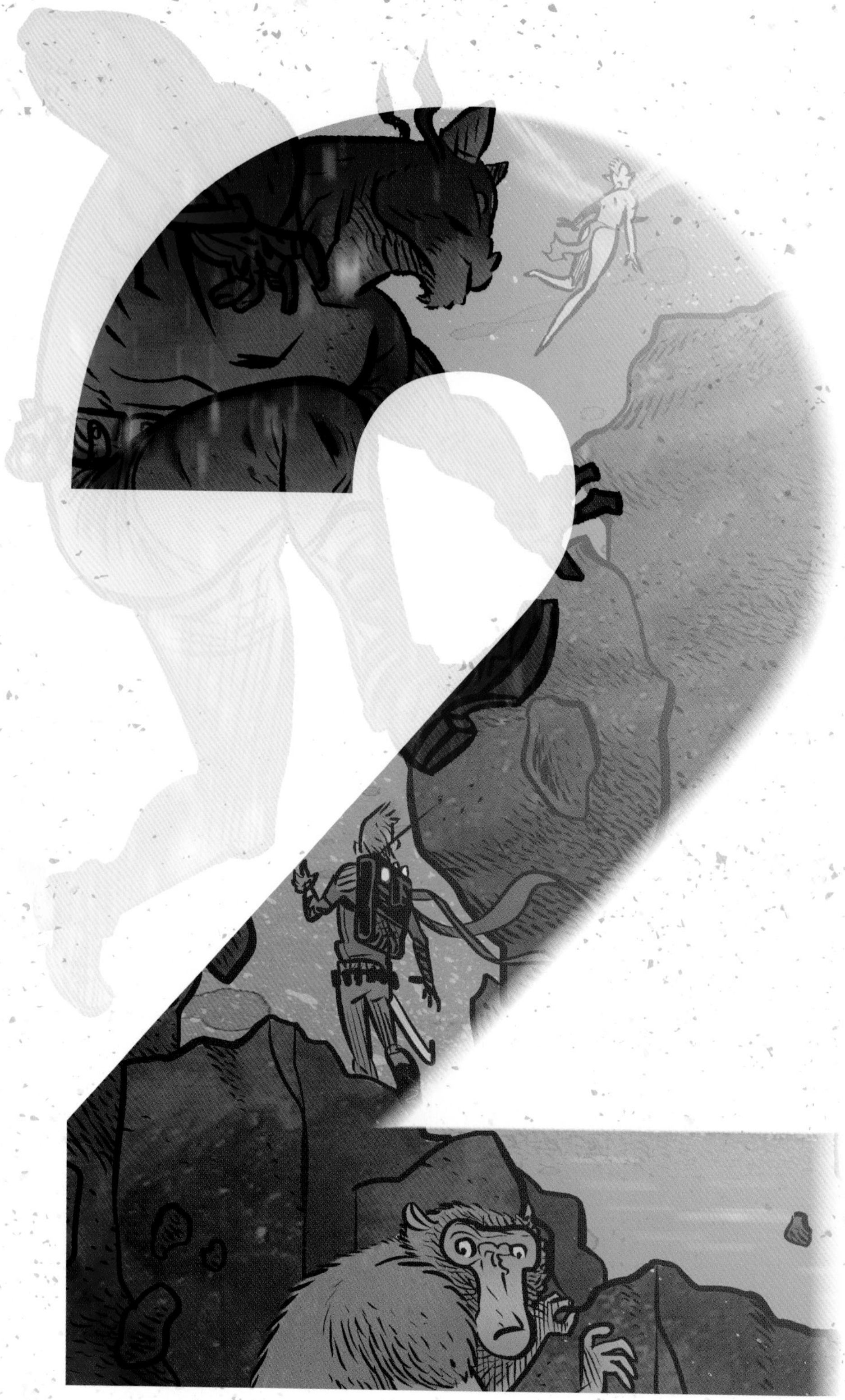

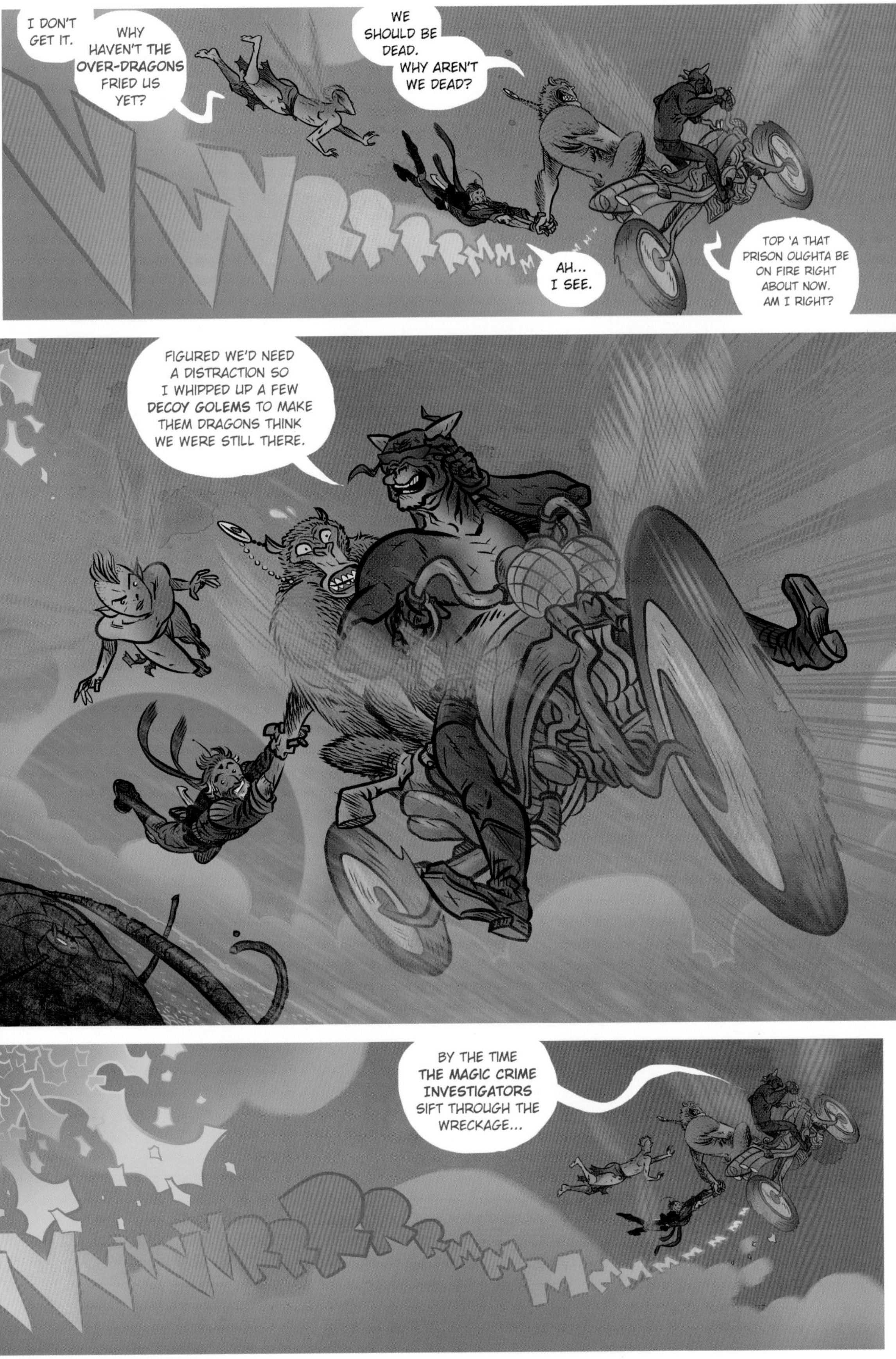
I DON'T GET IT.
WHY HAVEN'T THE OVER-DRAGONS FRIED US YET?
WE SHOULD BE DEAD.
WHY AREN'T WE DEAD?
VVVRRRRMMMMMM
AH... I SEE.
TOP 'A THAT PRISON OUGHTA BE ON FIRE RIGHT ABOUT NOW. AM I RIGHT?
FIGURED WE'D NEED A DISTRACTION SO I WHIPPED UP A FEW DECOY GOLEMS TO MAKE THEM DRAGONS THINK WE WERE STILL THERE.
BY THE TIME THE MAGIC CRIME INVESTIGATORS SIFT THROUGH THE WRECKAGE...
VVVRRRRMMMMMMMM

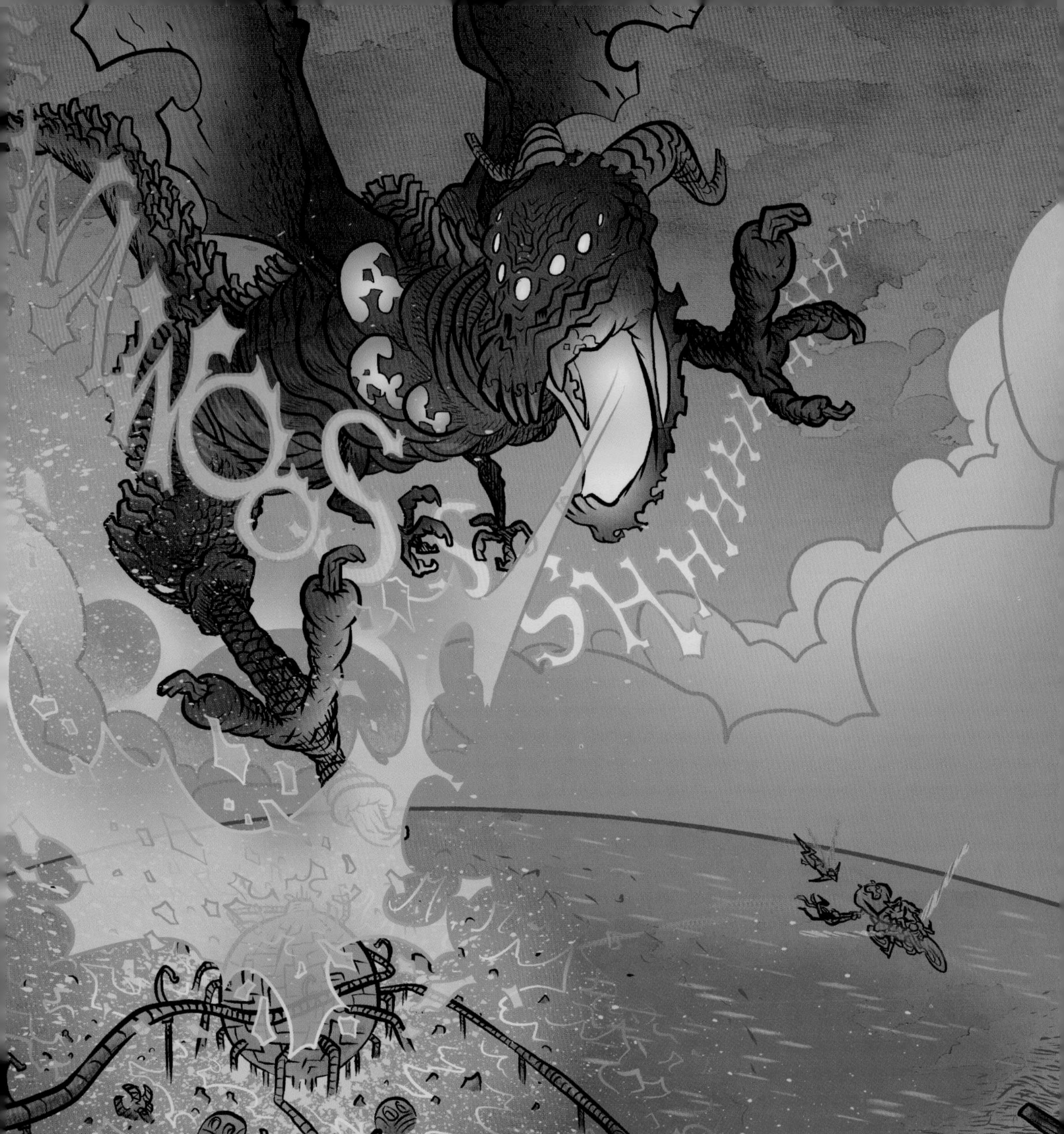

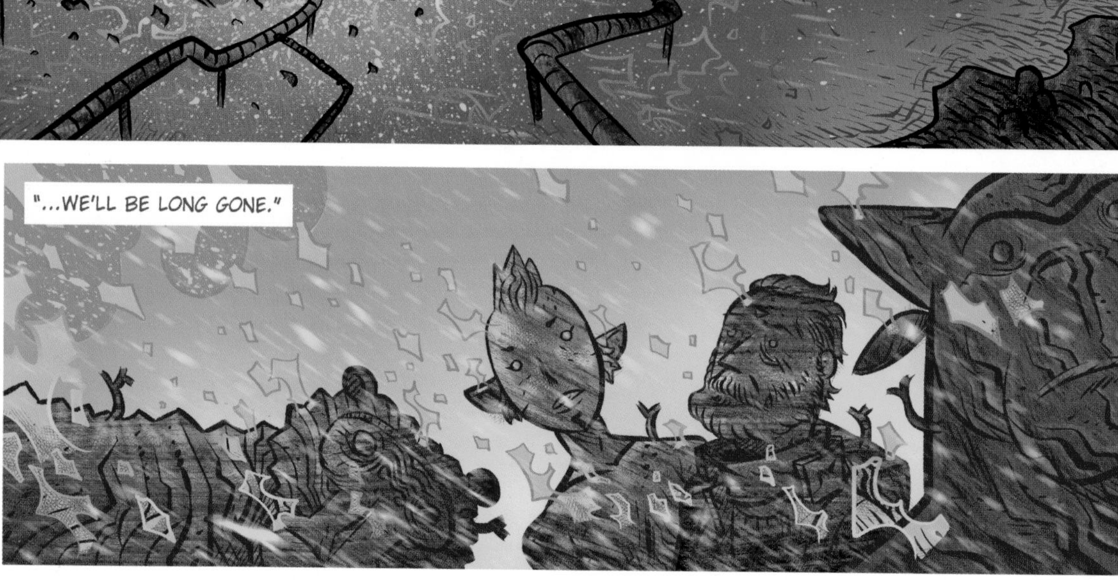
"...WE'LL BE LONG GONE."

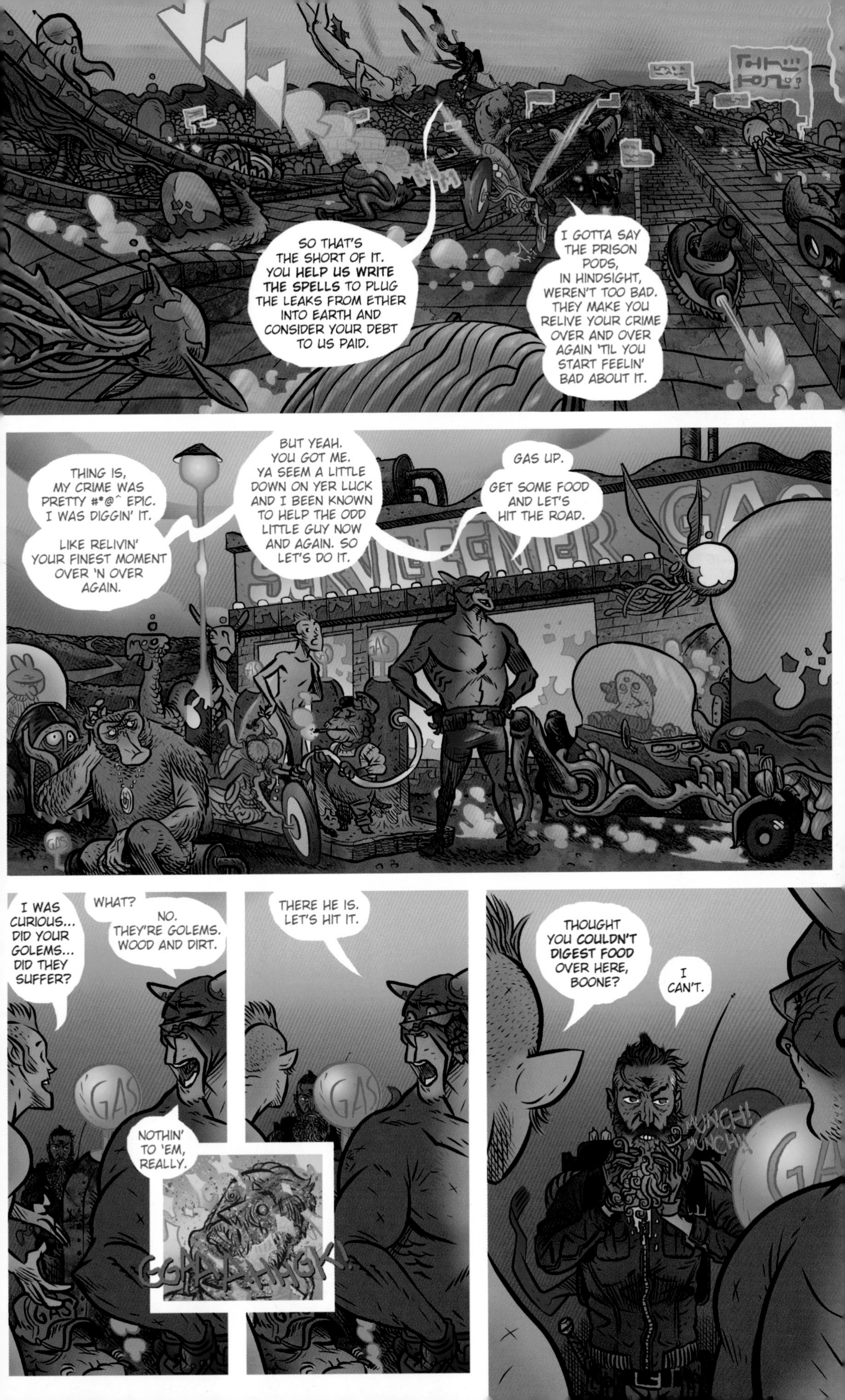
SO THAT'S THE SHORT OF IT. YOU HELP US WRITE THE SPELLS TO PLUG THE LEAKS FROM ETHER INTO EARTH AND CONSIDER YOUR DEBT TO US PAID.
I GOTTA SAY THE PRISON PODS, IN HINDSIGHT, WEREN'T TOO BAD. THEY MAKE YOU RELIVE YOUR CRIME OVER AND OVER AGAIN 'TIL YOU START FEELIN' BAD ABOUT IT.
THING IS, MY CRIME WAS PRETTY #*@^ EPIC. I WAS DIGGIN' IT.
LIKE RELIVIN' YOUR FINEST MOMENT OVER 'N OVER AGAIN.
BUT YEAH. YOU GOT ME. YA SEEM A LITTLE DOWN ON YER LUCK AND I BEEN KNOWN TO HELP THE ODD LITTLE GUY NOW AND AGAIN. SO LET'S DO IT.
GAS UP.
GET SOME FOOD AND LET'S HIT THE ROAD.
I WAS CURIOUS... DID YOUR GOLEMS... DID THEY SUFFER?
WHAT?
NO. THEY'RE GOLEMS. WOOD AND DIRT.
NOTHIN' TO 'EM, REALLY.
GGRAAHHGK!
THERE HE IS. LET'S HIT IT.
THOUGHT YOU COULDN'T DIGEST FOOD OVER HERE, BOONE?
I CAN'T.
MUNCH! MUNCH!

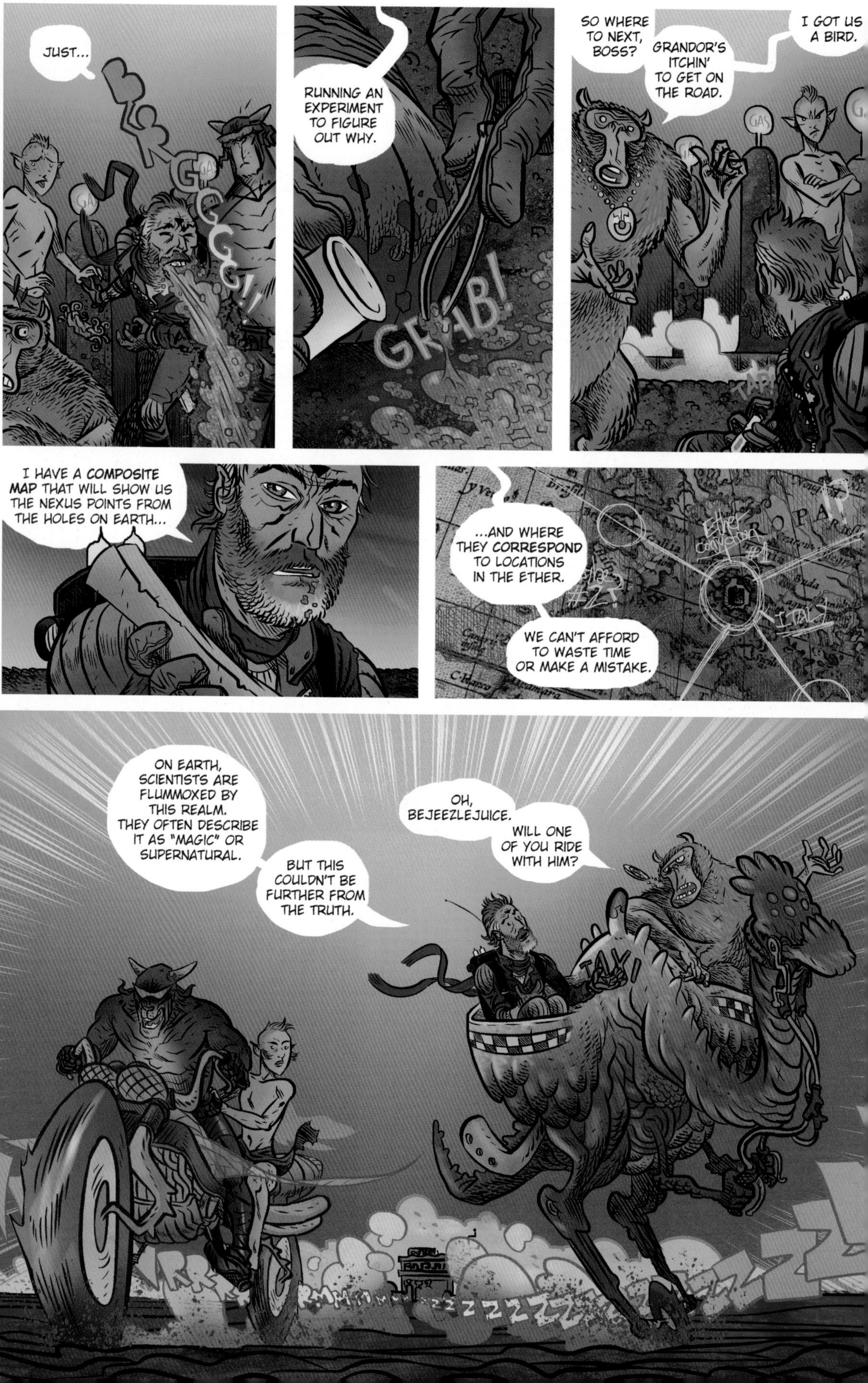
JUST...
RUNNING AN EXPERIMENT TO FIGURE OUT WHY.
GRAB!
SO WHERE TO NEXT, BOSS?
GRANDOR'S ITCHIN' TO GET ON THE ROAD.
I GOT US A BIRD.
I HAVE A COMPOSITE MAP THAT WILL SHOW US THE NEXUS POINTS FROM THE HOLES ON EARTH...
...AND WHERE THEY CORRESPOND TO LOCATIONS IN THE ETHER.
WE CAN'T AFFORD TO WASTE TIME OR MAKE A MISTAKE.
ON EARTH, SCIENTISTS ARE FLUMMOXED BY THIS REALM. THEY OFTEN DESCRIBE IT AS "MAGIC" OR SUPERNATURAL.
BUT THIS COULDN'T BE FURTHER FROM THE TRUTH.
OH, BEJEEZLEJUICE.
WILL ONE OF YOU RIDE WITH HIM?
TAXI

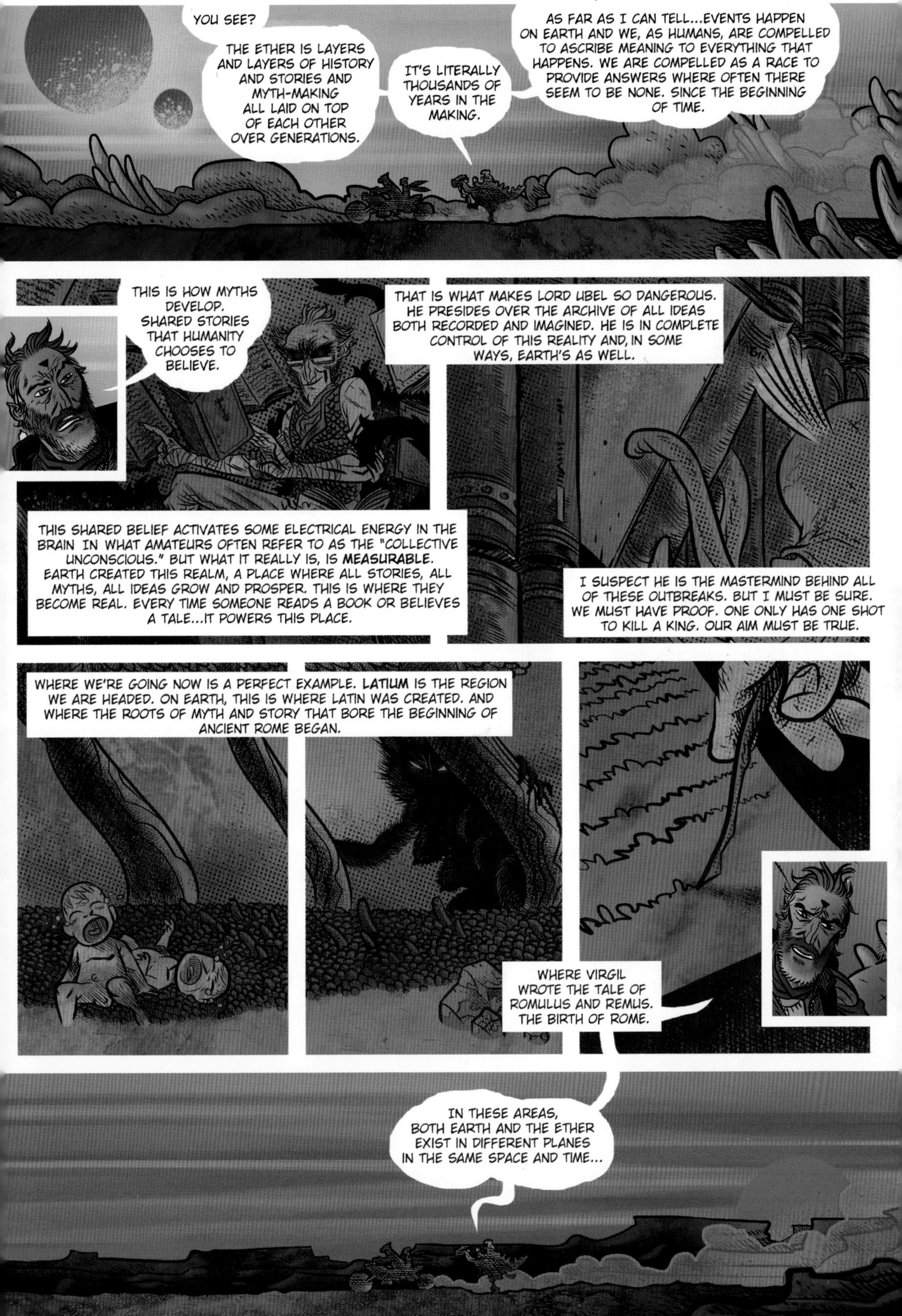
YOU SEE?
THE ETHER IS LAYERS AND LAYERS OF HISTORY AND STORIES AND MYTH-MAKING ALL LAID ON TOP OF EACH OTHER OVER GENERATIONS.
IT'S LITERALLY THOUSANDS OF YEARS IN THE MAKING.
AS FAR AS I CAN TELL...EVENTS HAPPEN ON EARTH AND WE, AS HUMANS, ARE COMPELLED TO ASCRIBE MEANING TO EVERYTHING THAT HAPPENS. WE ARE COMPELLED AS A RACE TO PROVIDE ANSWERS WHERE OFTEN THERE SEEM TO BE NONE. SINCE THE BEGINNING OF TIME.
THIS IS HOW MYTHS DEVELOP. SHARED STORIES THAT HUMANITY CHOOSES TO BELIEVE.
THIS SHARED BELIEF ACTIVATES SOME ELECTRICAL ENERGY IN THE BRAIN IN WHAT AMATEURS OFTEN REFER TO AS THE "COLLECTIVE UNCONSCIOUS." BUT WHAT IT REALLY IS, IS **MEASURABLE**. EARTH CREATED THIS REALM, A PLACE WHERE ALL STORIES, ALL MYTHS, ALL IDEAS GROW AND PROSPER. THIS IS WHERE THEY BECOME REAL. EVERY TIME SOMEONE READS A BOOK OR BELIEVES A TALE...IT POWERS THIS PLACE.
THAT IS WHAT MAKES LORD UBEL SO DANGEROUS. HE PRESIDES OVER THE ARCHIVE OF ALL IDEAS BOTH RECORDED AND IMAGINED. HE IS IN COMPLETE CONTROL OF THIS REALITY AND, IN SOME WAYS, EARTH'S AS WELL.
I SUSPECT HE IS THE MASTERMIND BEHIND ALL OF THESE OUTBREAKS. BUT I MUST BE SURE. WE MUST HAVE PROOF. ONE ONLY HAS ONE SHOT TO KILL A KING. OUR AIM MUST BE TRUE.
WHERE WE'RE GOING NOW IS A PERFECT EXAMPLE. **LATIUM** IS THE REGION WE ARE HEADED. ON EARTH, THIS IS WHERE LATIN WAS CREATED. AND WHERE THE ROOTS OF MYTH AND STORY THAT BORE THE BEGINNING OF ANCIENT ROME BEGAN.
WHERE VIRGIL WROTE THE TALE OF ROMULUS AND REMUS. THE BIRTH OF ROME.
IN THESE AREAS, BOTH EARTH AND THE ETHER EXIST IN DIFFERENT PLANES IN THE SAME SPACE AND TIME...

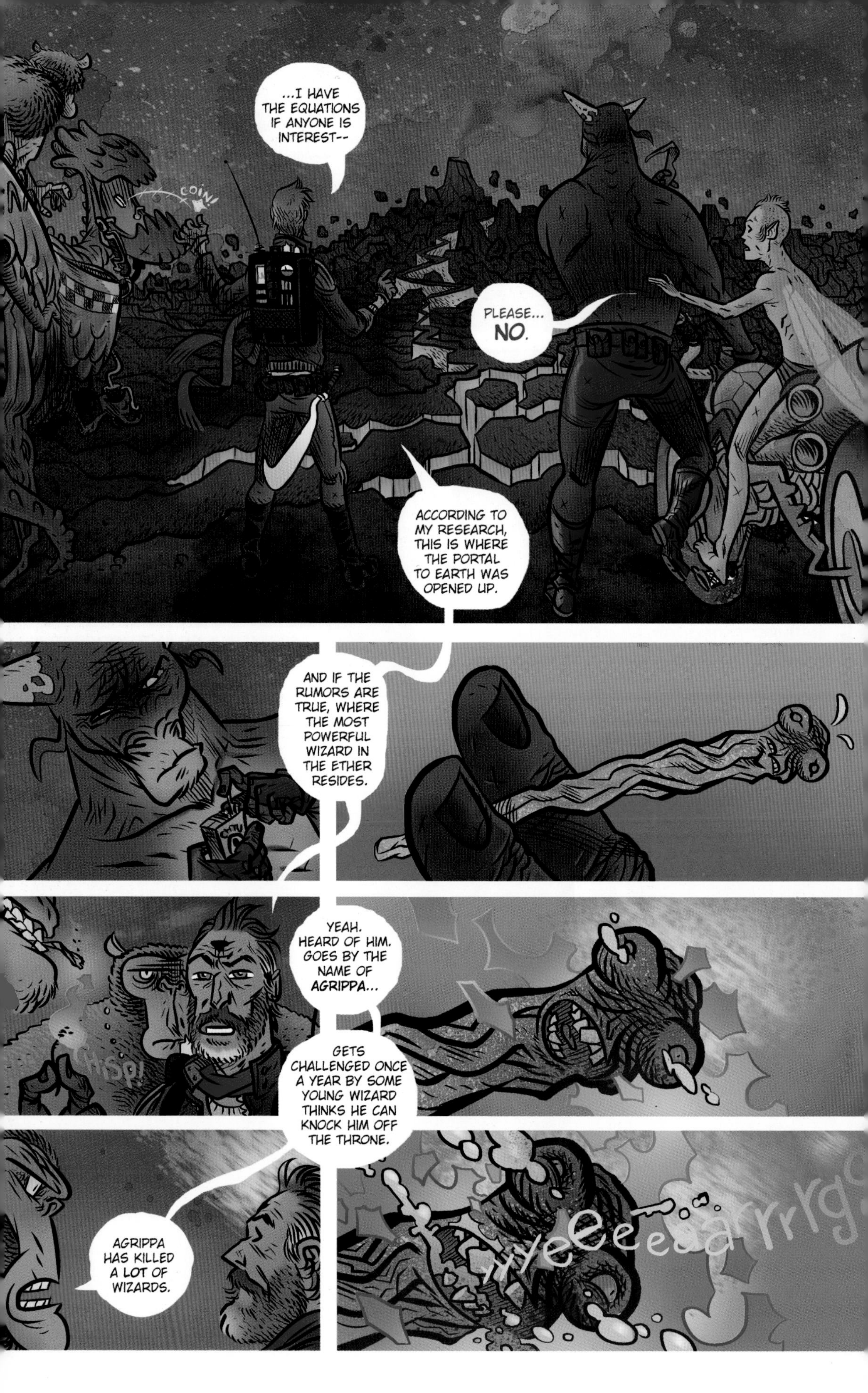
COIN!
...I HAVE THE EQUATIONS IF ANYONE IS INTEREST--
PLEASE... NO.
ACCORDING TO MY RESEARCH, THIS IS WHERE THE PORTAL TO EARTH WAS OPENED UP.
AND IF THE RUMORS ARE TRUE, WHERE THE MOST POWERFUL WIZARD IN THE ETHER RESIDES.
YEAH. HEARD OF HIM. GOES BY THE NAME OF **AGRIPPA**...
GETS CHALLENGED ONCE A YEAR BY SOME YOUNG WIZARD THINKS HE CAN KNOCK HIM OFF THE THRONE.
AGRIPPA HAS KILLED A LOT OF WIZARDS.

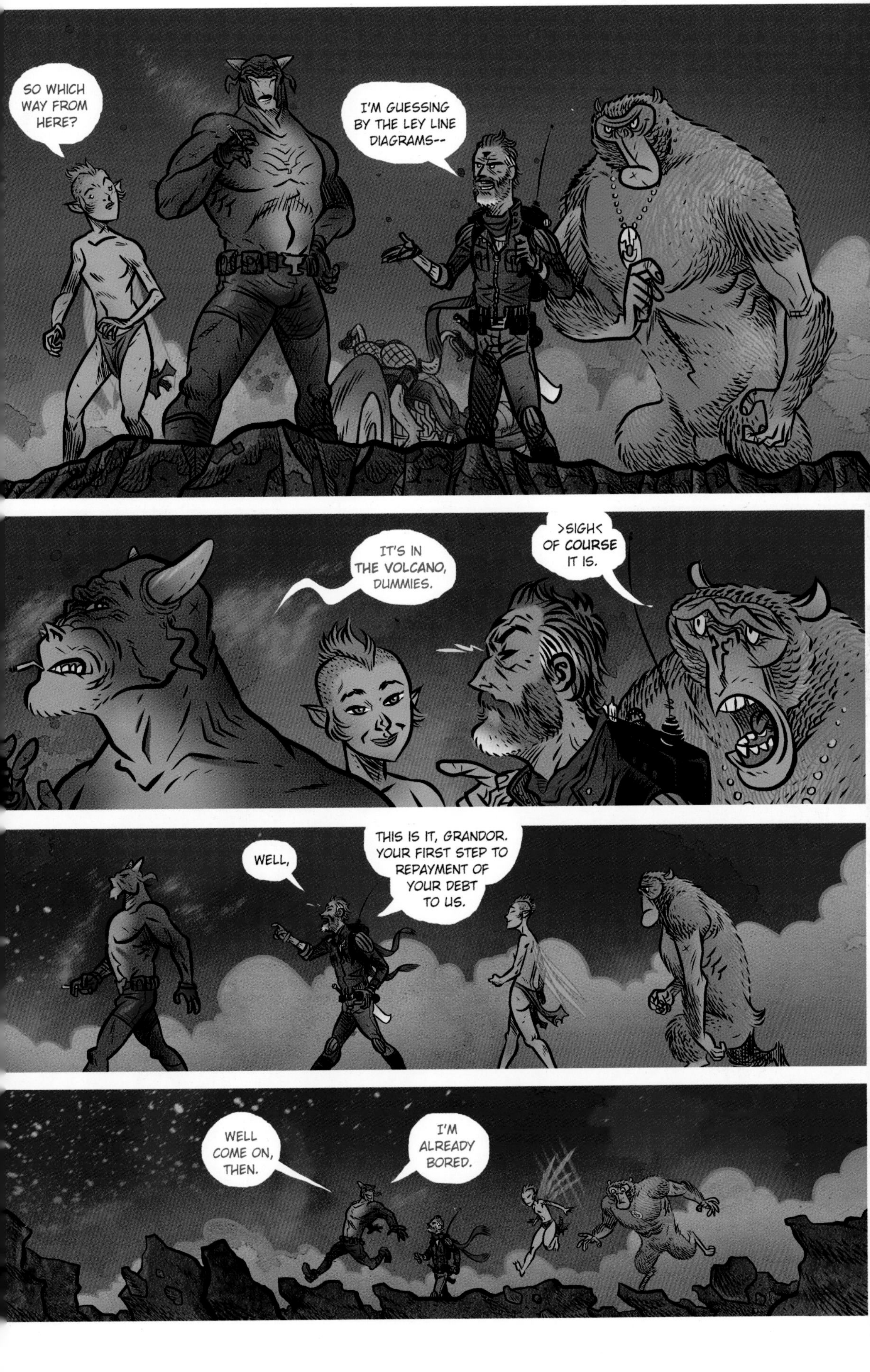
SO WHICH WAY FROM HERE?
I'M GUESSING BY THE LEY LINE DIAGRAMS--
IT'S IN THE VOLCANO, DUMMIES.
>SIGH< OF COURSE IT IS.
WELL,
THIS IS IT, GRANDOR. YOUR FIRST STEP TO REPAYMENT OF YOUR DEBT TO US.
WELL COME ON, THEN.
I'M ALREADY BORED.

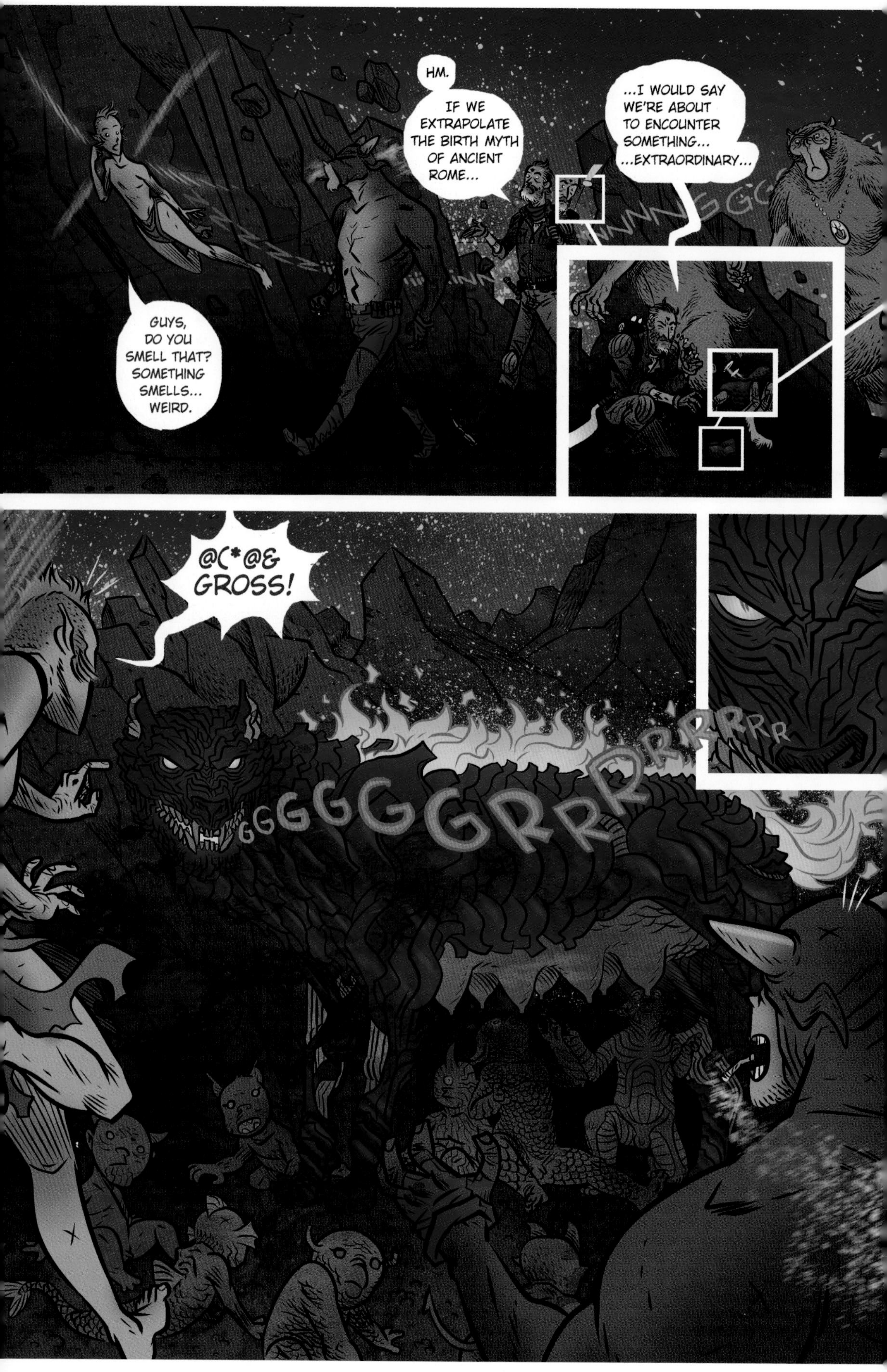
HM.
IF WE EXTRAPOLATE THE BIRTH MYTH OF ANCIENT ROME...
...I WOULD SAY WE'RE ABOUT TO ENCOUNTER SOMETHING... ...EXTRAORDINARY...
GUYS, DO YOU SMELL THAT? SOMETHING SMELLS... WEIRD.
@(*@& GROSS!
GGGGGGGRRRRRRRRRrr

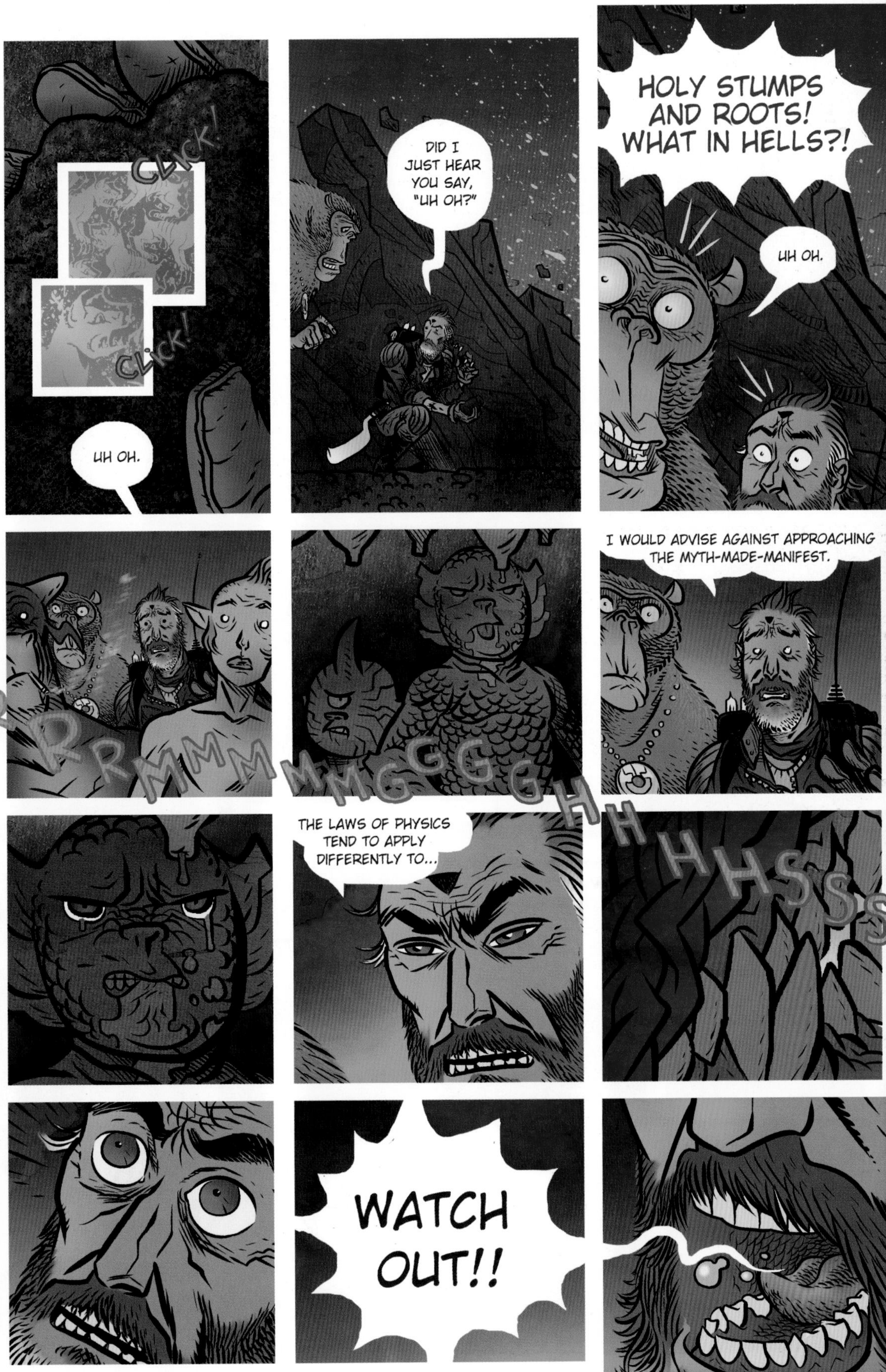
CLICK!
CLICK!
UH OH.
DID I JUST HEAR YOU SAY, "UH OH?"
HOLY STUMPS AND ROOTS! WHAT IN HELLS?!
UH OH.
RRRMMMMMMGGGGHHHHHSSS
I WOULD ADVISE AGAINST APPROACHING THE MYTH-MADE-MANIFEST.
THE LAWS OF PHYSICS TEND TO APPLY DIFFERENTLY TO...
WATCH OUT!!

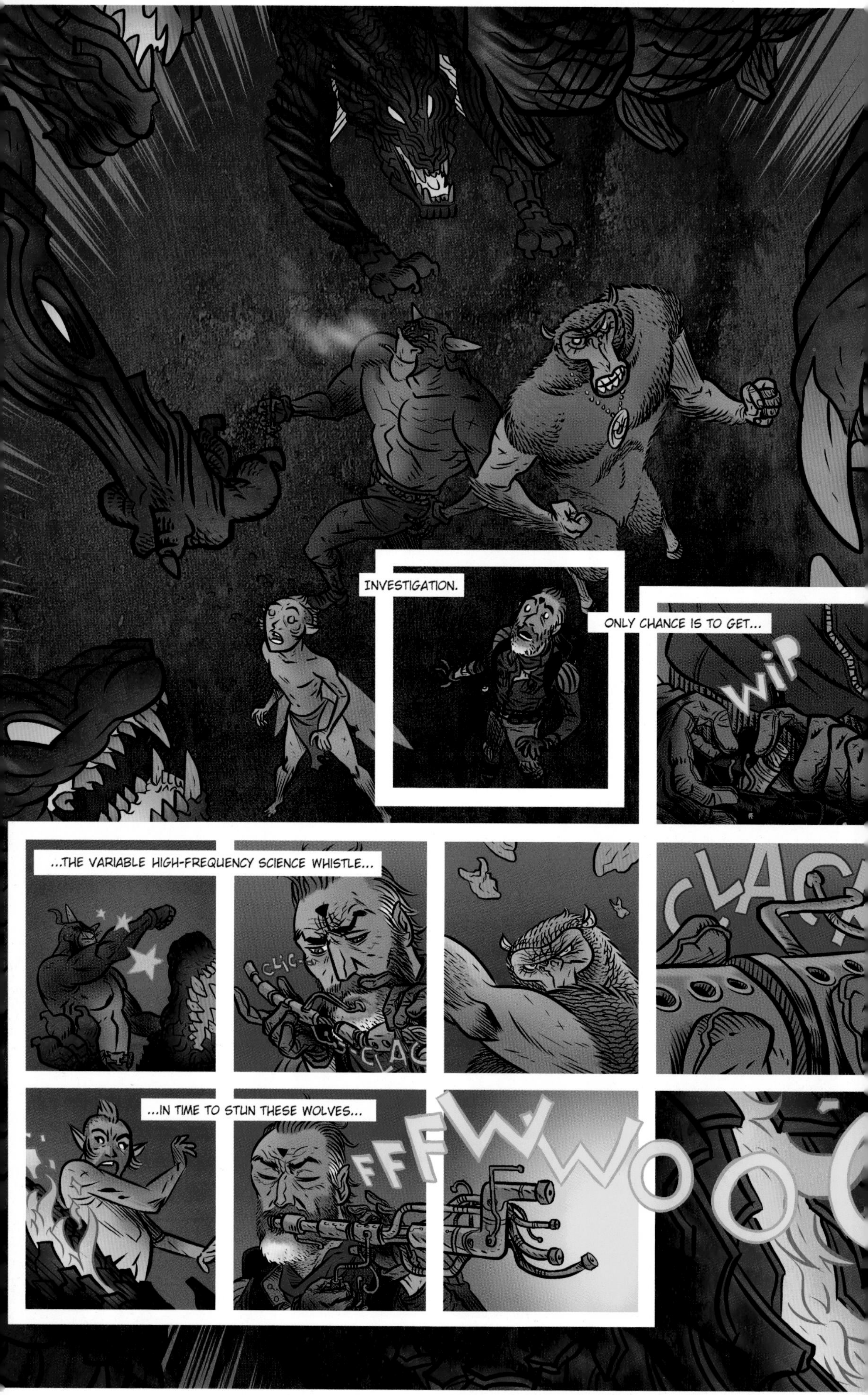
INVESTIGATION.
ONLY CHANCE IS TO GET...
WIP
...THE VARIABLE HIGH-FREQUENCY SCIENCE WHISTLE...
CLIC
CLAC
CLAC
...IN TIME TO STUN THESE WOLVES...
FFFWWOO

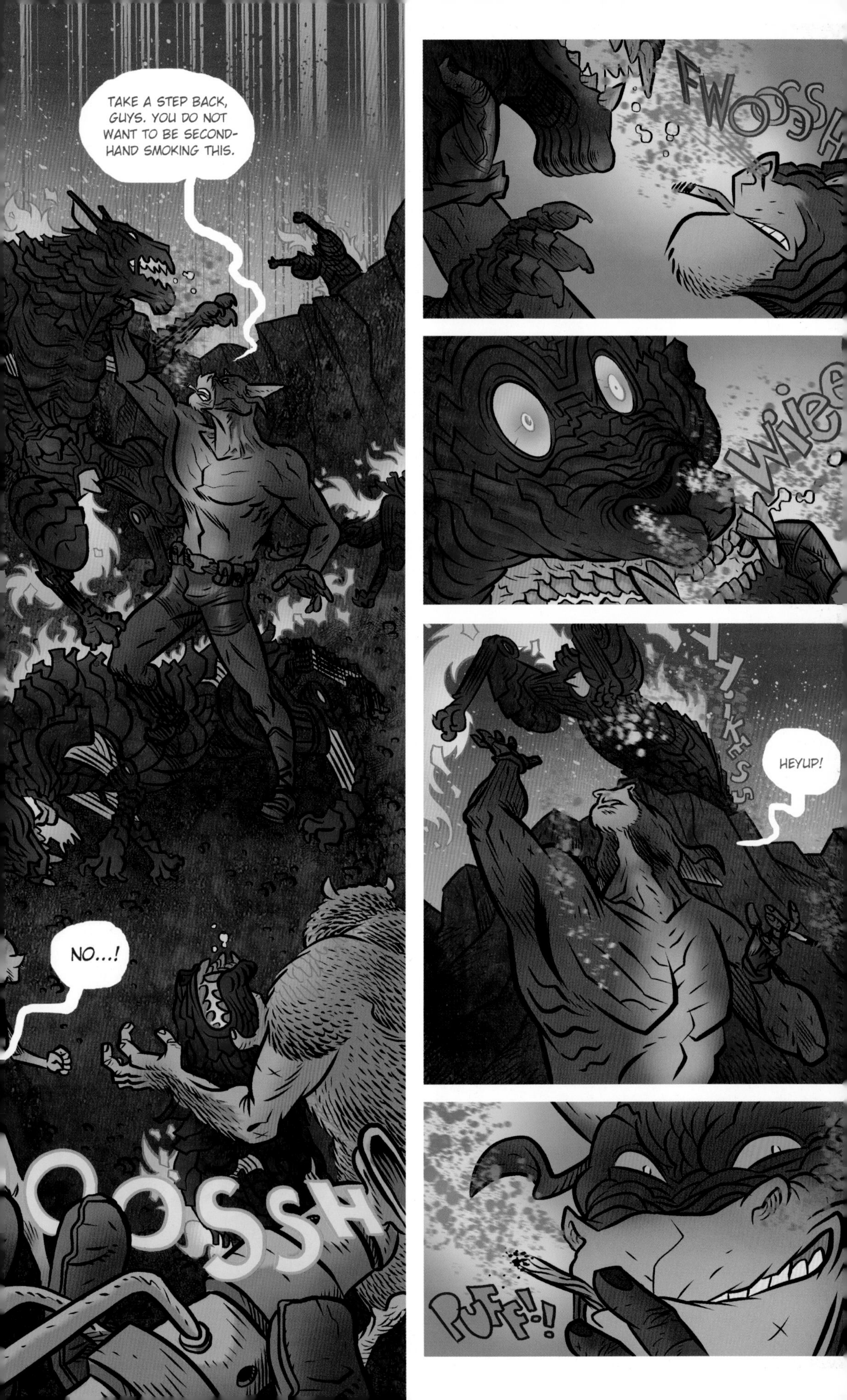
TAKE A STEP BACK, GUYS. YOU DO NOT WANT TO BE SECOND-HAND SMOKING THIS.
NO...!
OOSSH
FWOOSSH
WIEE
YIKESS
HEYUP!
PUFF!!

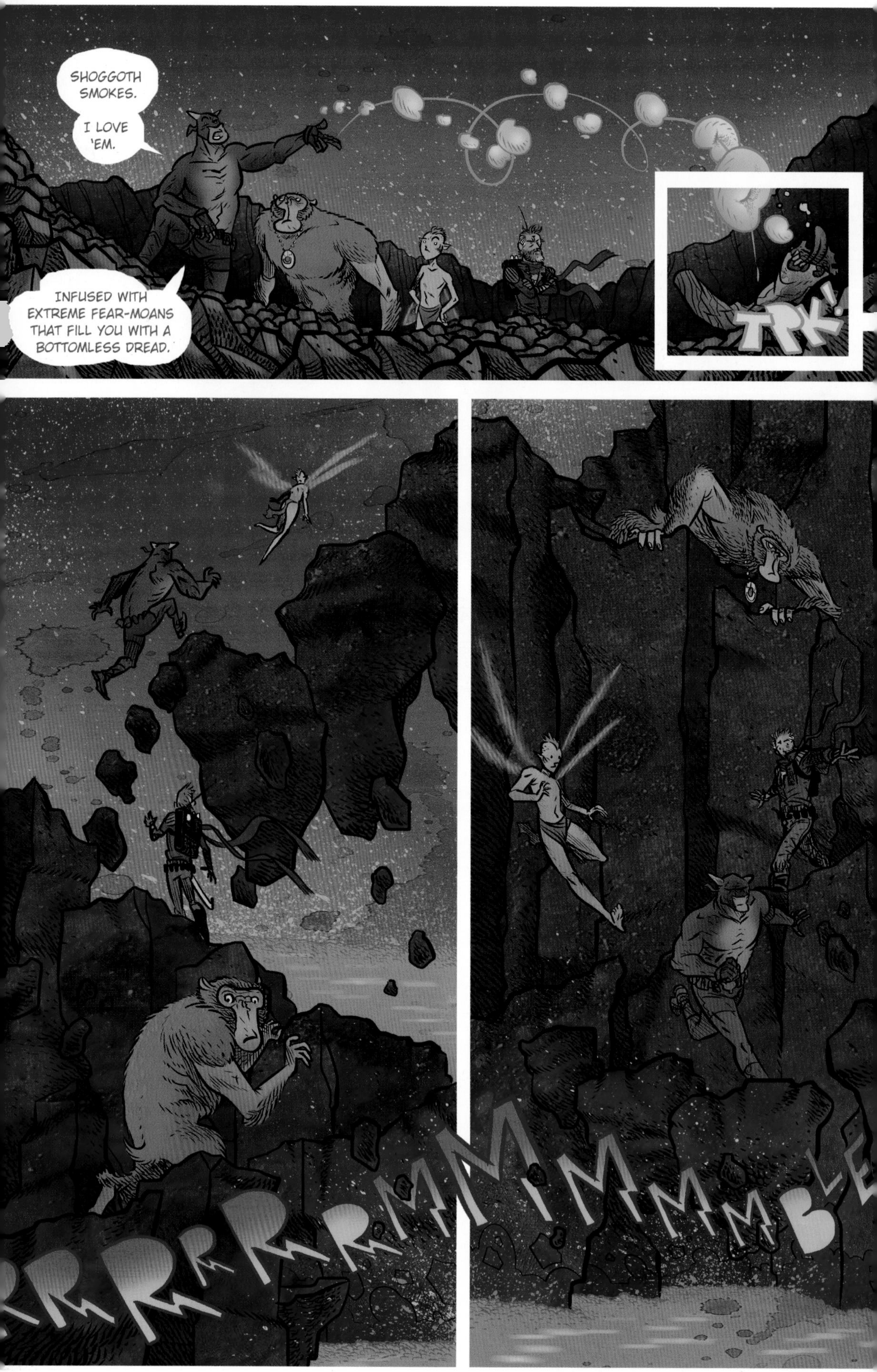
SHOGGOTH SMOKES.
I LOVE 'EM.
INFUSED WITH EXTREME FEAR-MOANS THAT FILL YOU WITH A BOTTOMLESS DREAD.
TPK!
RRRRRRRMMMMMMMBLE

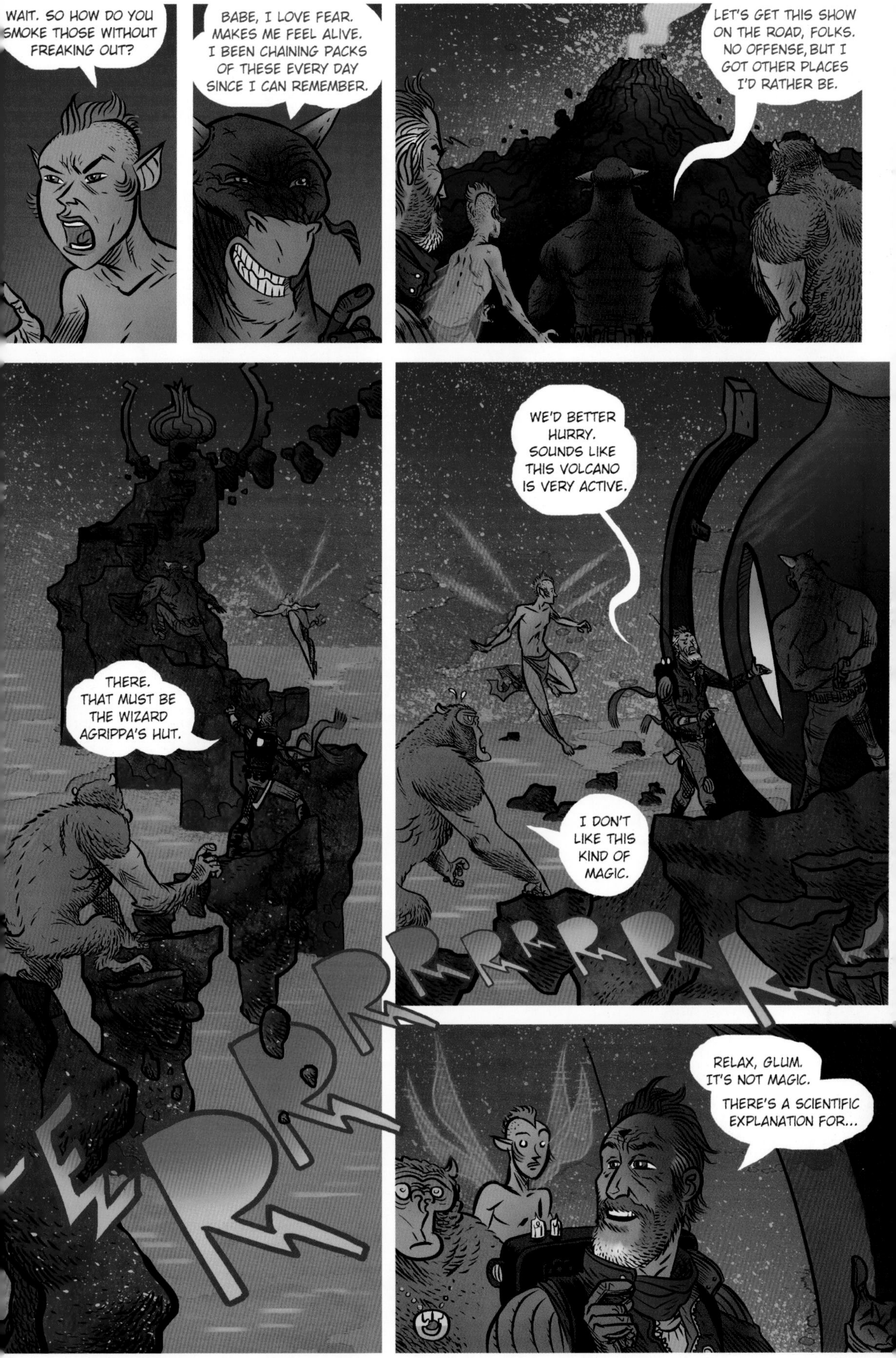
WAIT. SO HOW DO YOU SMOKE THOSE WITHOUT FREAKING OUT?
BABE, I LOVE FEAR. MAKES ME FEEL ALIVE. I BEEN CHAINING PACKS OF THESE EVERY DAY SINCE I CAN REMEMBER.
LET'S GET THIS SHOW ON THE ROAD, FOLKS. NO OFFENSE, BUT I GOT OTHER PLACES I'D RATHER BE.
THERE. THAT MUST BE THE WIZARD AGRIPPA'S HUT.
WE'D BETTER HURRY. SOUNDS LIKE THIS VOLCANO IS VERY ACTIVE.
I DON'T LIKE THIS KIND OF MAGIC.
RELAX, GLUM. IT'S NOT MAGIC.
THERE'S A SCIENTIFIC EXPLANATION FOR...

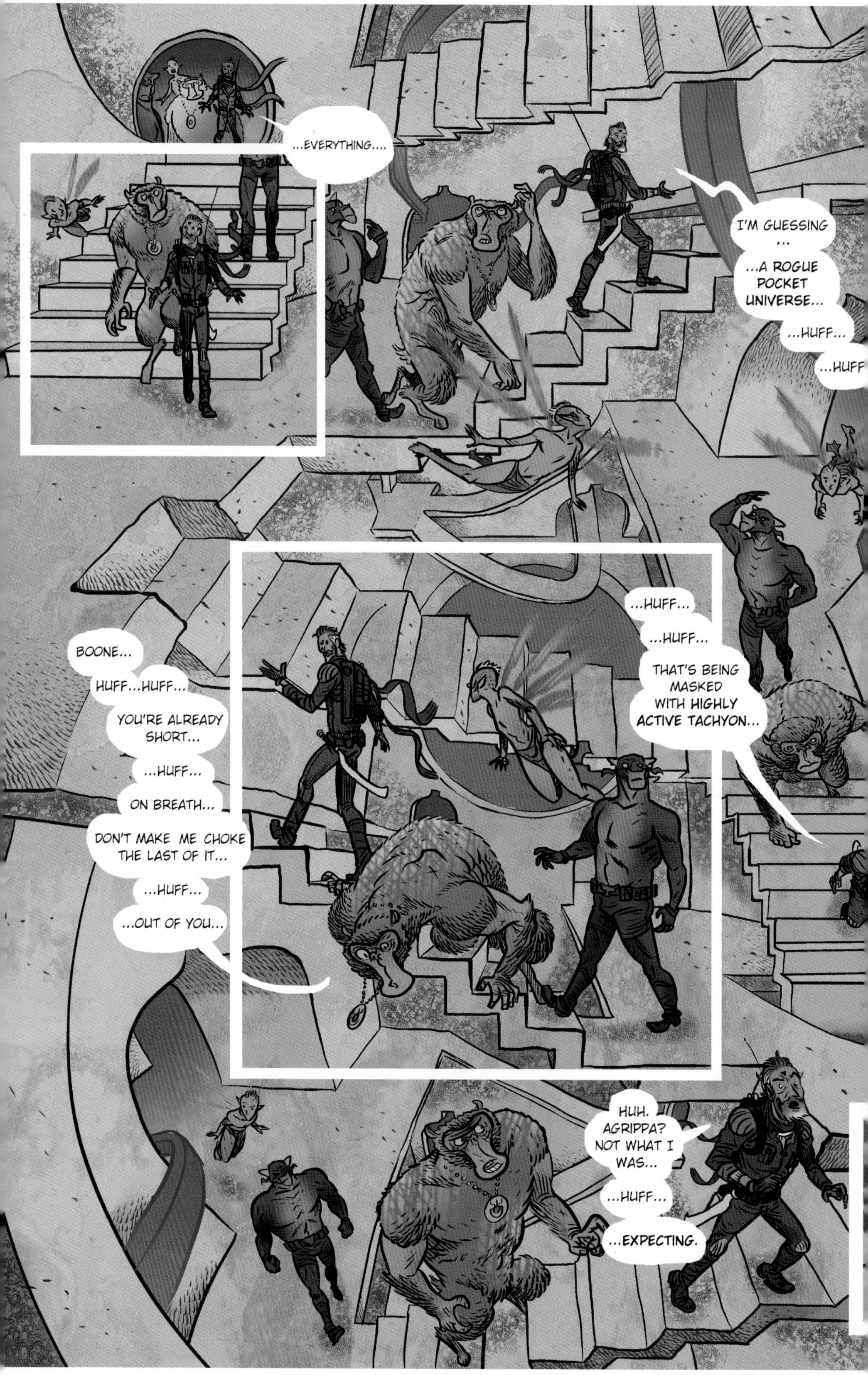
...EVERYTHING....
I'M GUESSING ...
...A ROGUE POCKET UNIVERSE...
...HUFF...
...HUFF
...HUFF...
...HUFF...
THAT'S BEING MASKED WITH HIGHLY ACTIVE TACHYON...
BOONE...
HUFF...HUFF...
YOU'RE ALREADY SHORT...
...HUFF...
ON BREATH...
DON'T MAKE ME CHOKE THE LAST OF IT...
...HUFF...
...OUT OF YOU...
HUH. AGRIPPA? NOT WHAT I WAS...
...HUFF...
...EXPECTING.

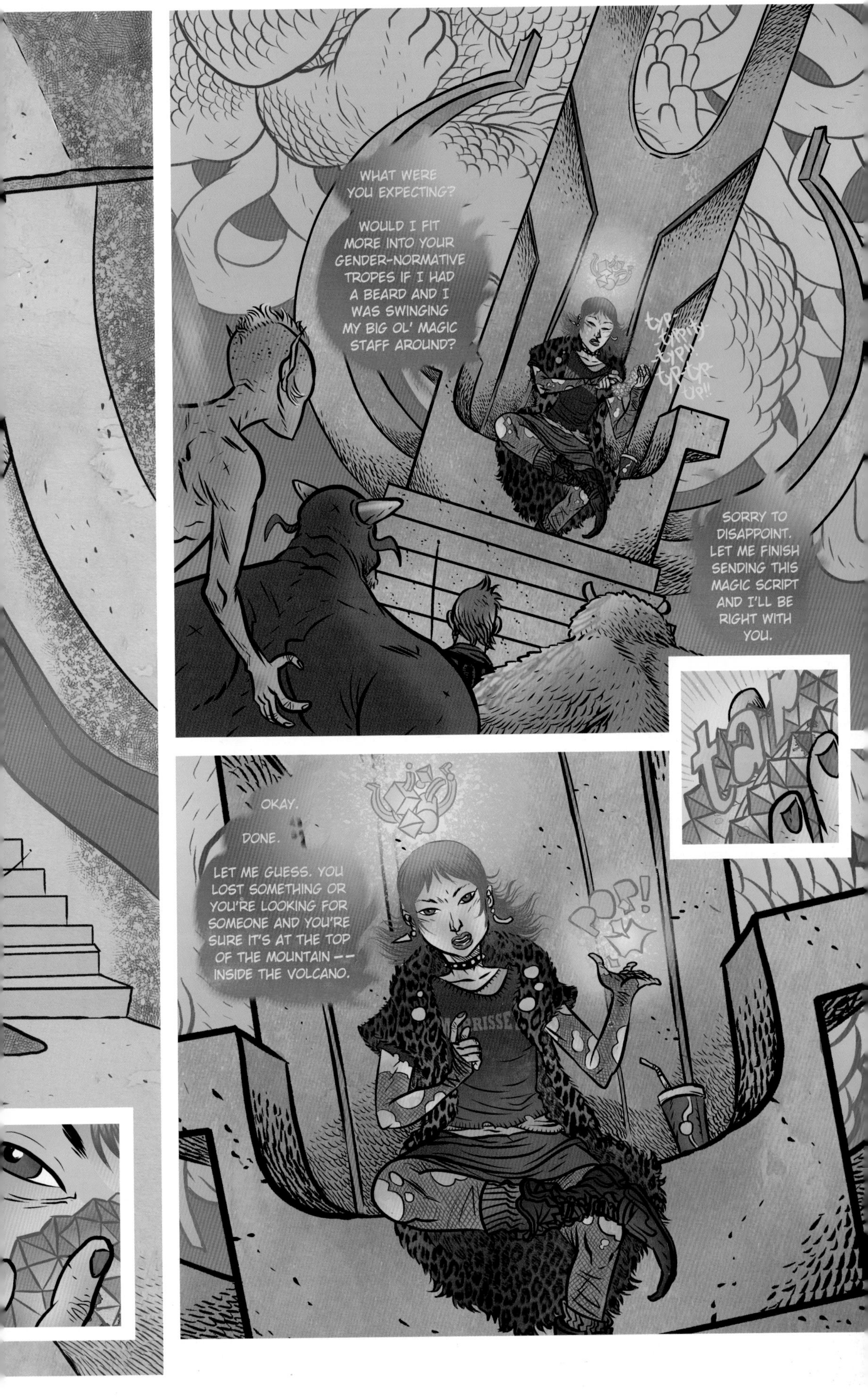
WHAT WERE YOU EXPECTING?
WOULD I FIT MORE INTO YOUR GENDER-NORMATIVE TROPES IF I HAD A BEARD AND I WAS SWINGING MY BIG OL' MAGIC STAFF AROUND?
TYP- TYPITY- TYP!! TYP-TYP- TUP!!
SORRY TO DISAPPOINT. LET ME FINISH SENDING THIS MAGIC SCRIPT AND I'LL BE RIGHT WITH YOU.
OKAY.
DONE.
LET ME GUESS. YOU LOST SOMETHING OR YOU'RE LOOKING FOR SOMEONE AND YOU'RE SURE IT'S AT THE TOP OF THE MOUNTAIN -- INSIDE THE VOLCANO.
POP!

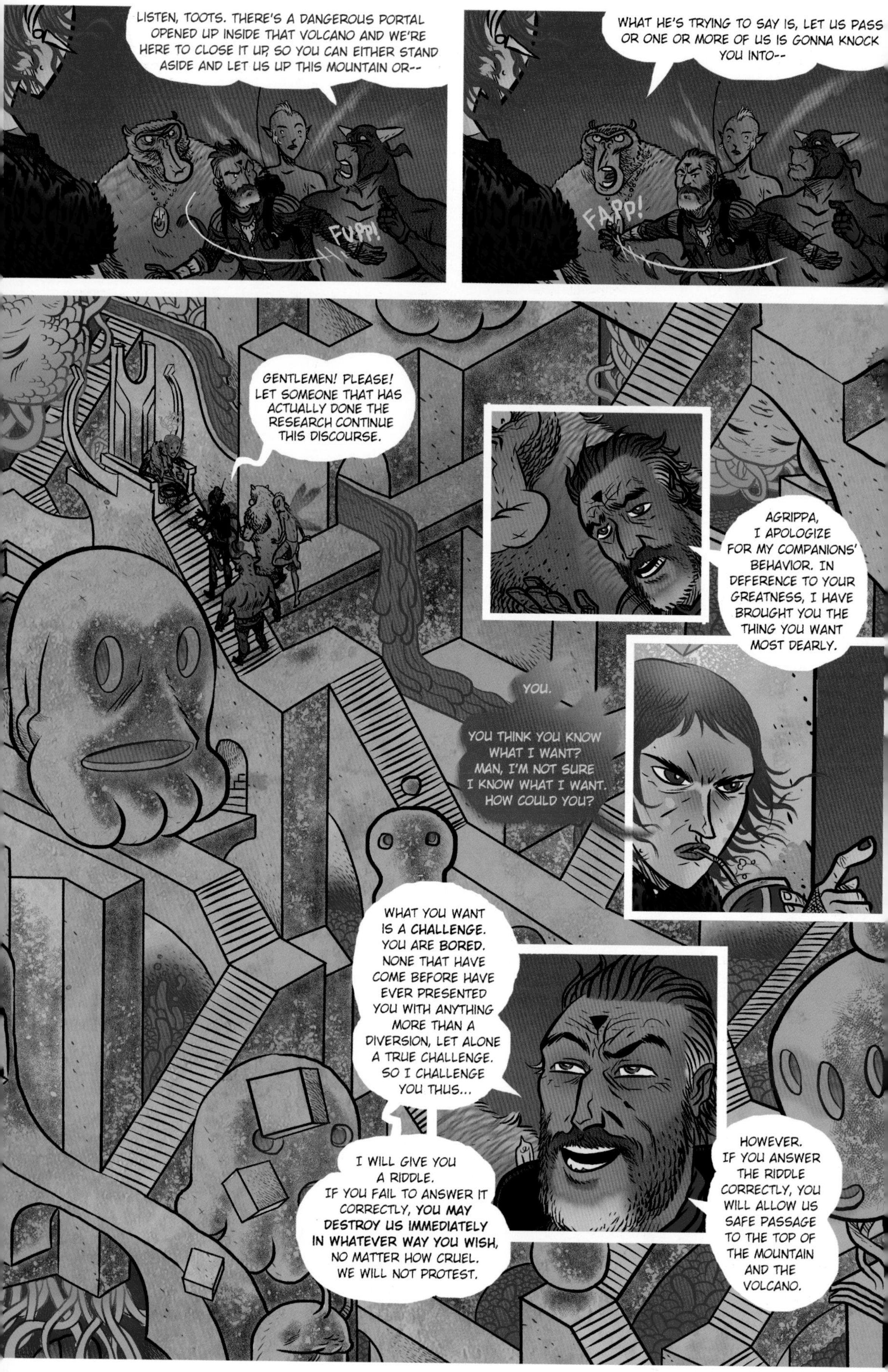
LISTEN, TOOTS. THERE'S A DANGEROUS PORTAL OPENED UP INSIDE THAT VOLCANO AND WE'RE HERE TO CLOSE IT UP, SO YOU CAN EITHER STAND ASIDE AND LET US UP THIS MOUNTAIN OR--
FUPP!
WHAT HE'S TRYING TO SAY IS, LET US PASS OR ONE OR MORE OF US IS GONNA KNOCK YOU INTO--
FAPP!
GENTLEMEN! PLEASE! LET SOMEONE THAT HAS ACTUALLY DONE THE RESEARCH CONTINUE THIS DISCOURSE.
AGRIPPA, I APOLOGIZE FOR MY COMPANIONS' BEHAVIOR. IN DEFERENCE TO YOUR GREATNESS, I HAVE BROUGHT YOU THE THING YOU WANT MOST DEARLY.
YOU.
YOU THINK YOU KNOW WHAT I WANT? MAN, I'M NOT SURE I KNOW WHAT I WANT. HOW COULD YOU?
WHAT YOU WANT IS A **CHALLENGE.** YOU ARE **BORED.** NONE THAT HAVE COME BEFORE HAVE EVER PRESENTED YOU WITH ANYTHING MORE THAN A DIVERSION, LET ALONE A TRUE CHALLENGE. SO I CHALLENGE YOU THUS...
I WILL GIVE YOU A RIDDLE. IF YOU FAIL TO ANSWER IT CORRECTLY, **YOU MAY DESTROY US IMMEDIATELY IN WHATEVER WAY YOU WISH,** NO MATTER HOW CRUEL. WE WILL NOT PROTEST.
HOWEVER. IF YOU ANSWER THE RIDDLE CORRECTLY, YOU WILL ALLOW US SAFE PASSAGE TO THE TOP OF THE MOUNTAIN AND THE VOLCANO.

AND NOW THAT I HAVE YOUR ATTENTION, I GIVE YOU...

THE RIDDLE!

THERE ARE FIVE CASTLES, WITH FIVE OCCUPANTS, EACH WITH A DIFFERENT COLOR CASTLE, DIFFERENT BEVERAGE OF CHOICE, DIFFERENT READING MATERIAL, AND A UNIQUE PET. THE GOAL IS TO FIGURE OUT WHO OWNS THE FISH. HERE IS ALL THE INFO YOU GET:

THE TROLL LIVES IN THE RED CASTLE.

THE ELF KEEPS DOGS.

THE DEMON DRINKS TEA.

THE GREEN CASTLE IS JUST TO THE LEFT OF THE WHITE ONE.

THE OWNER OF THE GREEN CASTLE DRINKS COFFEE.

THE ANCIENT MAGIC READER KEEPS BIRDS.

THE OWNER OF THE YELLOW CASTLE READS POISON RECIPES.

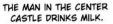

THE MAN IN THE CENTER CASTLE DRINKS MILK.

THE WIZARD LIVES IN THE FIRST CASTLE.

THE ANCIENT RUNE READER HAS A NEIGHBOR WHO KEEPS CATS.

THE MAN WHO READS DEATH GLYPHS DRINKS BEER.

THE MAN WHO KEEPS HORSES LIVES NEXT TO THE READER OF POISON RECIPES.

THE BARBARIAN READS DEAD SEA SCROLLS.

THE WIZARD LIVES NEXT TO THE BLUE CASTLE.

THE ANCIENT RUNE READER HAS A NEIGHBOR WHO DRINKS WATER.

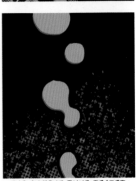

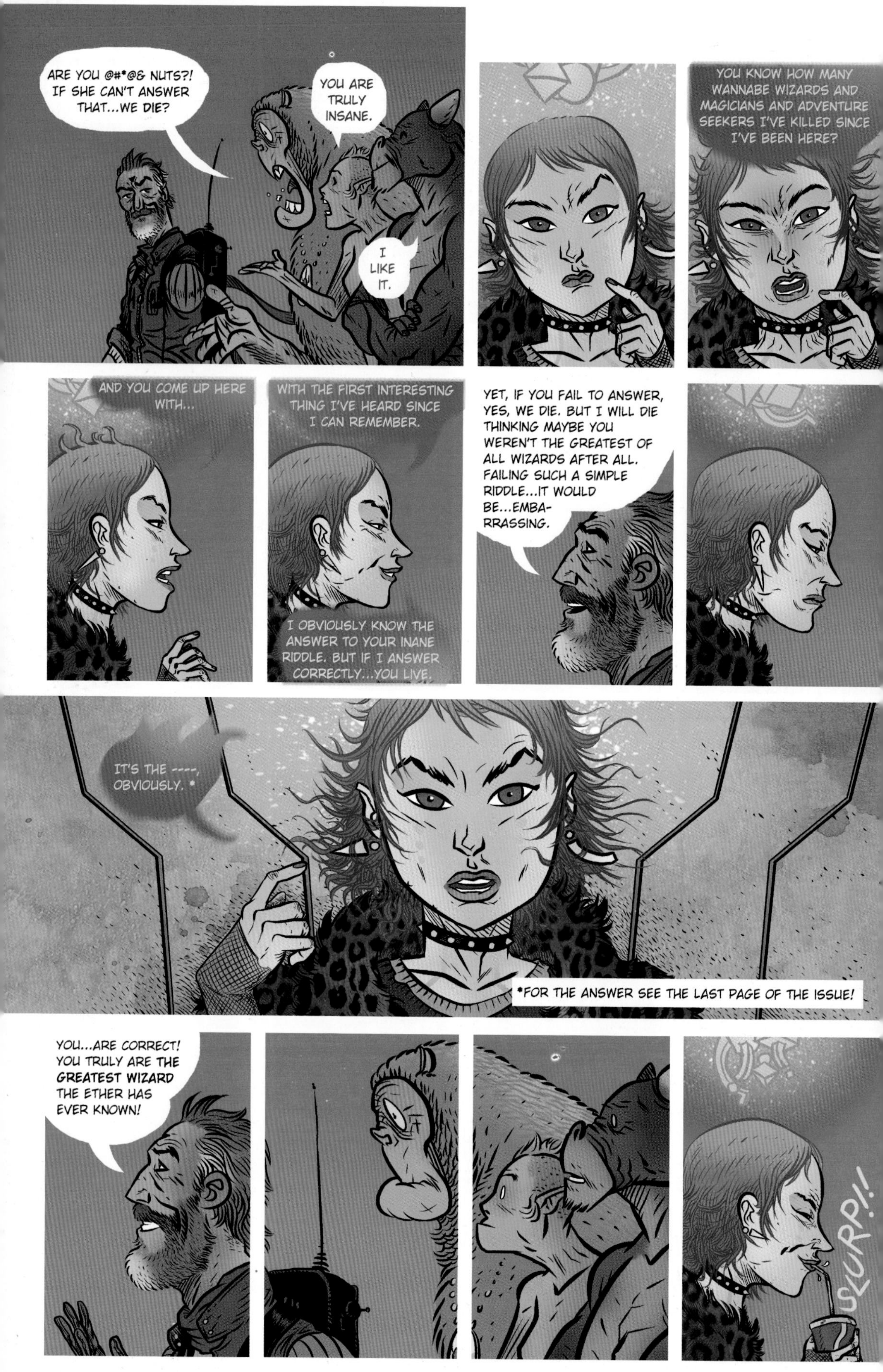
ARE YOU @#*@& NUTS?! IF SHE CAN'T ANSWER THAT...WE DIE?
YOU ARE TRULY INSANE.
I LIKE IT.
YOU KNOW HOW MANY WANNABE WIZARDS AND MAGICIANS AND ADVENTURE SEEKERS I'VE KILLED SINCE I'VE BEEN HERE?
AND YOU COME UP HERE WITH...
WITH THE FIRST INTERESTING THING I'VE HEARD SINCE I CAN REMEMBER.
I OBVIOUSLY KNOW THE ANSWER TO YOUR INANE RIDDLE. BUT IF I ANSWER CORRECTLY...YOU LIVE.
YET, IF YOU FAIL TO ANSWER, YES, WE DIE. BUT I WILL DIE THINKING MAYBE YOU WEREN'T THE GREATEST OF ALL WIZARDS AFTER ALL. FAILING SUCH A SIMPLE RIDDLE...IT WOULD BE...EMBARRASSING.
IT'S THE ----, OBVIOUSLY. *
*FOR THE ANSWER SEE THE LAST PAGE OF THE ISSUE!
YOU...ARE CORRECT! YOU TRULY ARE THE **GREATEST WIZARD** THE ETHER HAS EVER KNOWN!
SLURP!!

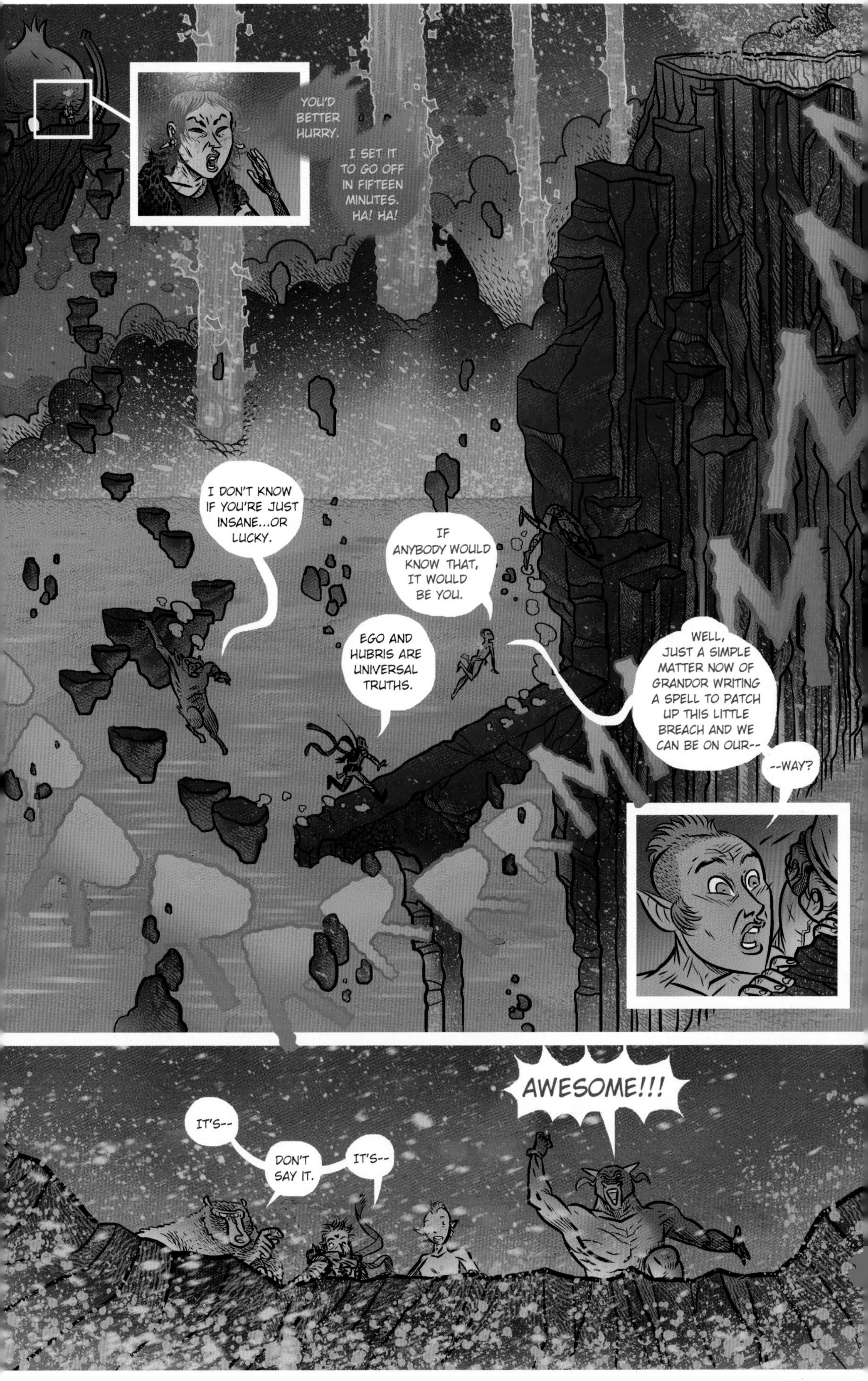
YOU'D BETTER HURRY.
I SET IT TO GO OFF IN FIFTEEN MINUTES. HA! HA!
I DON'T KNOW IF YOU'RE JUST INSANE...OR LUCKY.
IF ANYBODY WOULD KNOW THAT, IT WOULD BE YOU.
EGO AND HUBRIS ARE UNIVERSAL TRUTHS.
WELL, JUST A SIMPLE MATTER NOW OF GRANDOR WRITING A SPELL TO PATCH UP THIS LITTLE BREACH AND WE CAN BE ON OUR--
--WAY?
IT'S--
DON'T SAY IT.
IT'S--
AWESOME!!!

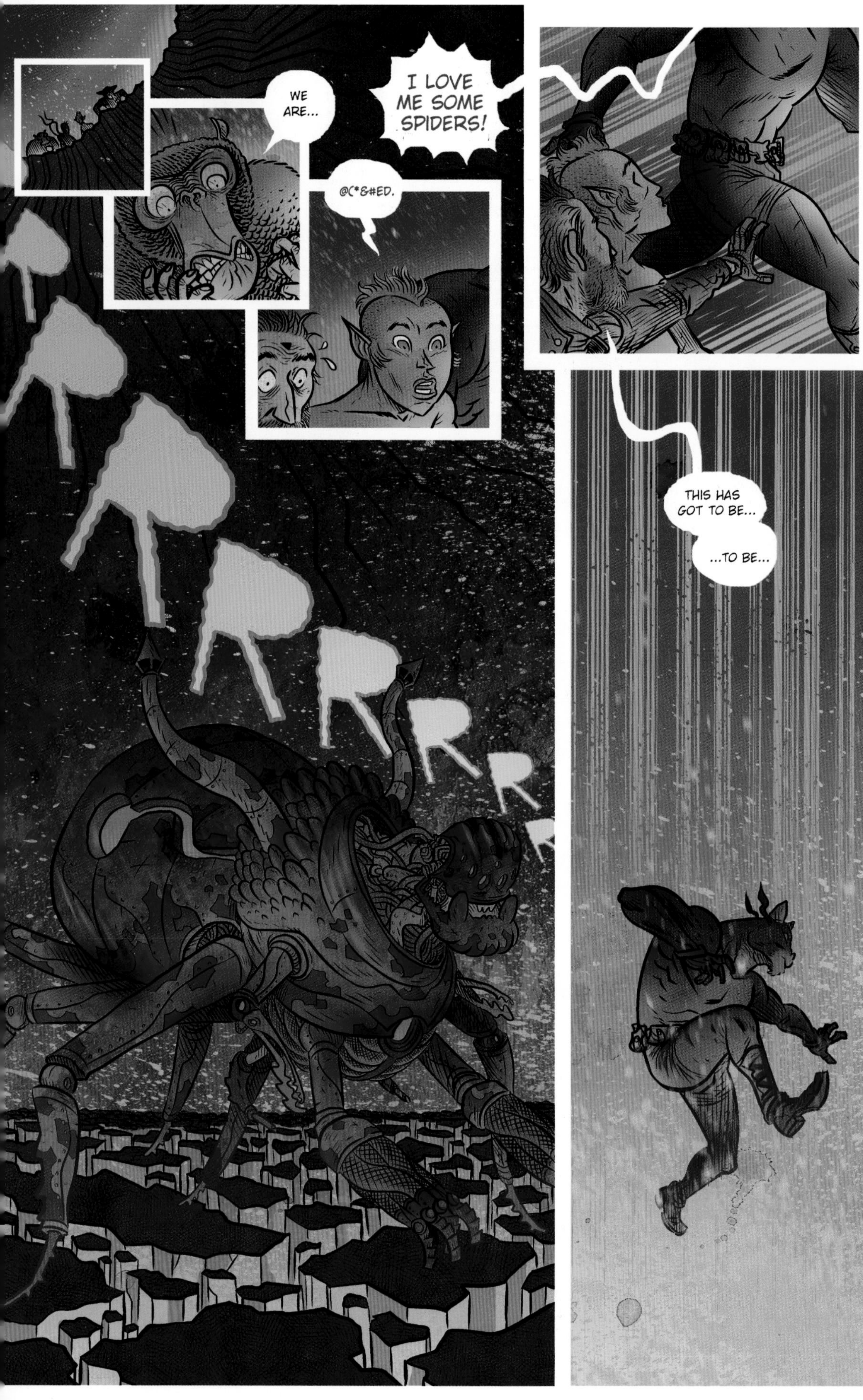

WE ARE...
@C*&#ED.
I LOVE ME SOME SPIDERS!
THIS HAS GOT TO BE...
...TO BE...
RRRRRRRR

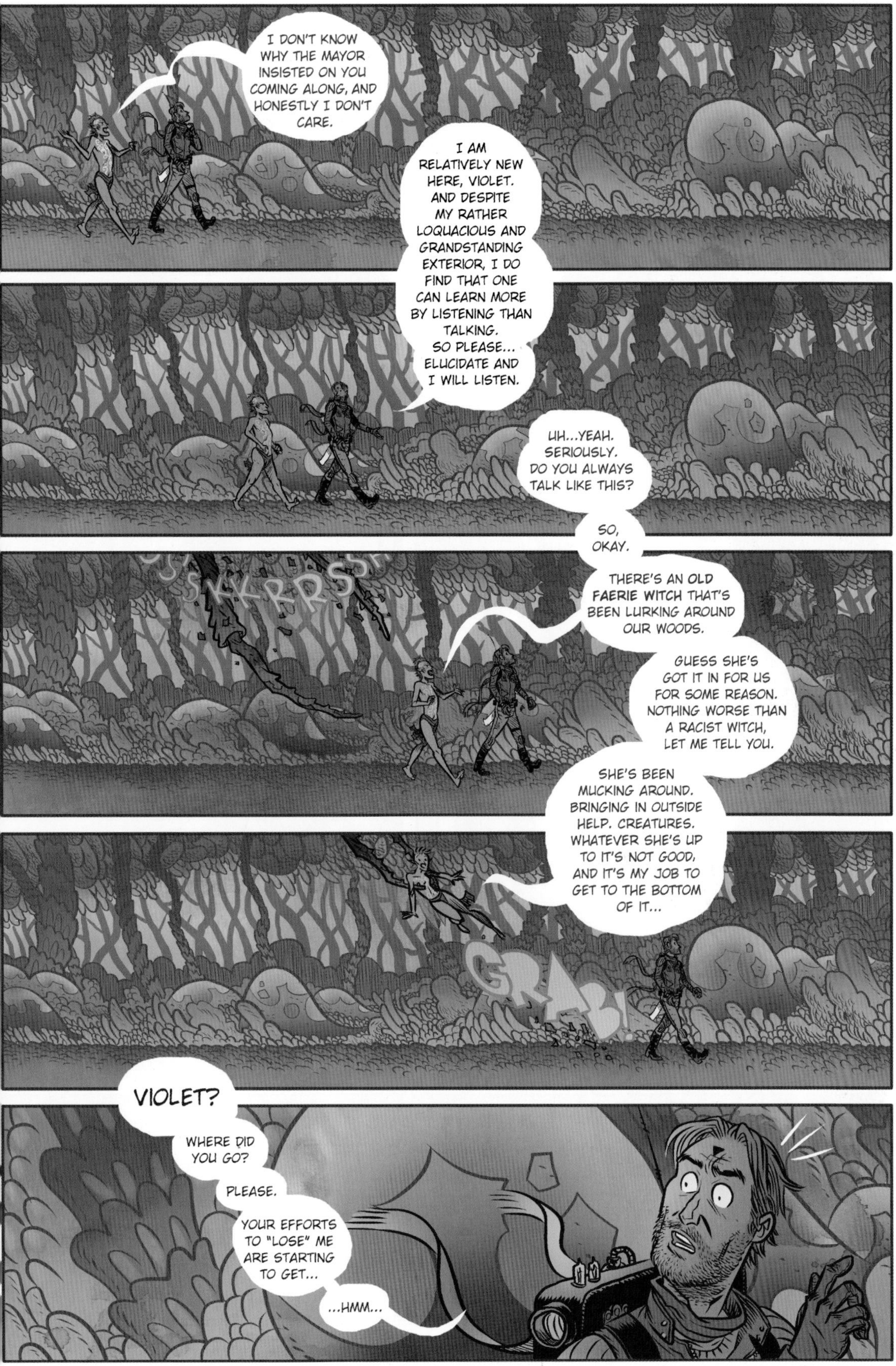
I DON'T KNOW WHY THE MAYOR INSISTED ON YOU COMING ALONG, AND HONESTLY I DON'T CARE.
I AM RELATIVELY NEW HERE, VIOLET. AND DESPITE MY RATHER LOQUACIOUS AND GRANDSTANDING EXTERIOR, I DO FIND THAT ONE CAN LEARN MORE BY LISTENING THAN TALKING. SO PLEASE... ELUCIDATE AND I WILL LISTEN.
UH...YEAH. SERIOUSLY. DO YOU ALWAYS TALK LIKE THIS?
SO, OKAY.
SKKRRSS
THERE'S AN OLD **FAERIE WITCH** THAT'S BEEN LURKING AROUND OUR WOODS.
GUESS SHE'S GOT IT IN FOR US FOR SOME REASON. NOTHING WORSE THAN A RACIST WITCH, LET ME TELL YOU.
SHE'S BEEN MUCKING AROUND. BRINGING IN OUTSIDE HELP. CREATURES. WHATEVER SHE'S UP TO IT'S NOT GOOD, AND IT'S MY JOB TO GET TO THE BOTTOM OF IT...
GRAB!
VIOLET?
WHERE DID YOU GO?
PLEASE.
YOUR EFFORTS TO "LOSE" ME ARE STARTING TO GET...
...HMM...

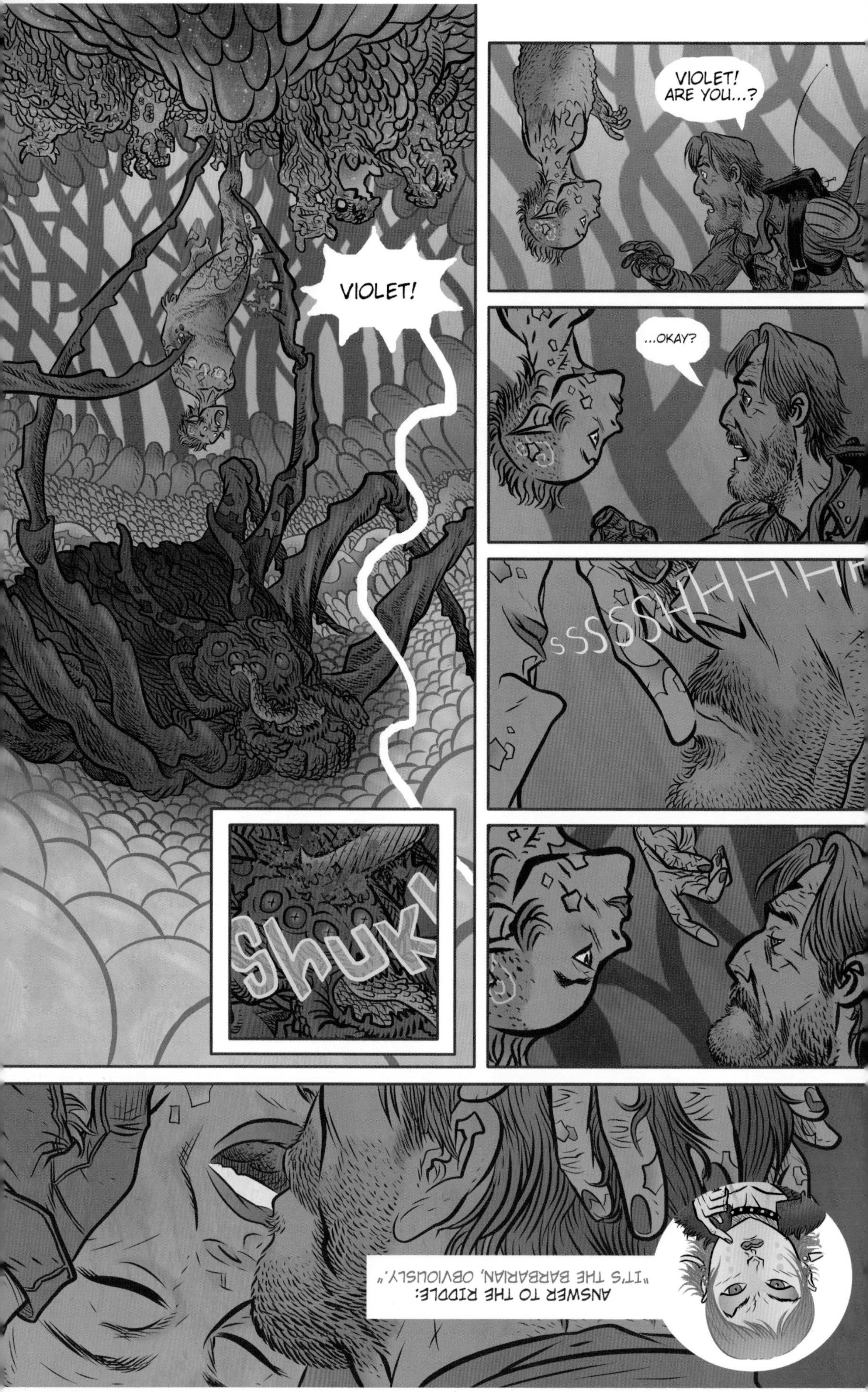
VIOLET!
SHUK!
VIOLET! ARE YOU...?
...OKAY?
sSSSSHHHHH
ANSWER TO THE RIDDLE: "IT'S THE BARBARIAN, OBVIOUSLY."

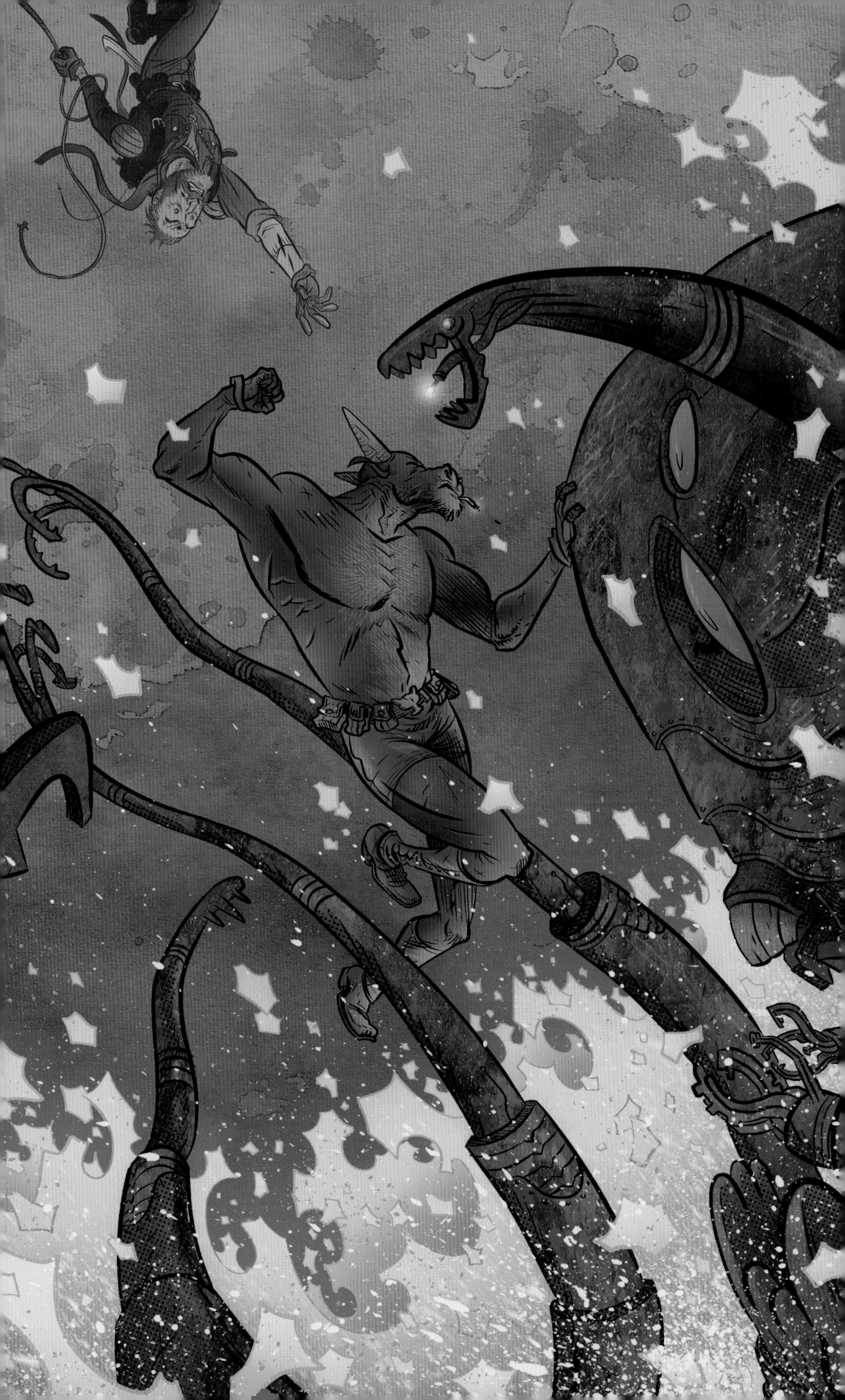

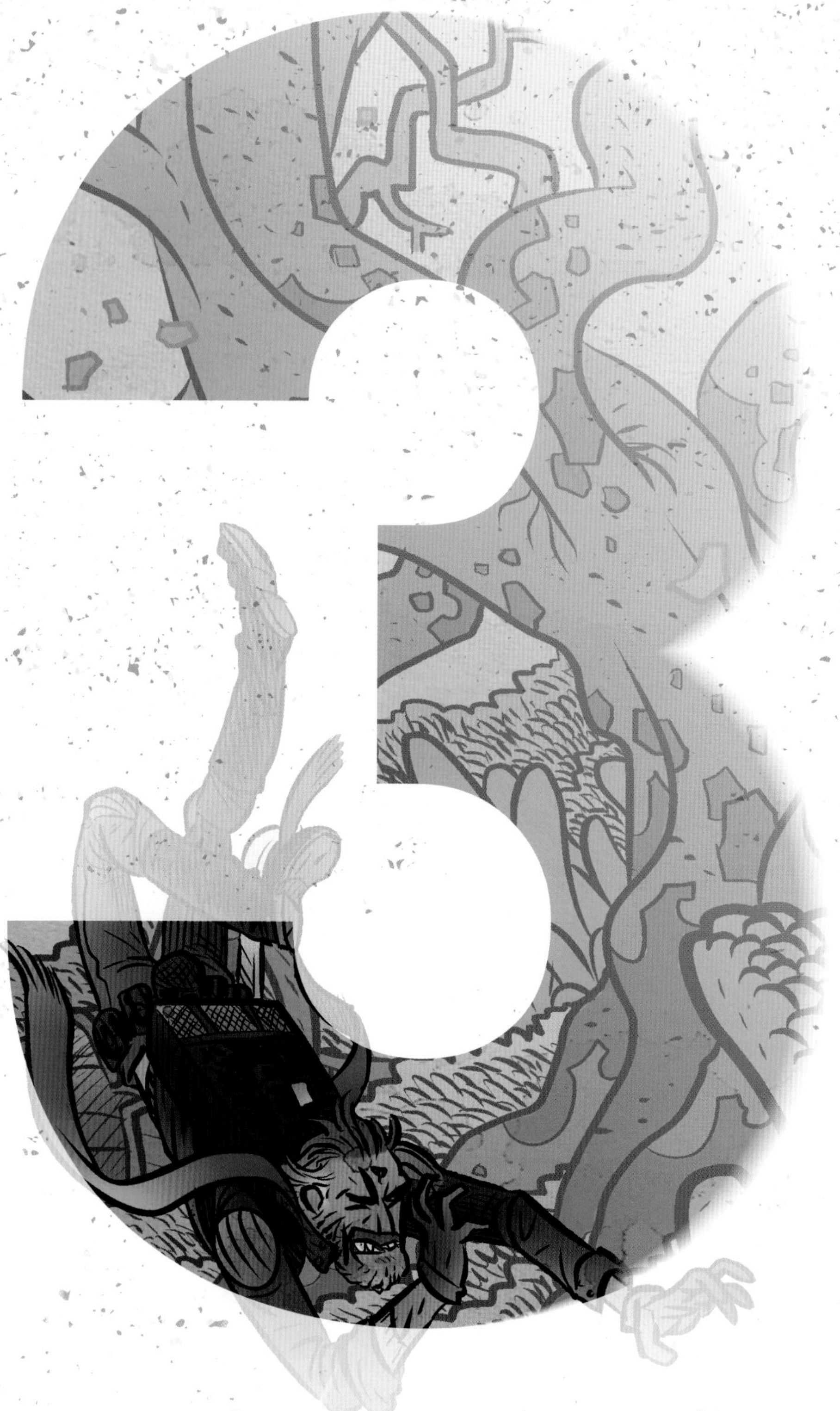

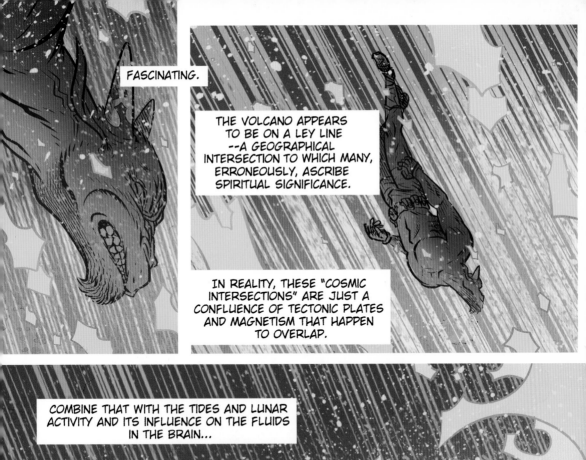

FASCINATING.

THE VOLCANO APPEARS TO BE ON A LEY LINE --A GEOGRAPHICAL INTERSECTION TO WHICH MANY, ERRONEOUSLY, ASCRIBE SPIRITUAL SIGNIFICANCE.

IN REALITY, THESE "COSMIC INTERSECTIONS" ARE JUST A CONFLUENCE OF TECTONIC PLATES AND MAGNETISM THAT HAPPEN TO OVERLAP.

COMBINE THAT WITH THE TIDES AND LUNAR ACTIVITY AND ITS INFLUENCE ON THE FLUIDS IN THE BRAIN...

WELL, LET'S JUST SAY...

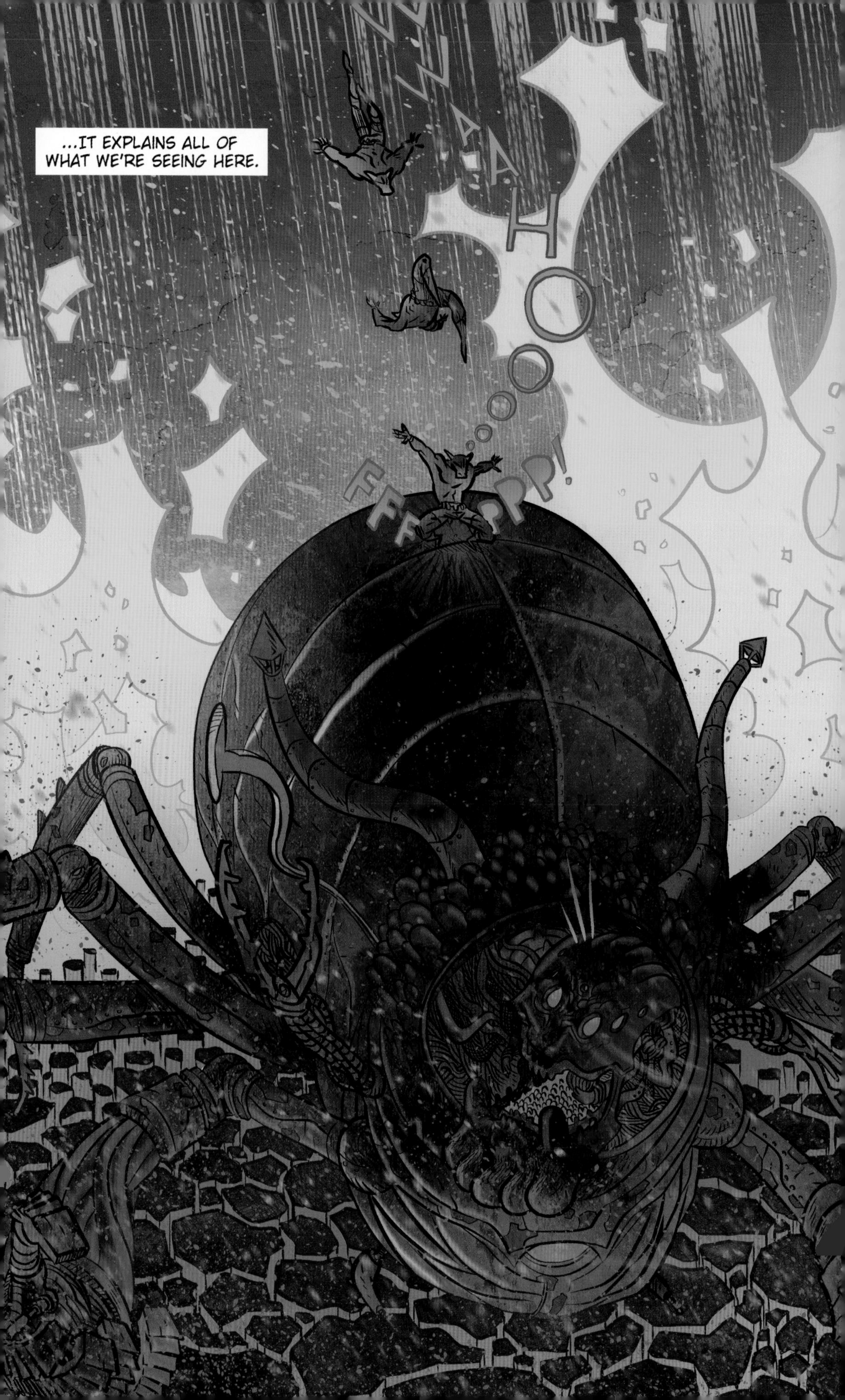
...IT EXPLAINS ALL OF WHAT WE'RE SEEING HERE.
WWAAHOOOOO
FFFPPPP!

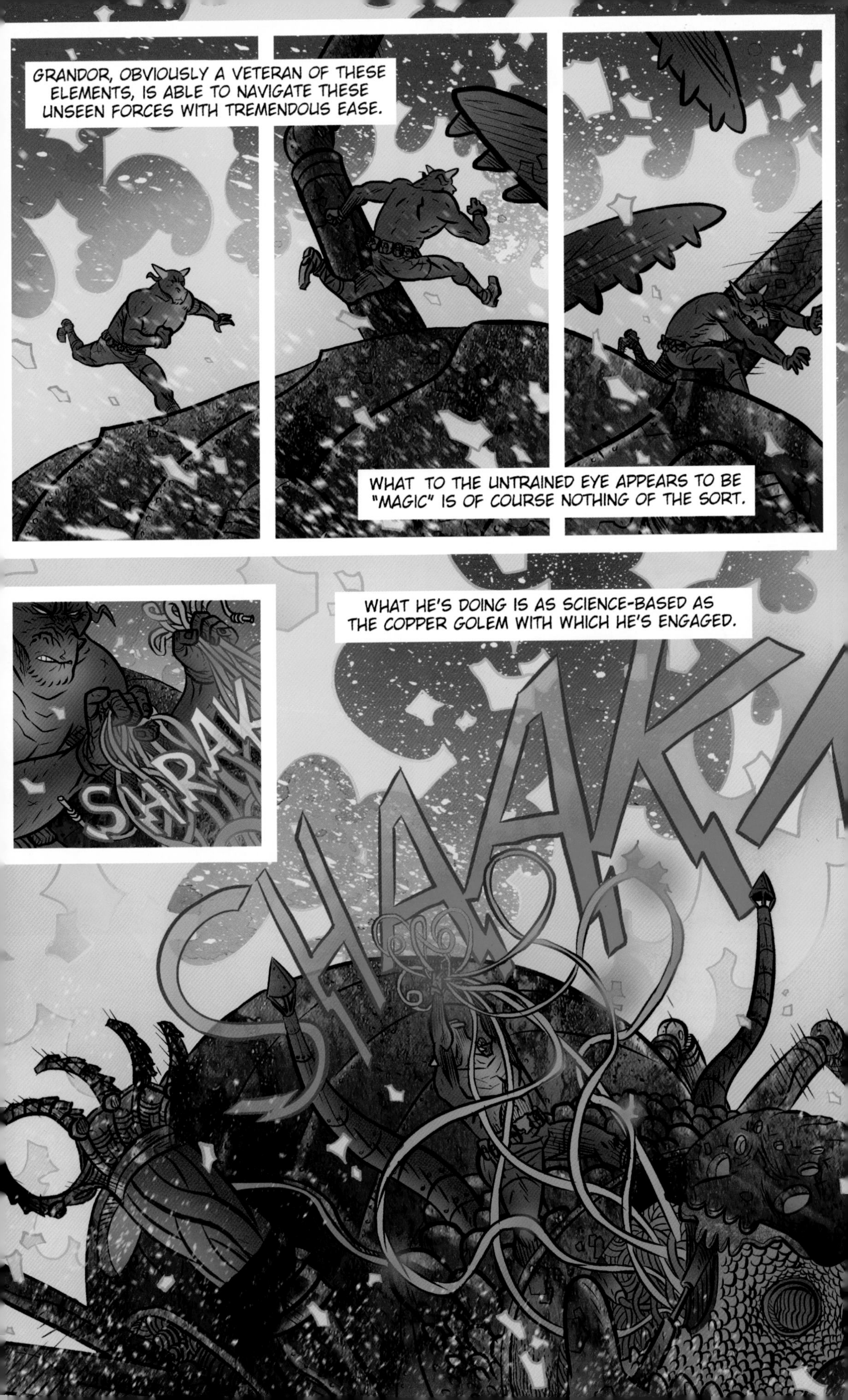
GRANDOR, OBVIOUSLY A VETERAN OF THESE ELEMENTS, IS ABLE TO NAVIGATE THESE UNSEEN FORCES WITH TREMENDOUS EASE.
WHAT TO THE UNTRAINED EYE APPEARS TO BE "MAGIC" IS OF COURSE NOTHING OF THE SORT.
SHRAK
WHAT HE'S DOING IS AS SCIENCE-BASED AS THE COPPER GOLEM WITH WHICH HE'S ENGAGED.
SHAAK

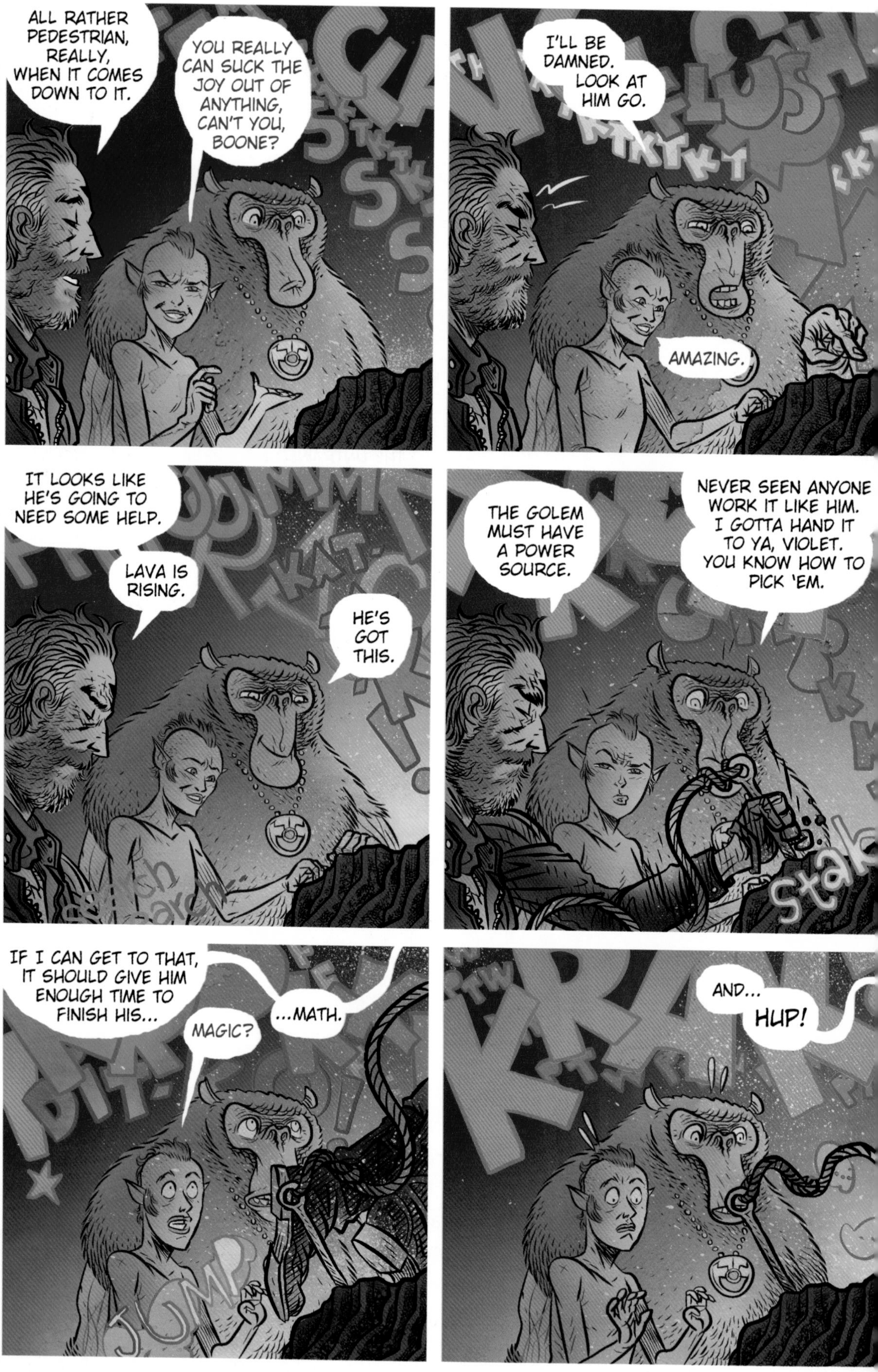
ALL RATHER PEDESTRIAN, REALLY, WHEN IT COMES DOWN TO IT.
YOU REALLY CAN SUCK THE JOY OUT OF ANYTHING, CAN'T YOU, BOONE?
I'LL BE DAMNED.
LOOK AT HIM GO.
AMAZING.
IT LOOKS LIKE HE'S GOING TO NEED SOME HELP.
LAVA IS RISING.
HE'S GOT THIS.
THE GOLEM MUST HAVE A POWER SOURCE.
NEVER SEEN ANYONE WORK IT LIKE HIM. I GOTTA HAND IT TO YA, VIOLET. YOU KNOW HOW TO PICK 'EM.
IF I CAN GET TO THAT, IT SHOULD GIVE HIM ENOUGH TIME TO FINISH HIS...
MAGIC?
...MATH.
AND...
HUP!

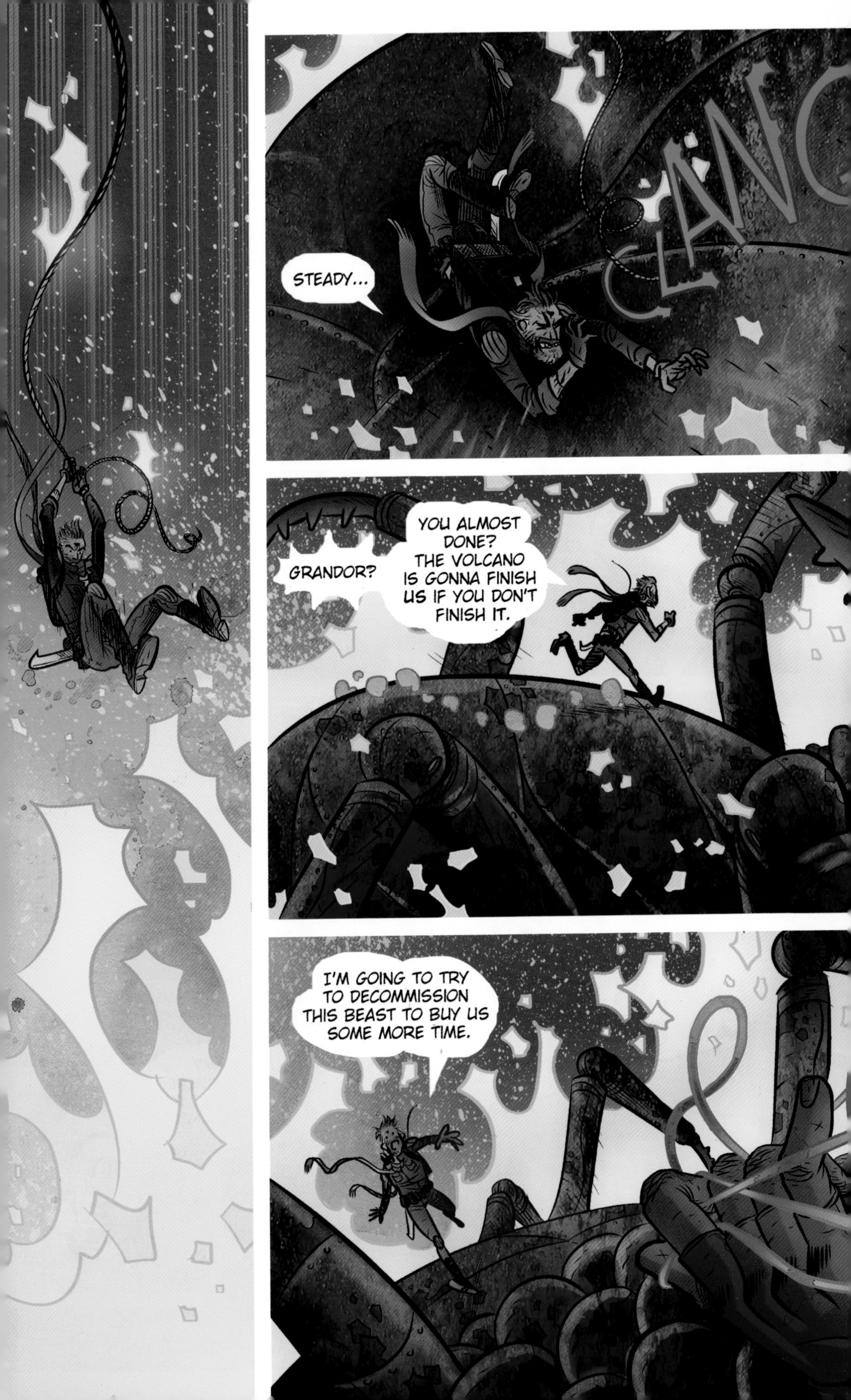
STEADY...
CLANG
GRANDOR?
YOU ALMOST DONE? THE VOLCANO IS GONNA FINISH US IF YOU DON'T FINISH IT.
I'M GOING TO TRY TO DECOMMISSION THIS BEAST TO BUY US SOME MORE TIME.

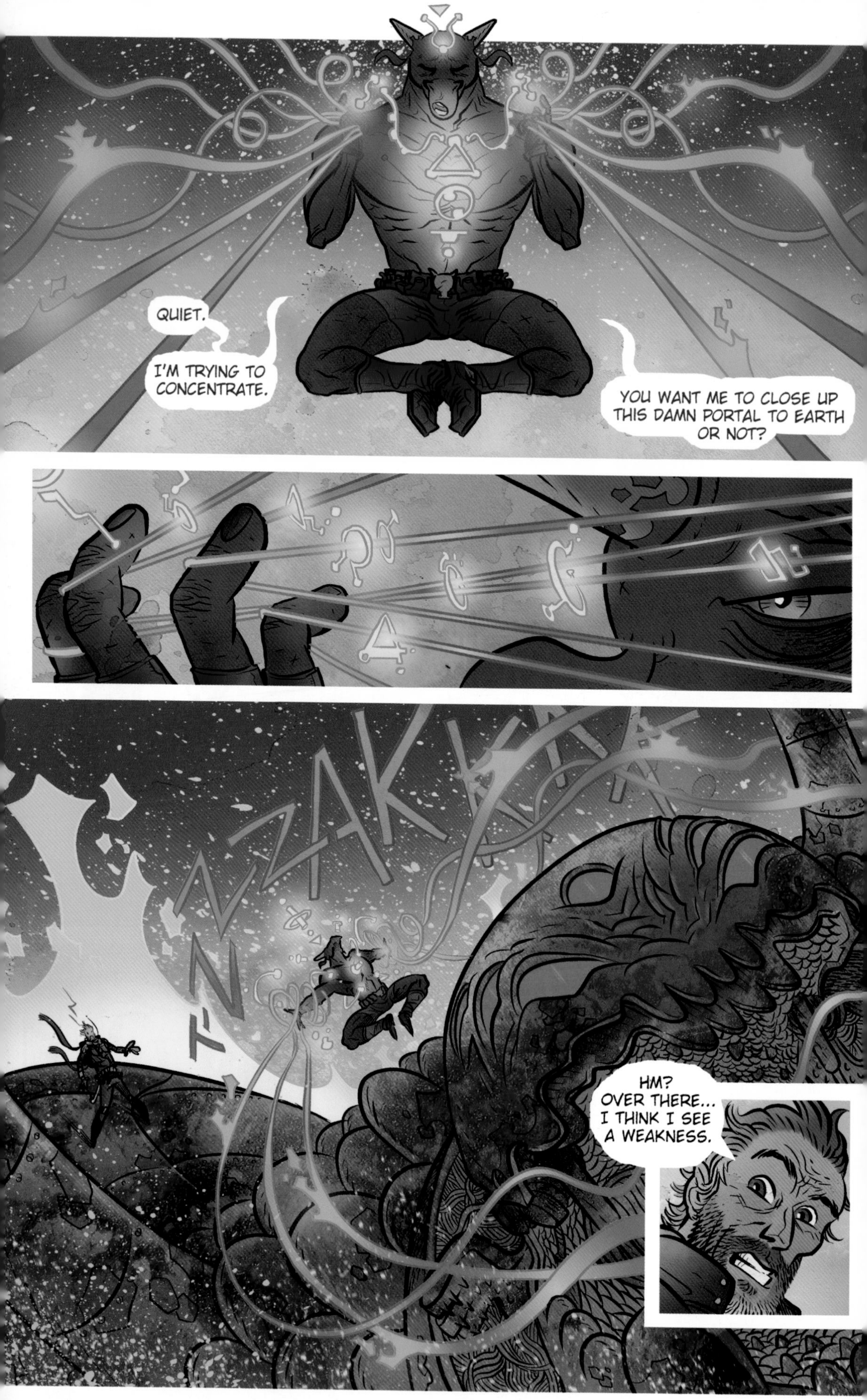
QUIET.
I'M TRYING TO CONCENTRATE.
YOU WANT ME TO CLOSE UP THIS DAMN PORTAL TO EARTH OR NOT?
ZZAK
HM? OVER THERE... I THINK I SEE A WEAKNESS.

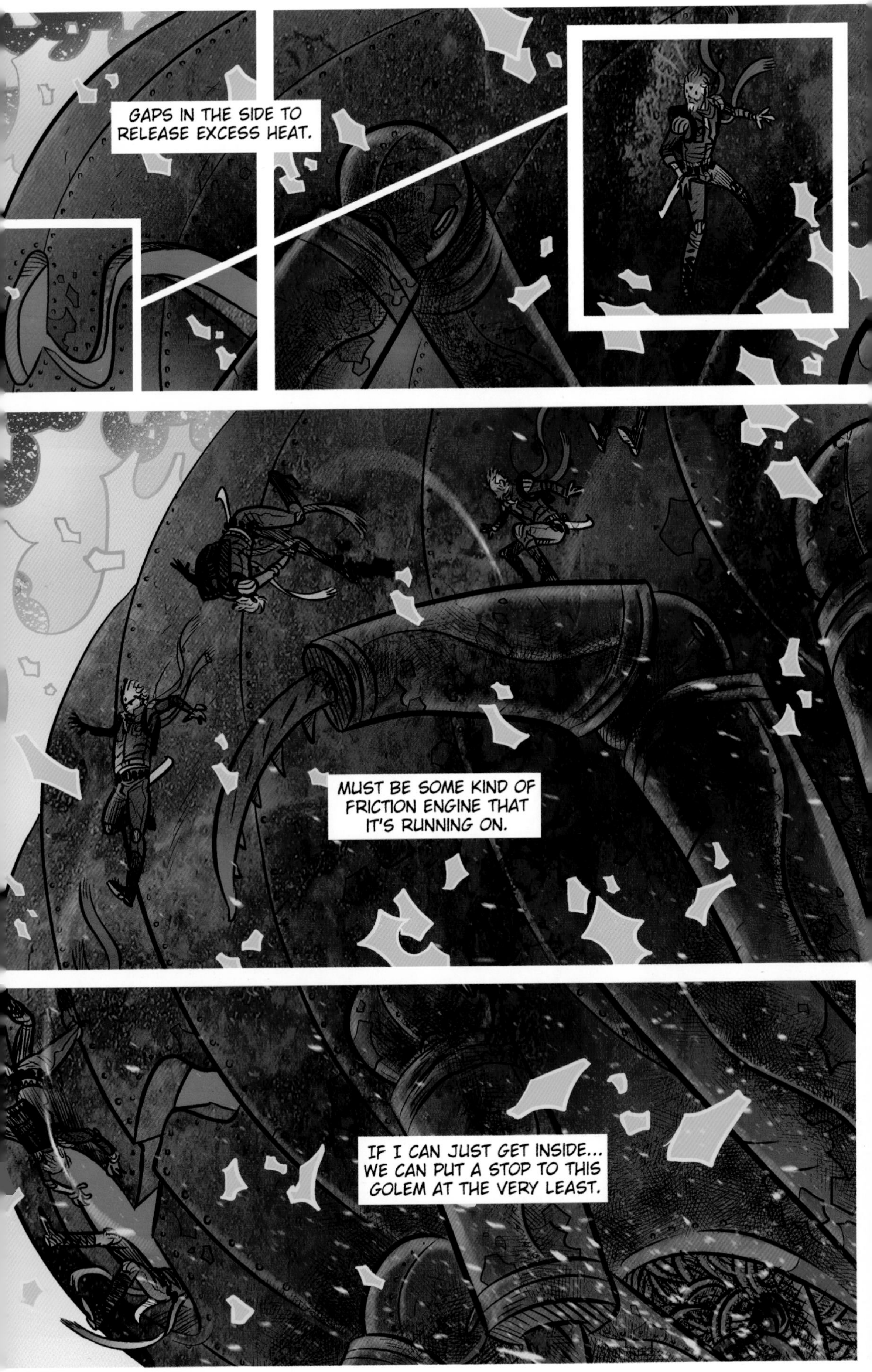
GAPS IN THE SIDE TO
RELEASE EXCESS HEAT.
MUST BE SOME KIND OF
FRICTION ENGINE THAT
IT'S RUNNING ON.
IF I CAN JUST GET INSIDE...
WE CAN PUT A STOP TO THIS
GOLEM AT THE VERY LEAST.

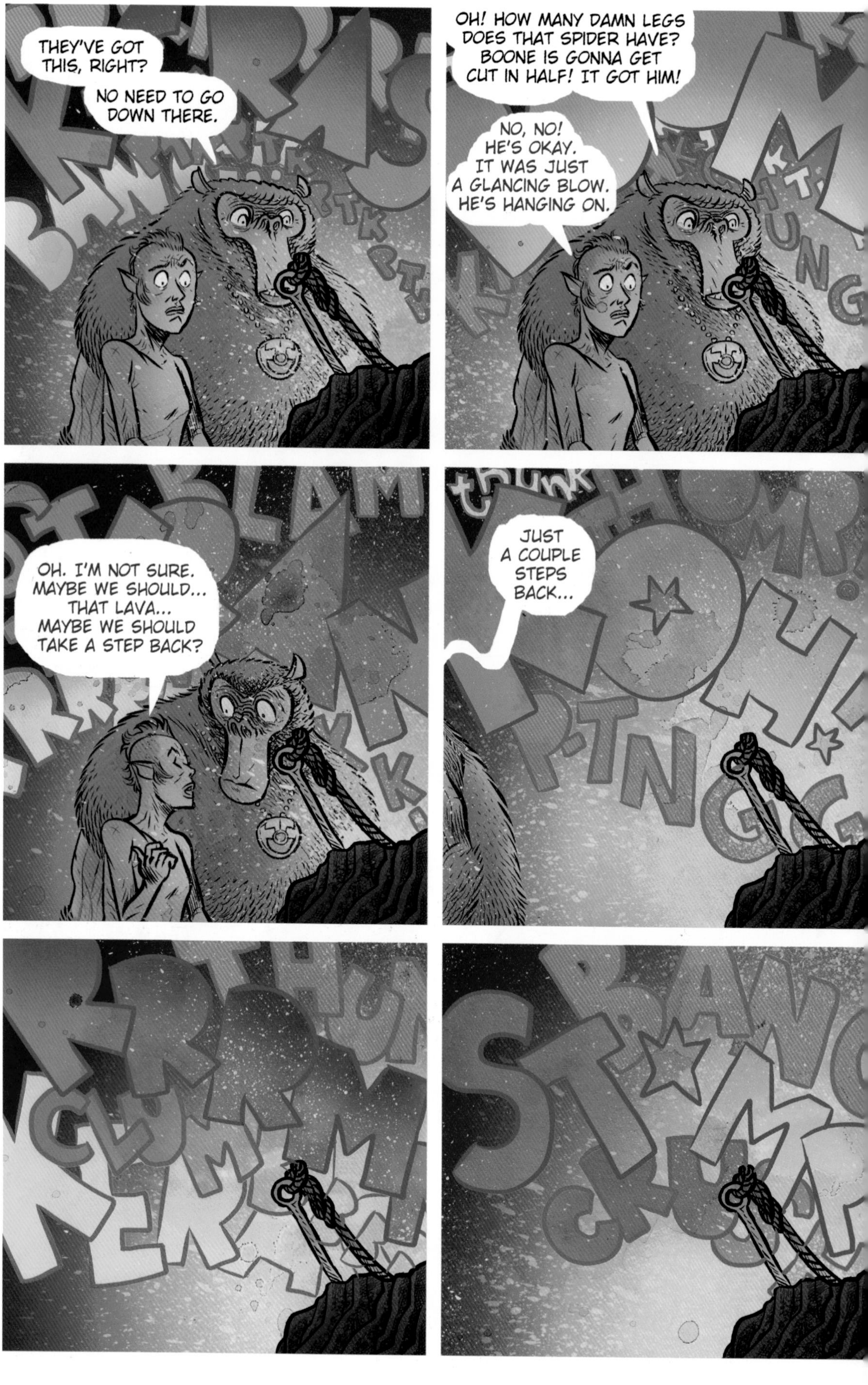
THEY'VE GOT THIS, RIGHT?
NO NEED TO GO DOWN THERE.
OH! HOW MANY DAMN LEGS DOES THAT SPIDER HAVE? BOONE IS GONNA GET CUT IN HALF! IT GOT HIM!
NO, NO! HE'S OKAY. IT WAS JUST A GLANCING BLOW. HE'S HANGING ON.
OH. I'M NOT SURE. MAYBE WE SHOULD... THAT LAVA... MAYBE WE SHOULD TAKE A STEP BACK?
thunk
JUST A COUPLE STEPS BACK...

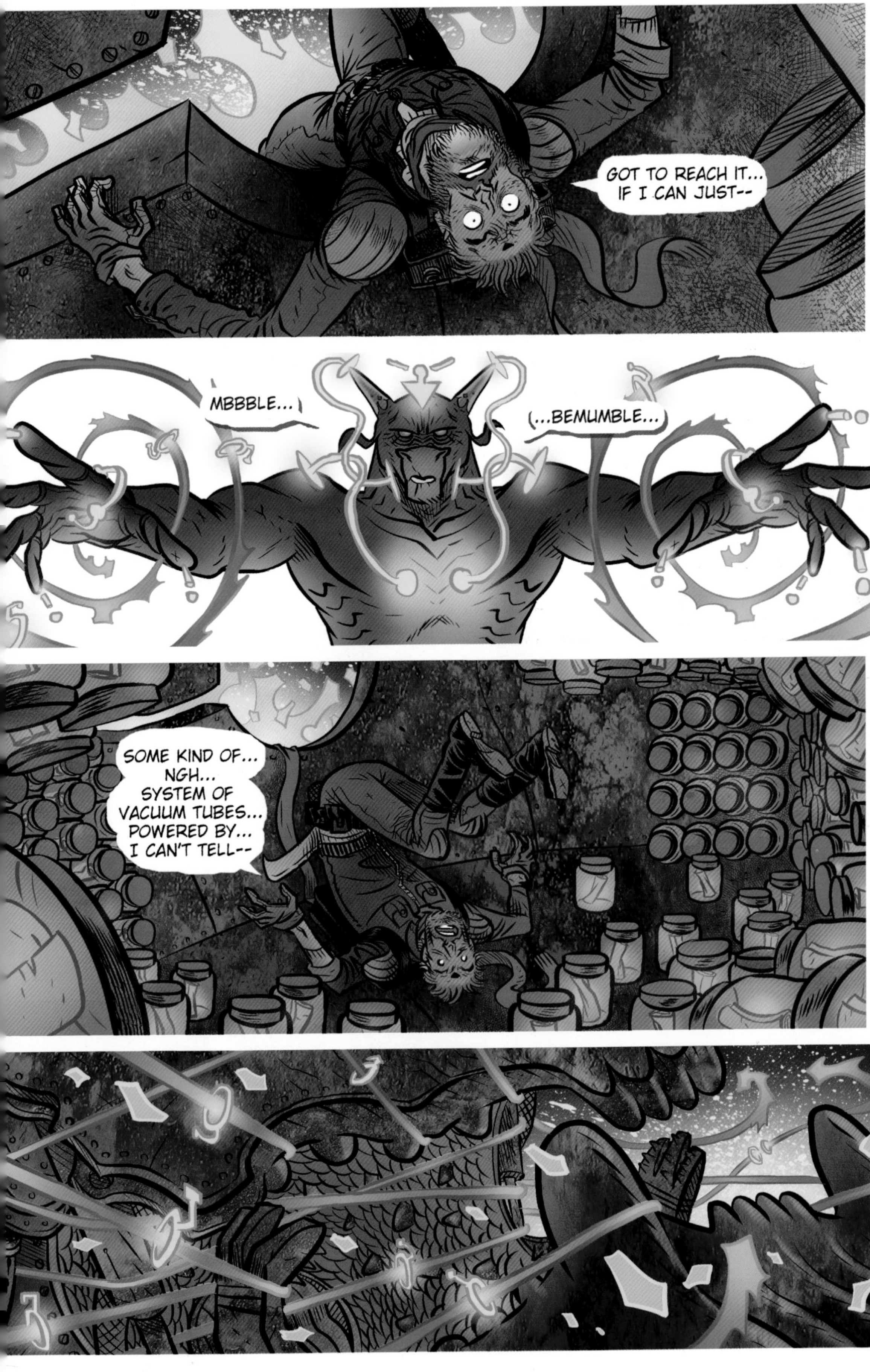
GOT TO REACH IT... IF I CAN JUST--
MBBBLE...
(...BEMUMBLE...
SOME KIND OF... NGH... SYSTEM OF VACUUM TUBES... POWERED BY... I CAN'T TELL--

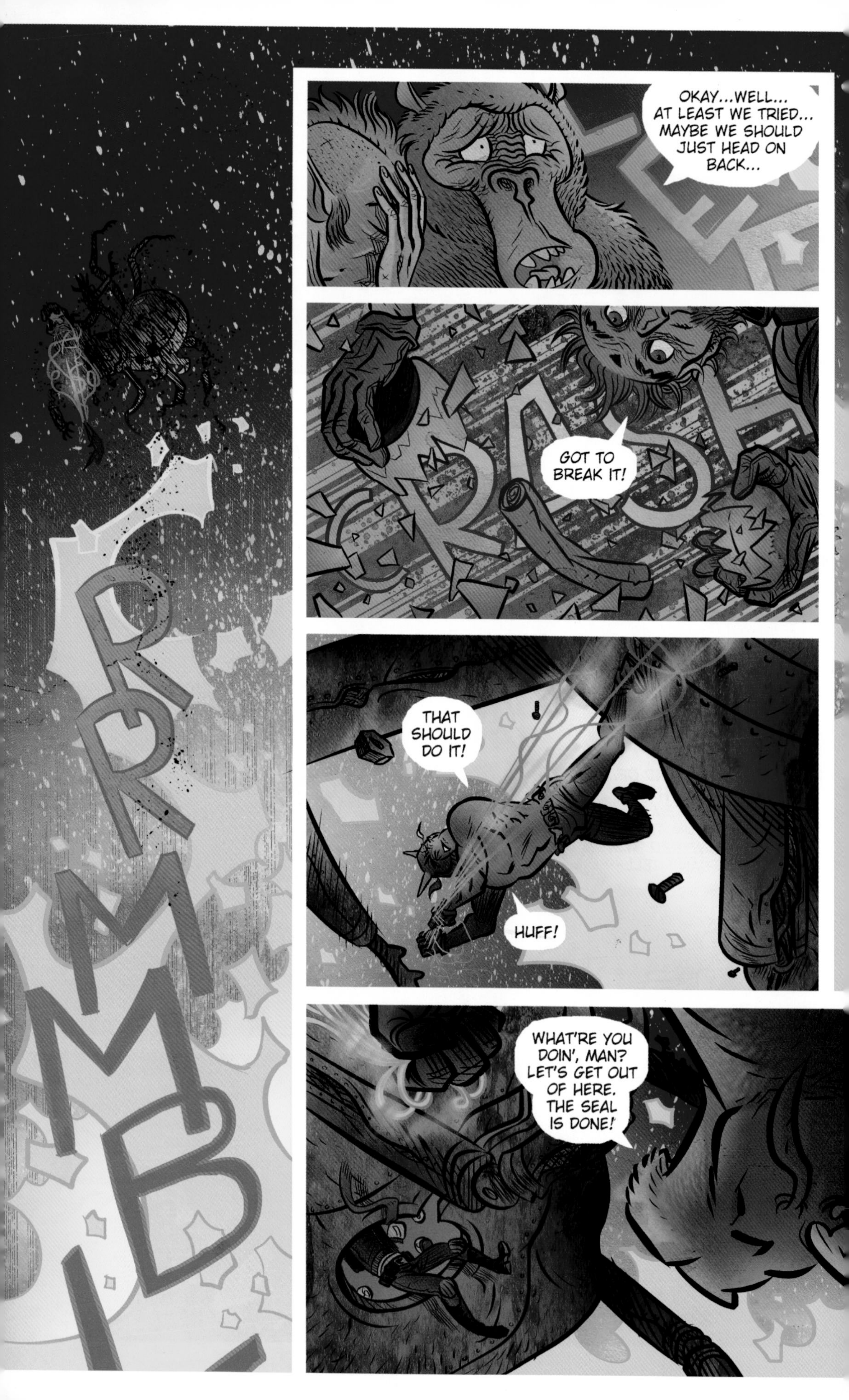
OKAY...WELL... AT LEAST WE TRIED... MAYBE WE SHOULD JUST HEAD ON BACK...
GOT TO BREAK IT!
CRASH
THAT SHOULD DO IT!
HUFF!
WHAT'RE YOU DOIN', MAN? LET'S GET OUT OF HERE. THE SEAL IS DONE!
RRRMMB

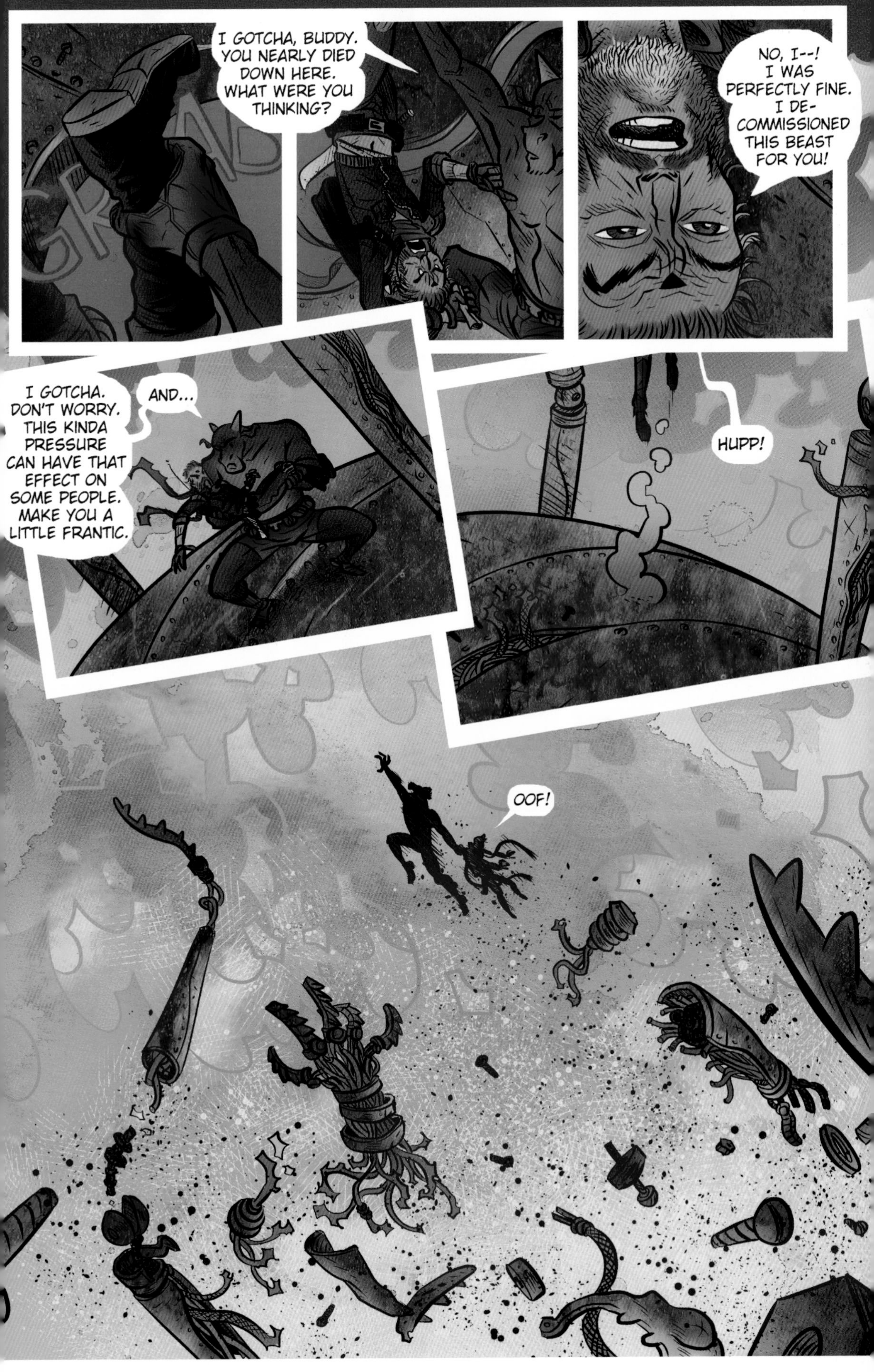
I GOTCHA, BUDDY. YOU NEARLY DIED DOWN HERE. WHAT WERE YOU THINKING?
NO, I--! I WAS PERFECTLY FINE. I DE-COMMISSIONED THIS BEAST FOR YOU!
I GOTCHA. DON'T WORRY. THIS KINDA PRESSURE CAN HAVE THAT EFFECT ON SOME PEOPLE. MAKE YOU A LITTLE FRANTIC.
AND...
HUPP!
OOF!

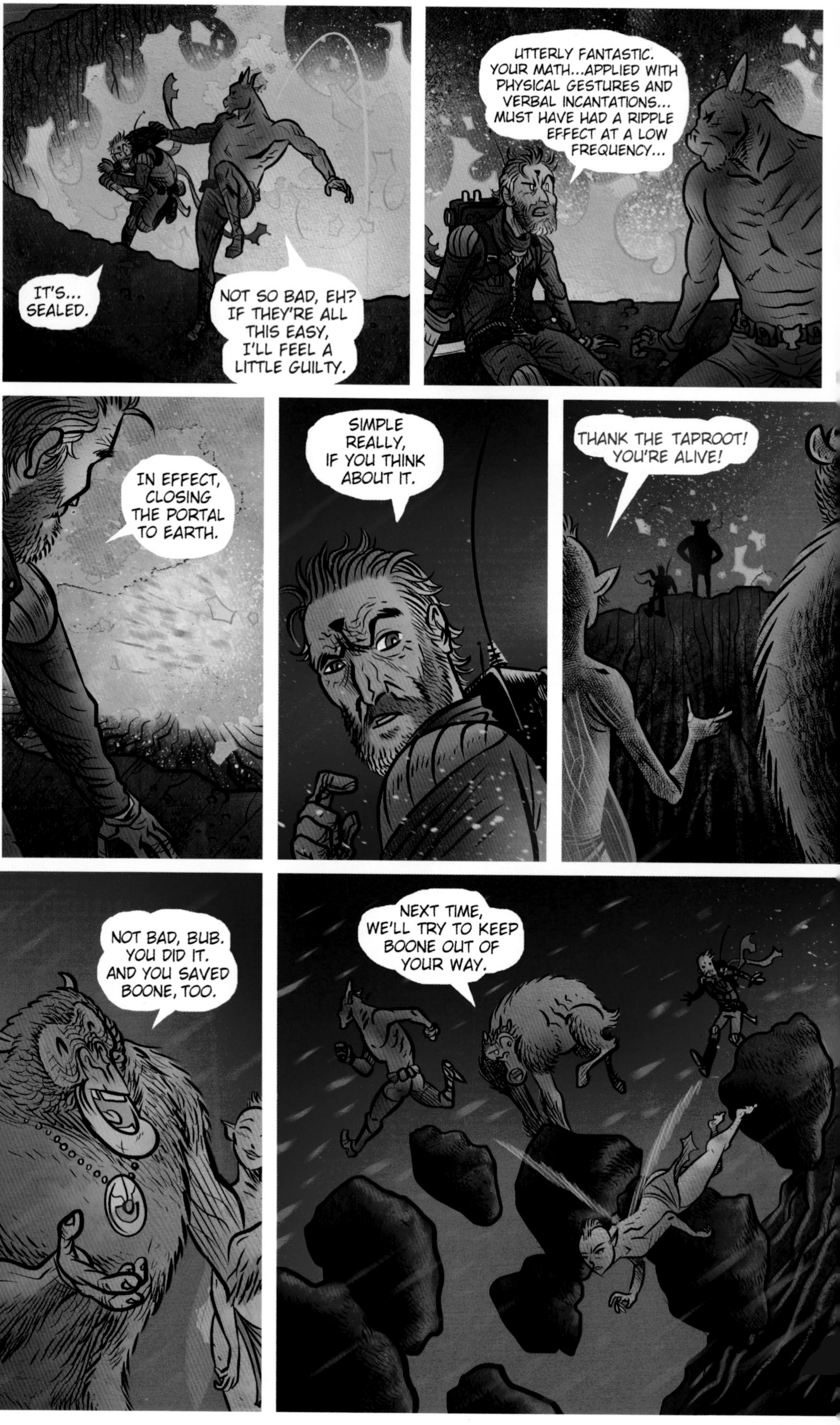
IT'S... SEALED.
NOT SO BAD, EH? IF THEY'RE ALL THIS EASY, I'LL FEEL A LITTLE GUILTY.
UTTERLY FANTASTIC. YOUR MATH...APPLIED WITH PHYSICAL GESTURES AND VERBAL INCANTATIONS... MUST HAVE HAD A RIPPLE EFFECT AT A LOW FREQUENCY...
IN EFFECT, CLOSING THE PORTAL TO EARTH.
SIMPLE REALLY, IF YOU THINK ABOUT IT.
THANK THE TAPROOT! YOU'RE ALIVE!
NOT BAD, BUB. YOU DID IT. AND YOU SAVED BOONE, TOO.
NEXT TIME, WE'LL TRY TO KEEP BOONE OUT OF YOUR WAY.

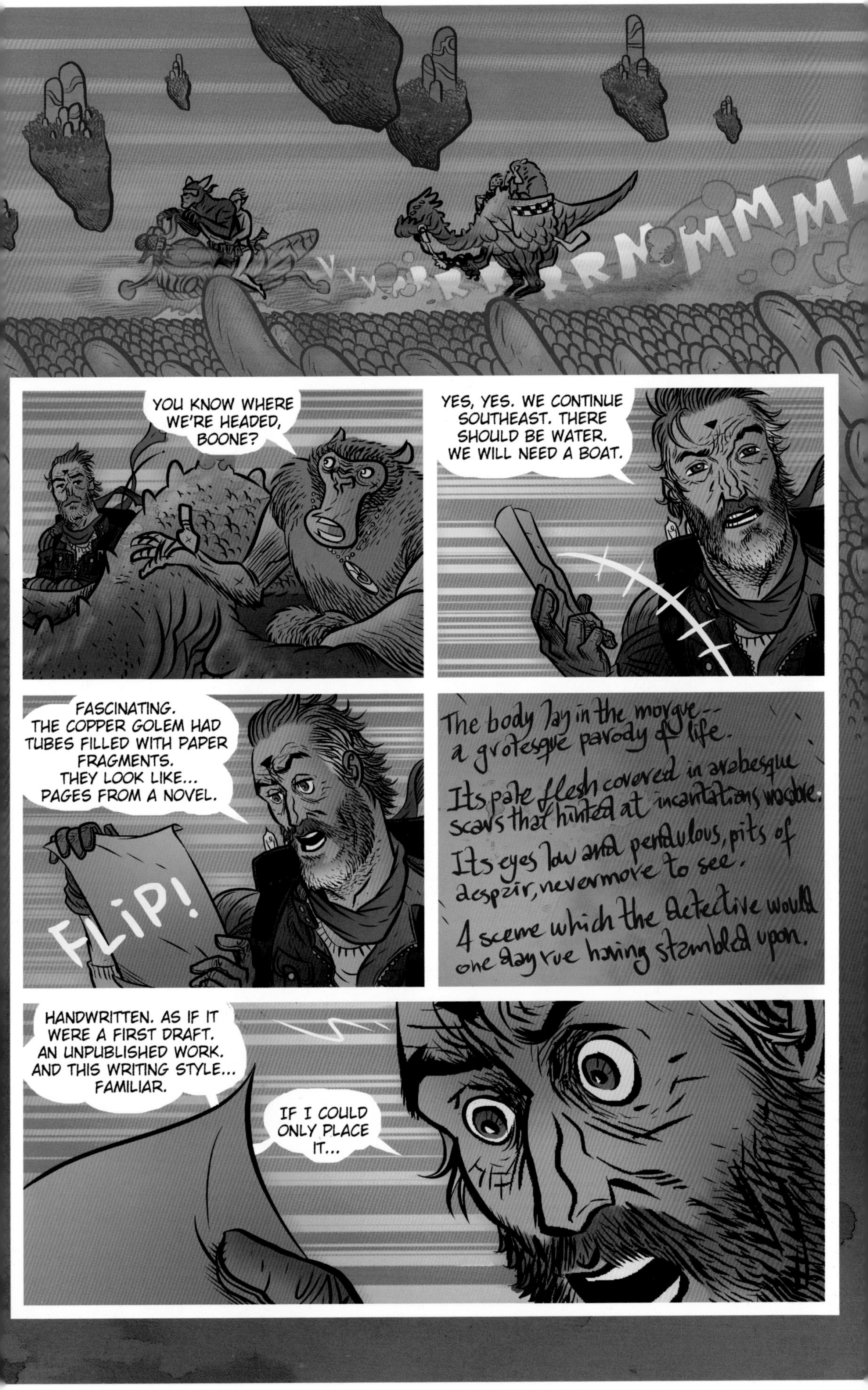
YOU KNOW WHERE WE'RE HEADED, BOONE?
YES, YES. WE CONTINUE SOUTHEAST. THERE SHOULD BE WATER. WE WILL NEED A BOAT.
FASCINATING. THE COPPER GOLEM HAD TUBES FILLED WITH PAPER FRAGMENTS. THEY LOOK LIKE... PAGES FROM A NOVEL.
FLIP!
The body lay in the morgue-- a grotesque parody of life.
Its pale flesh covered in arabesque scars that hinted at incantations macabre.
Its eyes low and pendulous, pits of despair, nevermore to see.
A scene which the detective would one day rue having stumbled upon.
HANDWRITTEN. AS IF IT WERE A FIRST DRAFT. AN UNPUBLISHED WORK. AND THIS WRITING STYLE... FAMILIAR.
IF I COULD ONLY PLACE IT...

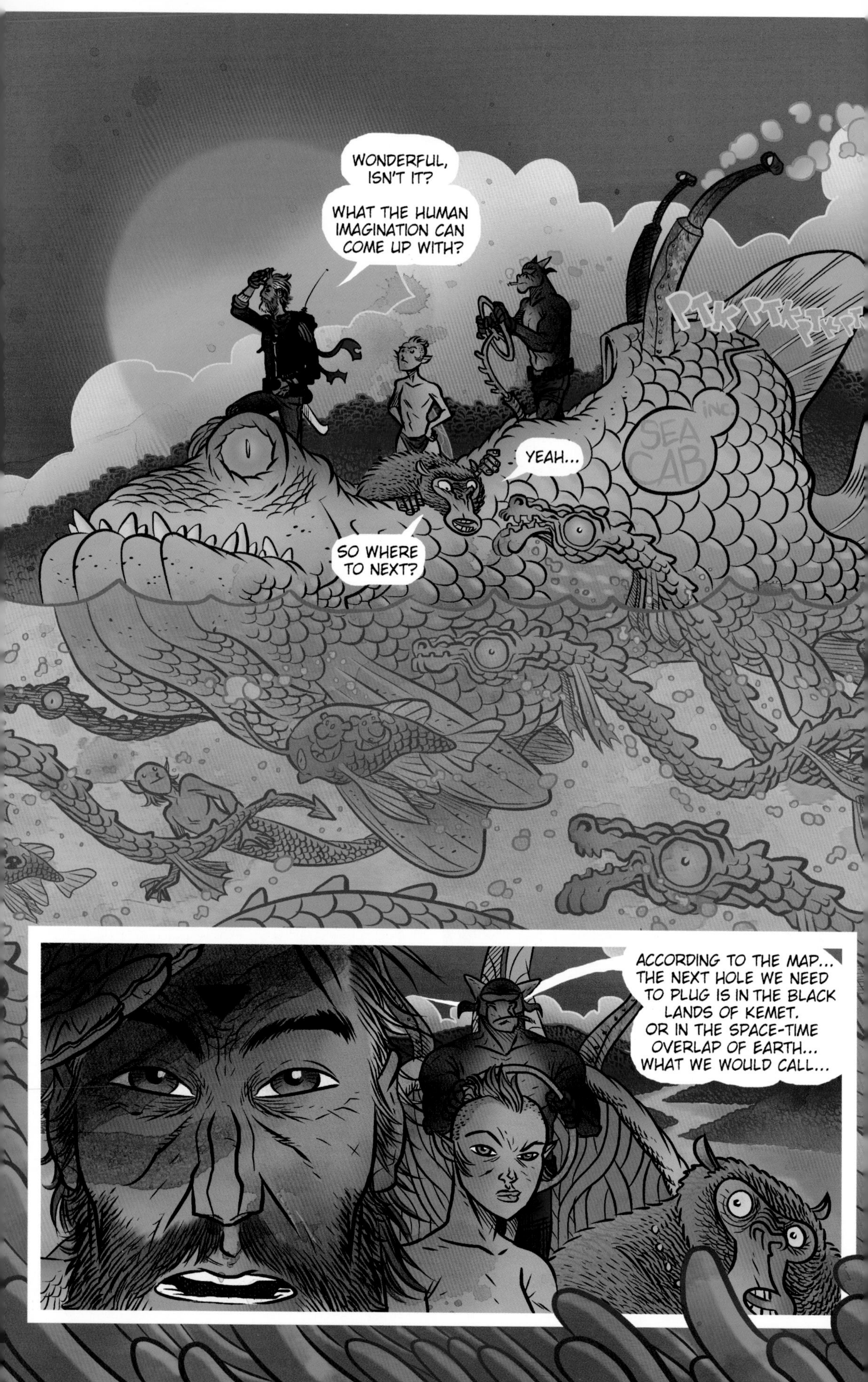
WONDERFUL, ISN'T IT?
WHAT THE HUMAN IMAGINATION CAN COME UP WITH?
PTK PTK PTK
SEA CAB inc.
YEAH...
SO WHERE TO NEXT?
ACCORDING TO THE MAP... THE NEXT HOLE WE NEED TO PLUG IS IN THE BLACK LANDS OF KEMET. OR IN THE SPACE-TIME OVERLAP OF EARTH... WHAT WE WOULD CALL...

...EGYPT.

VIOLET...I'M...I'M GLAD YOU CAME WITH US.

PLEASE. DID I HAVE A CHOICE?

I'D LIKE TO THINK SO.

WHAT ARE YOU DOING, BOONE?

I'M TRYING TO MAKE THINGS RIGHT. THE WAY WE LEFT THINGS, I REALIZE I... I COULD HAVE DONE IT DIFFERENTLY.

JUST FOCUS ON THE MISSION. OUR PAST... IS PAST.

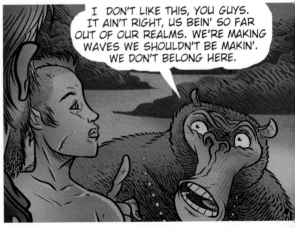

I DON'T LIKE THIS, YOU GUYS. IT AIN'T RIGHT, US BEIN' SO FAR OUT OF OUR REALMS. WE'RE MAKING WAVES WE SHOULDN'T BE MAKIN'. WE DON'T BELONG HERE.

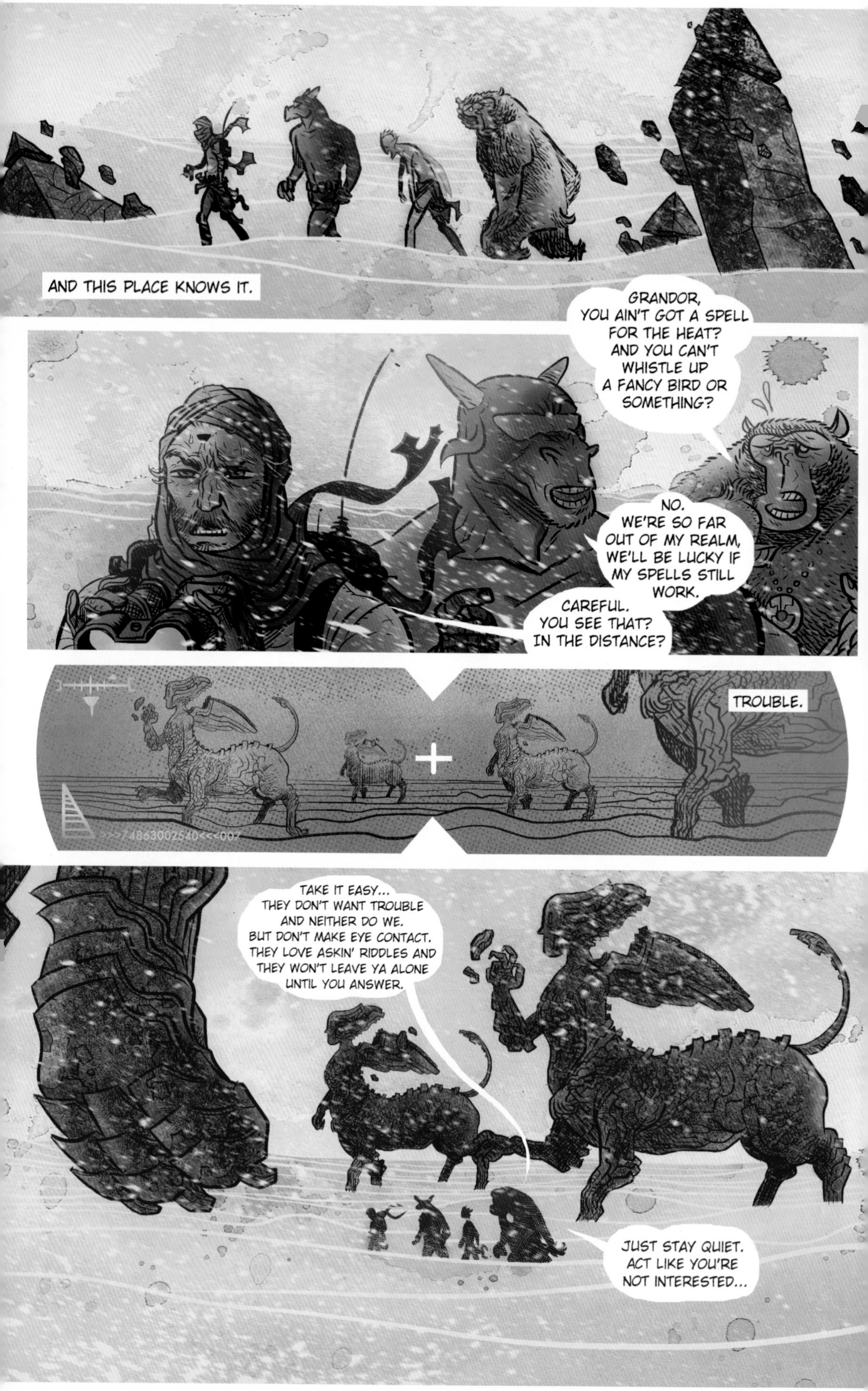

AND THIS PLACE KNOWS IT.
GRANDOR, YOU AIN'T GOT A SPELL FOR THE HEAT? AND YOU CAN'T WHISTLE UP A FANCY BIRD OR SOMETHING?
NO. WE'RE SO FAR OUT OF MY REALM, WE'LL BE LUCKY IF MY SPELLS STILL WORK.
CAREFUL. YOU SEE THAT? IN THE DISTANCE?
TROUBLE.
TAKE IT EASY... THEY DON'T WANT TROUBLE AND NEITHER DO WE. BUT DON'T MAKE EYE CONTACT. THEY LOVE ASKIN' RIDDLES AND THEY WON'T LEAVE YA ALONE UNTIL YOU ANSWER.
JUST STAY QUIET. ACT LIKE YOU'RE NOT INTERESTED...

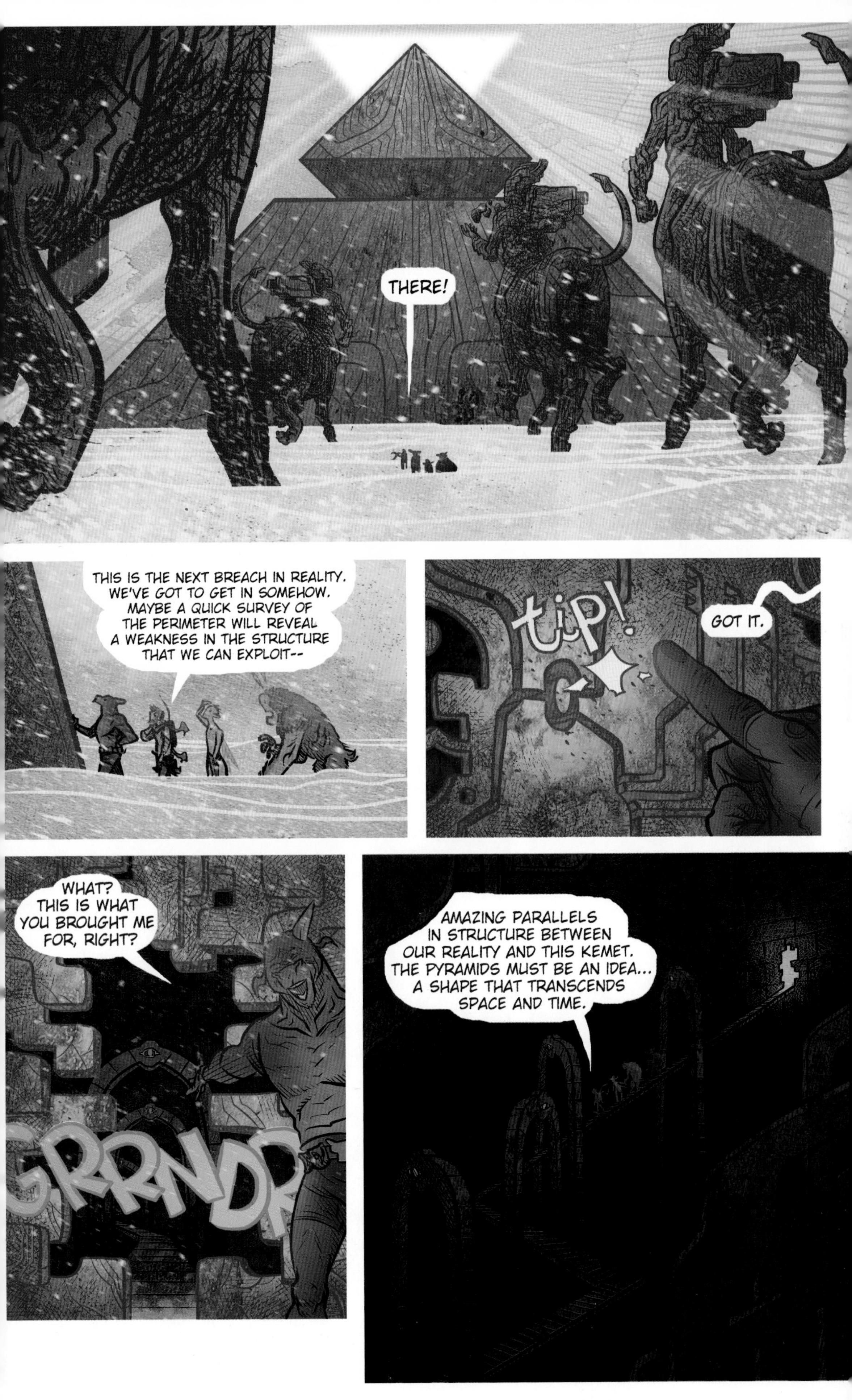
THERE!
THIS IS THE NEXT BREACH IN REALITY. WE'VE GOT TO GET IN SOMEHOW. MAYBE A QUICK SURVEY OF THE PERIMETER WILL REVEAL A WEAKNESS IN THE STRUCTURE THAT WE CAN EXPLOIT--
tip!
GOT IT.
WHAT? THIS IS WHAT YOU BROUGHT ME FOR, RIGHT?
GRRNDR
AMAZING PARALLELS IN STRUCTURE BETWEEN OUR REALITY AND THIS KEMET. THE PYRAMIDS MUST BE AN IDEA... A SHAPE THAT TRANSCENDS SPACE AND TIME.

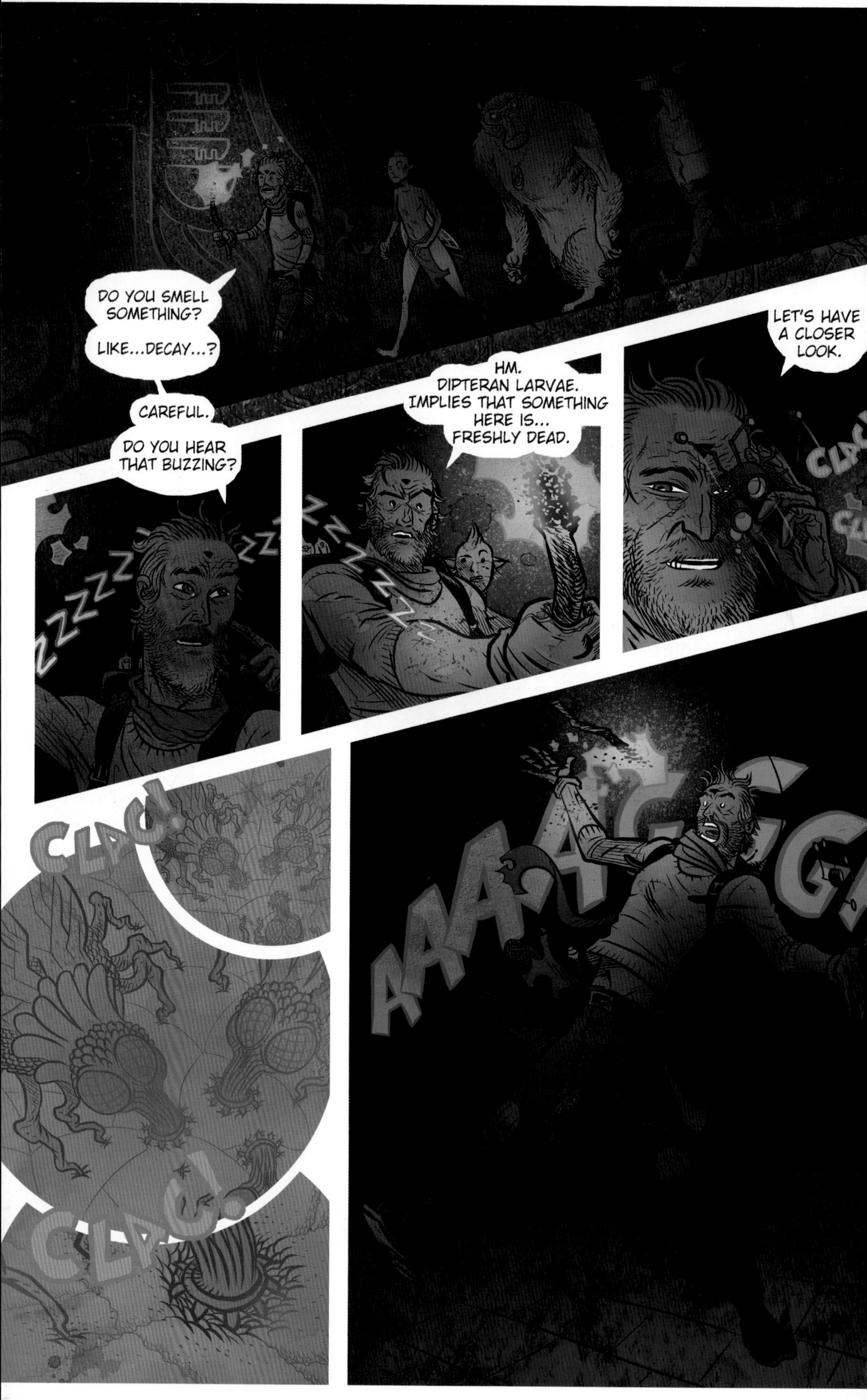
DO YOU SMELL SOMETHING?
LIKE...DECAY...?
CAREFUL.
DO YOU HEAR THAT BUZZING?
ZZZZZ
HM. DIPTERAN LARVAE. IMPLIES THAT SOMETHING HERE IS... FRESHLY DEAD.
LET'S HAVE A CLOSER LOOK.
CLAC!
CLAC!
AAAAAGG

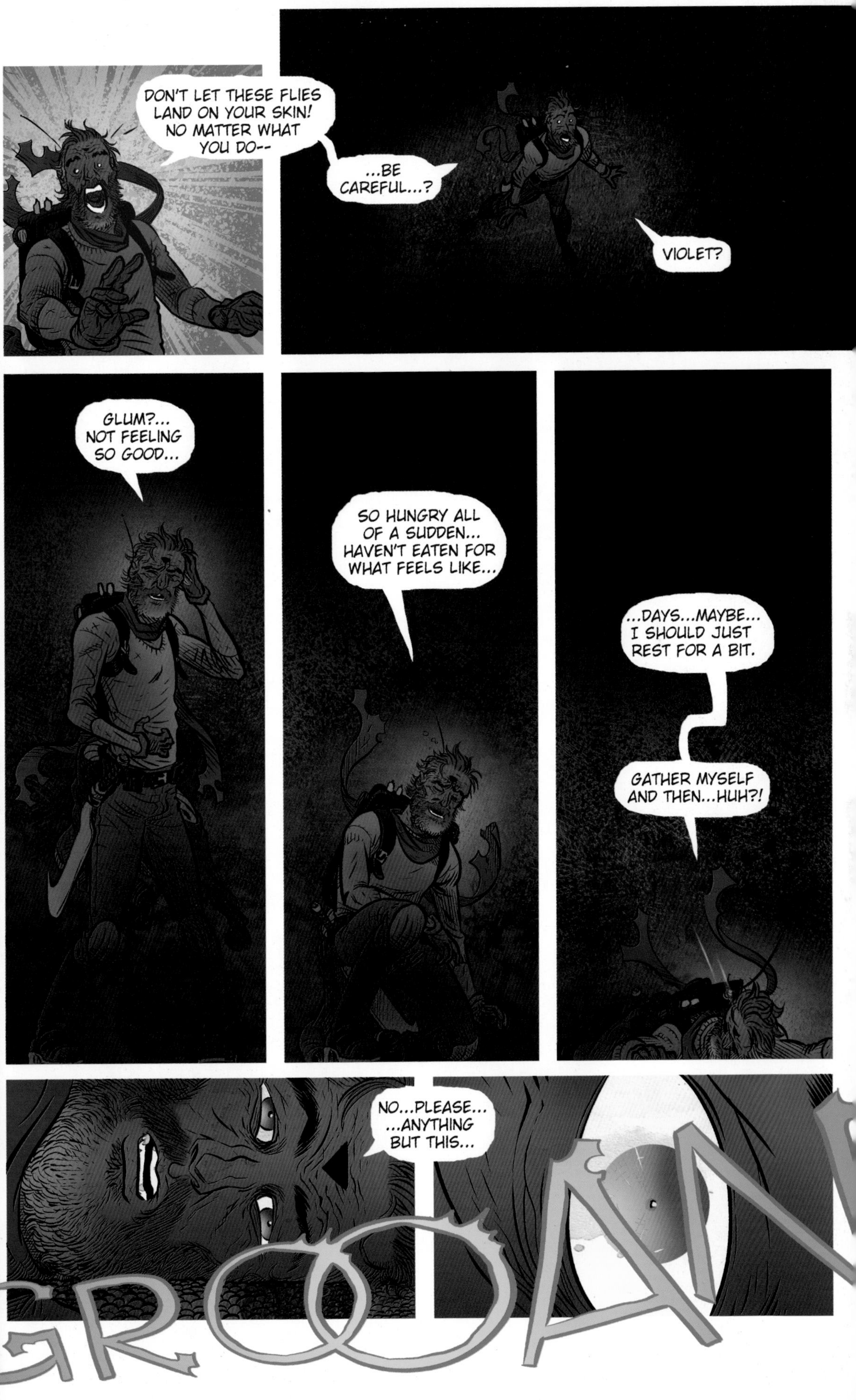
DON'T LET THESE FLIES LAND ON YOUR SKIN! NO MATTER WHAT YOU DO--
...BE CAREFUL...?
VIOLET?
GLUM?... NOT FEELING SO GOOD...
SO HUNGRY ALL OF A SUDDEN... HAVEN'T EATEN FOR WHAT FEELS LIKE...
...DAYS...MAYBE... I SHOULD JUST REST FOR A BIT.
GATHER MYSELF AND THEN...HUH?!
NO...PLEASE... ...ANYTHING BUT THIS...
GROAN

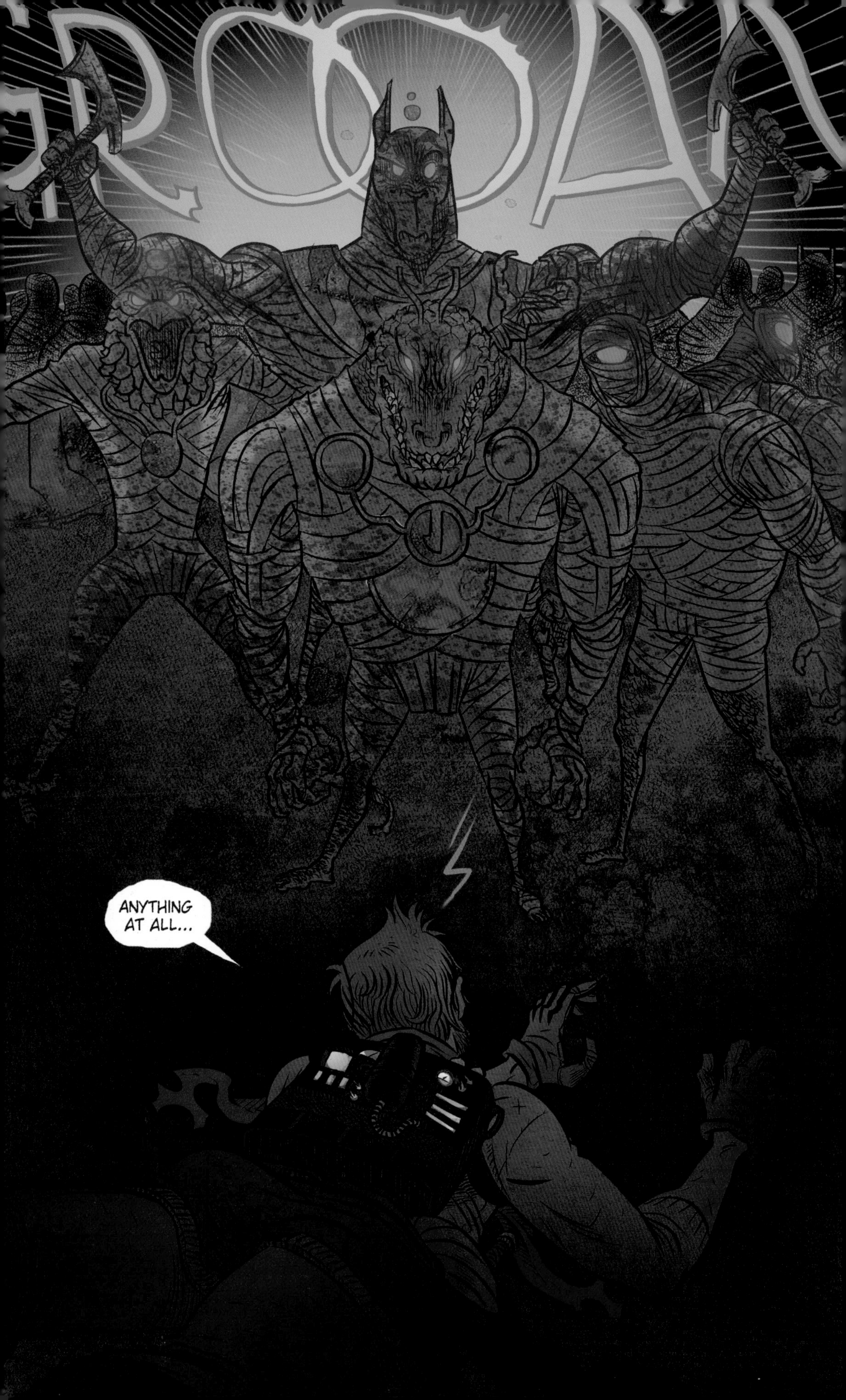
GROAR
ANYTHING AT ALL...

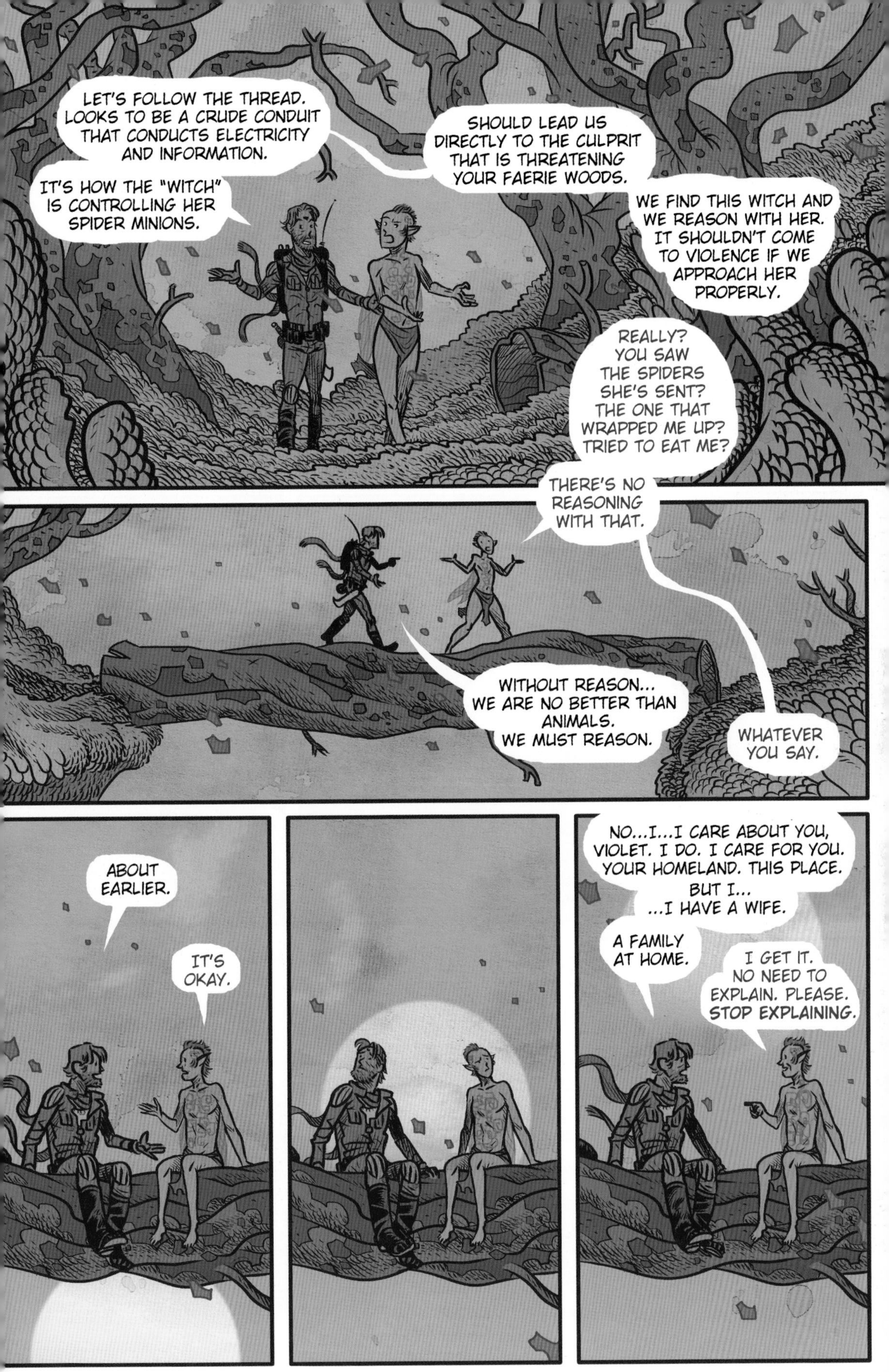

LET'S FOLLOW THE THREAD. LOOKS TO BE A CRUDE CONDUIT THAT CONDUCTS ELECTRICITY AND INFORMATION.
IT'S HOW THE "WITCH" IS CONTROLLING HER SPIDER MINIONS.
SHOULD LEAD US DIRECTLY TO THE CULPRIT THAT IS THREATENING YOUR FAERIE WOODS.
WE FIND THIS WITCH AND WE REASON WITH HER. IT SHOULDN'T COME TO VIOLENCE IF WE APPROACH HER PROPERLY.
REALLY? YOU SAW THE SPIDERS SHE'S SENT? THE ONE THAT WRAPPED ME UP? TRIED TO EAT ME?
THERE'S NO REASONING WITH THAT.
WITHOUT REASON... WE ARE NO BETTER THAN ANIMALS. WE MUST REASON.
WHATEVER YOU SAY.
ABOUT EARLIER.
IT'S OKAY.
NO...I...I CARE ABOUT YOU, VIOLET. I DO. I CARE FOR YOU. YOUR HOMELAND. THIS PLACE.
BUT I... ...I HAVE A WIFE.
A FAMILY AT HOME.
I GET IT. NO NEED TO EXPLAIN. PLEASE. STOP EXPLAINING.

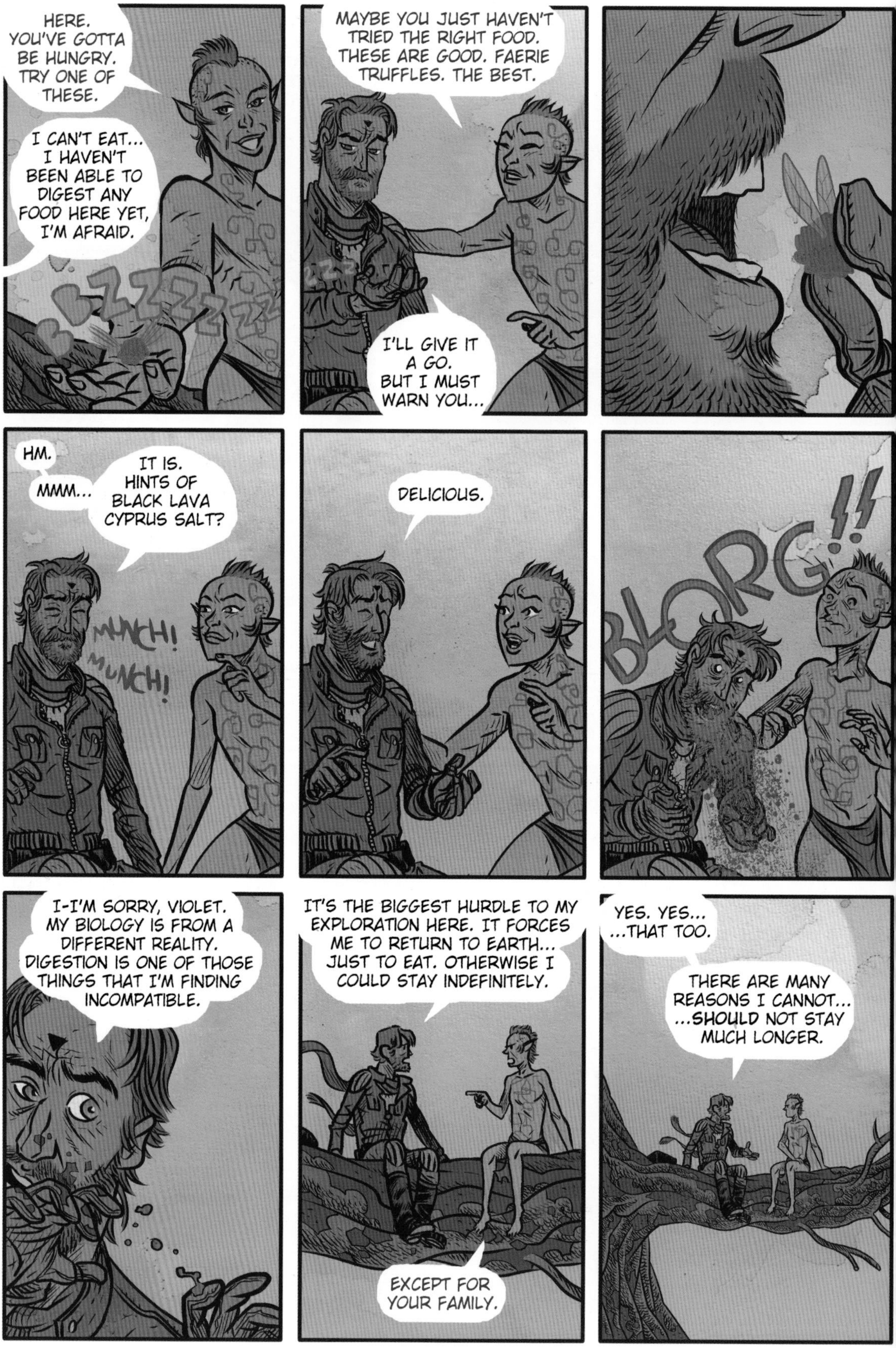
HERE. YOU'VE GOTTA BE HUNGRY. TRY ONE OF THESE.
I CAN'T EAT... I HAVEN'T BEEN ABLE TO DIGEST ANY FOOD HERE YET, I'M AFRAID.
MAYBE YOU JUST HAVEN'T TRIED THE RIGHT FOOD. THESE ARE GOOD. FAERIE TRUFFLES. THE BEST.
I'LL GIVE IT A GO. BUT I MUST WARN YOU...
HM.
MMM...
IT IS. HINTS OF BLACK LAVA CYPRUS SALT?
MUNCH!
MUNCH!
DELICIOUS.
BLORG!!
I-I'M SORRY, VIOLET. MY BIOLOGY IS FROM A DIFFERENT REALITY. DIGESTION IS ONE OF THOSE THINGS THAT I'M FINDING INCOMPATIBLE.
IT'S THE BIGGEST HURDLE TO MY EXPLORATION HERE. IT FORCES ME TO RETURN TO EARTH... JUST TO EAT. OTHERWISE I COULD STAY INDEFINITELY.
EXCEPT FOR YOUR FAMILY.
YES. YES... ...THAT TOO.
THERE ARE MANY REASONS I CANNOT... ...SHOULD NOT STAY MUCH LONGER.

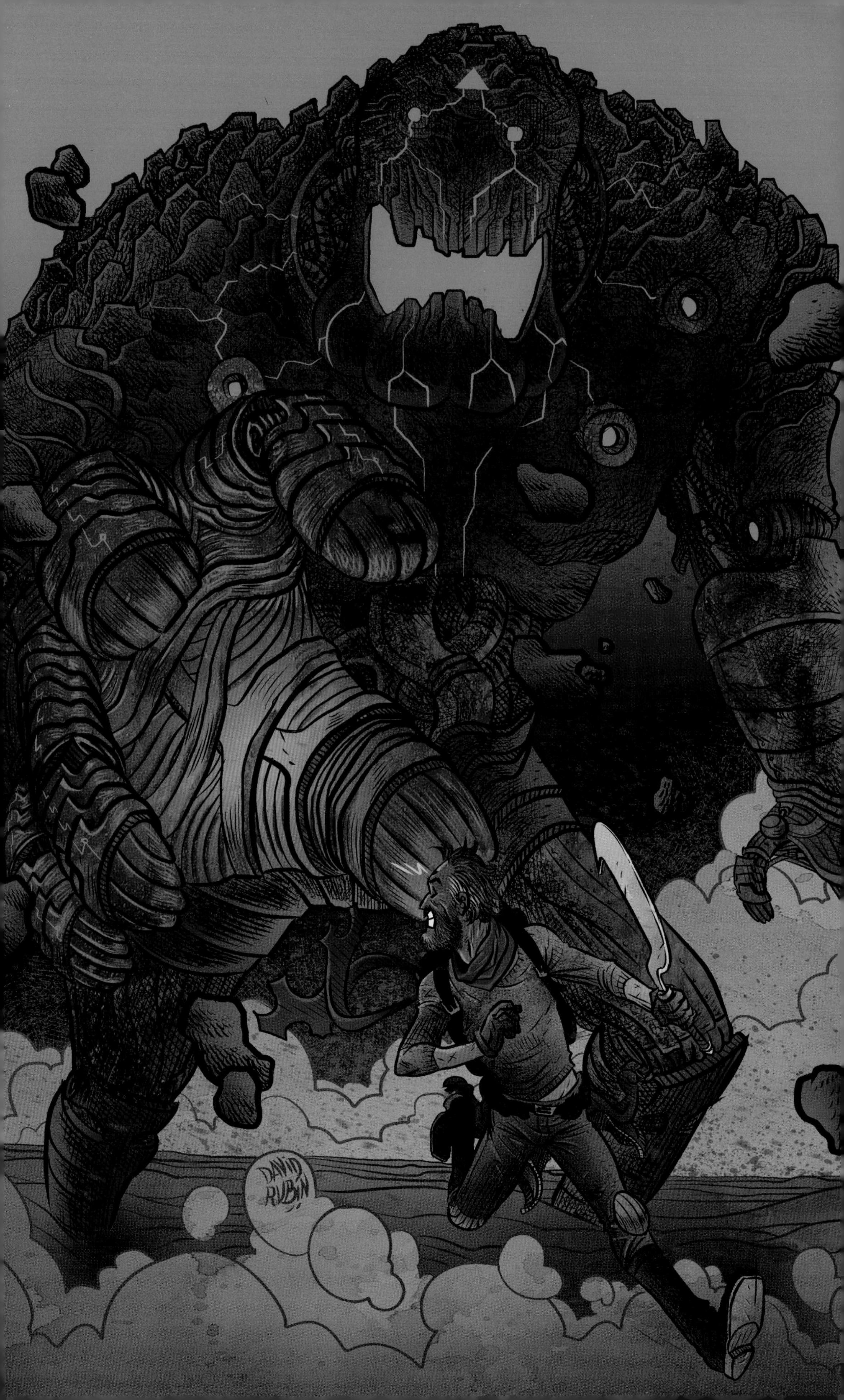
DAVID RUBIN

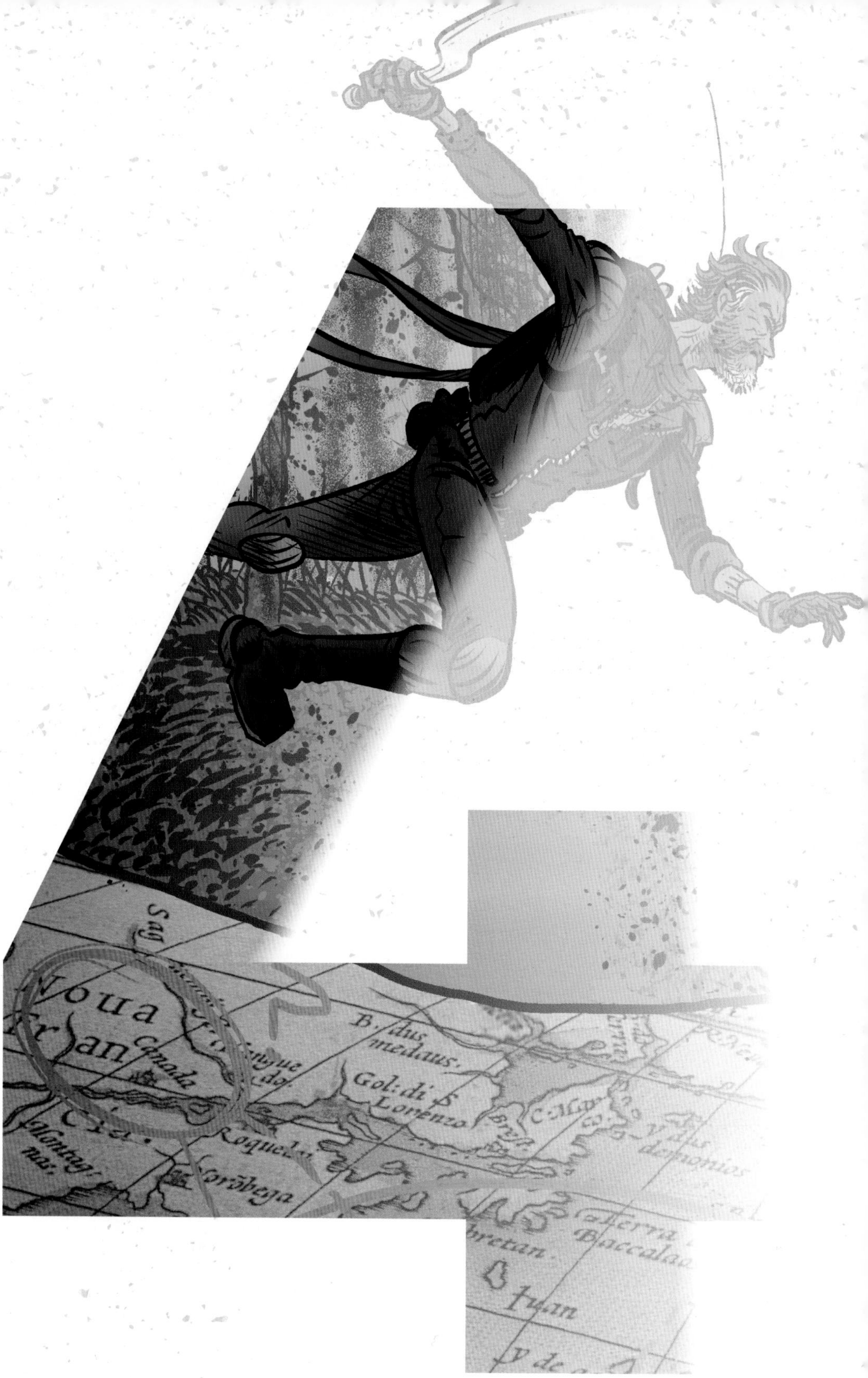
Noua
Canada
Gol: di S
Lorenzo
Norõbega
bretan.

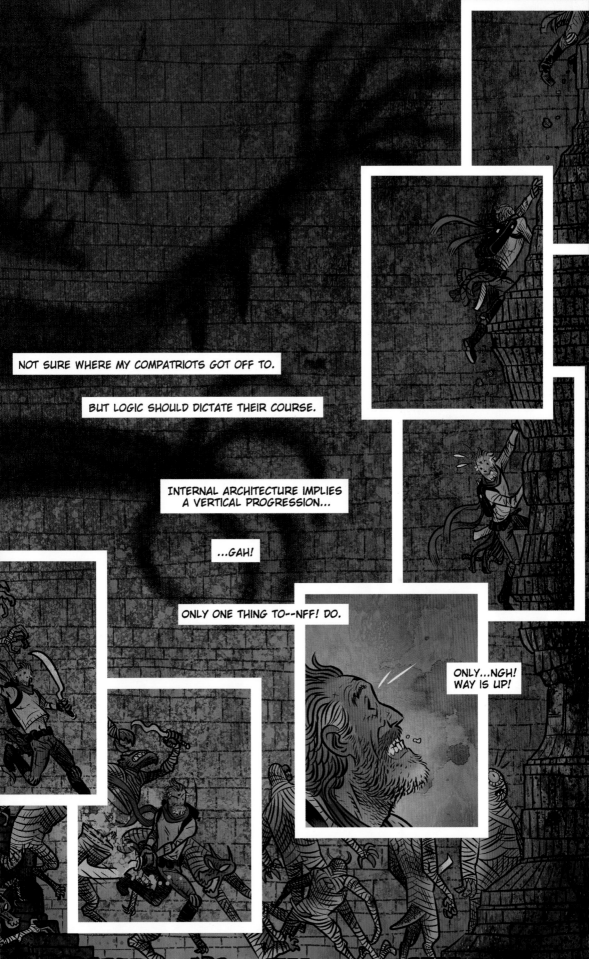

NOT SURE WHERE MY COMPATRIOTS GOT OFF TO.

BUT LOGIC SHOULD DICTATE THEIR COURSE.

INTERNAL ARCHITECTURE IMPLIES
A VERTICAL PROGRESSION...

...GAH!

ONLY ONE THING TO--NFF! DO.

ONLY...NGH!
WAY IS UP!

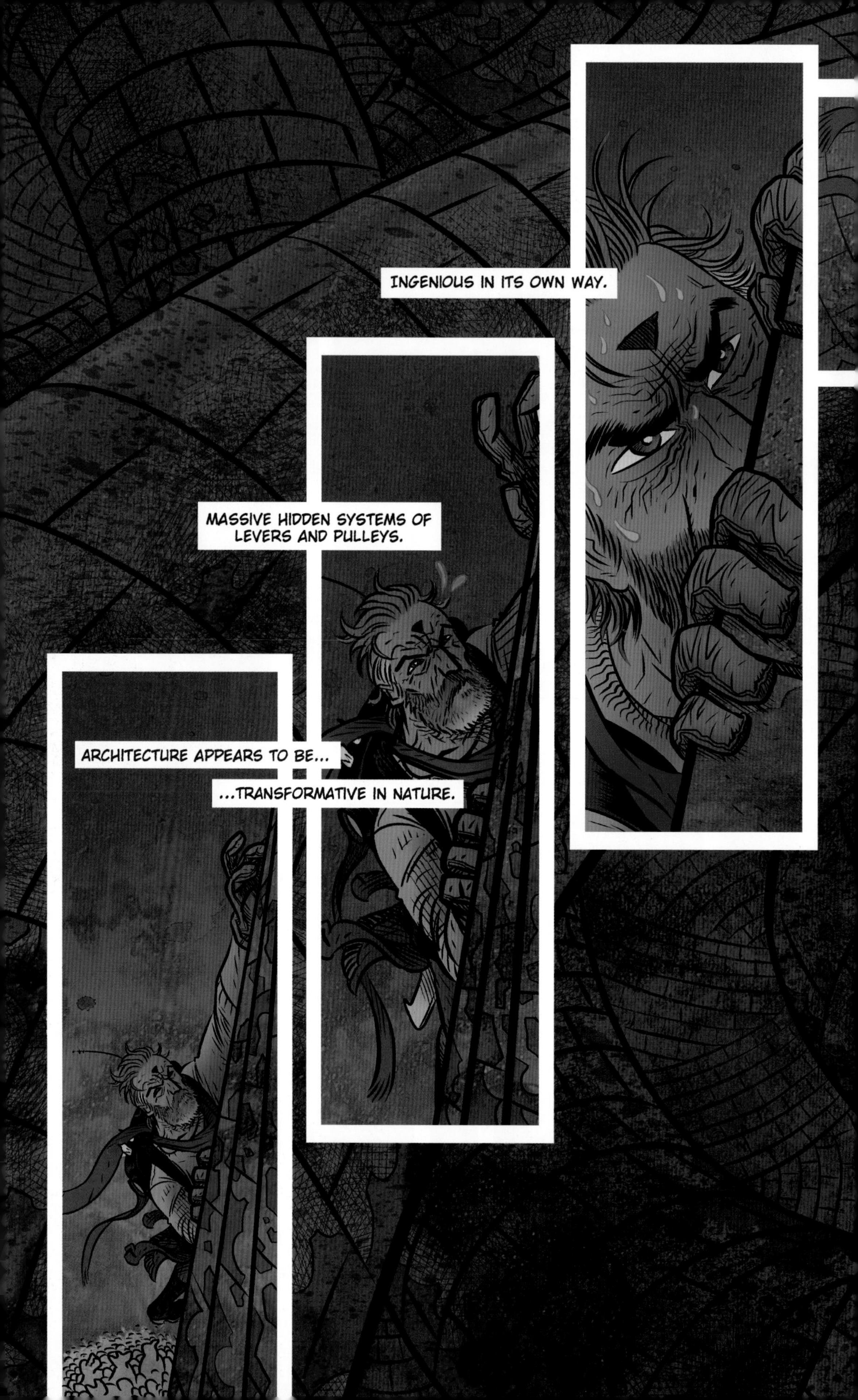
INGENIOUS IN ITS OWN WAY.
MASSIVE HIDDEN SYSTEMS OF LEVERS AND PULLEYS.
ARCHITECTURE APPEARS TO BE...
...TRANSFORMATIVE IN NATURE.

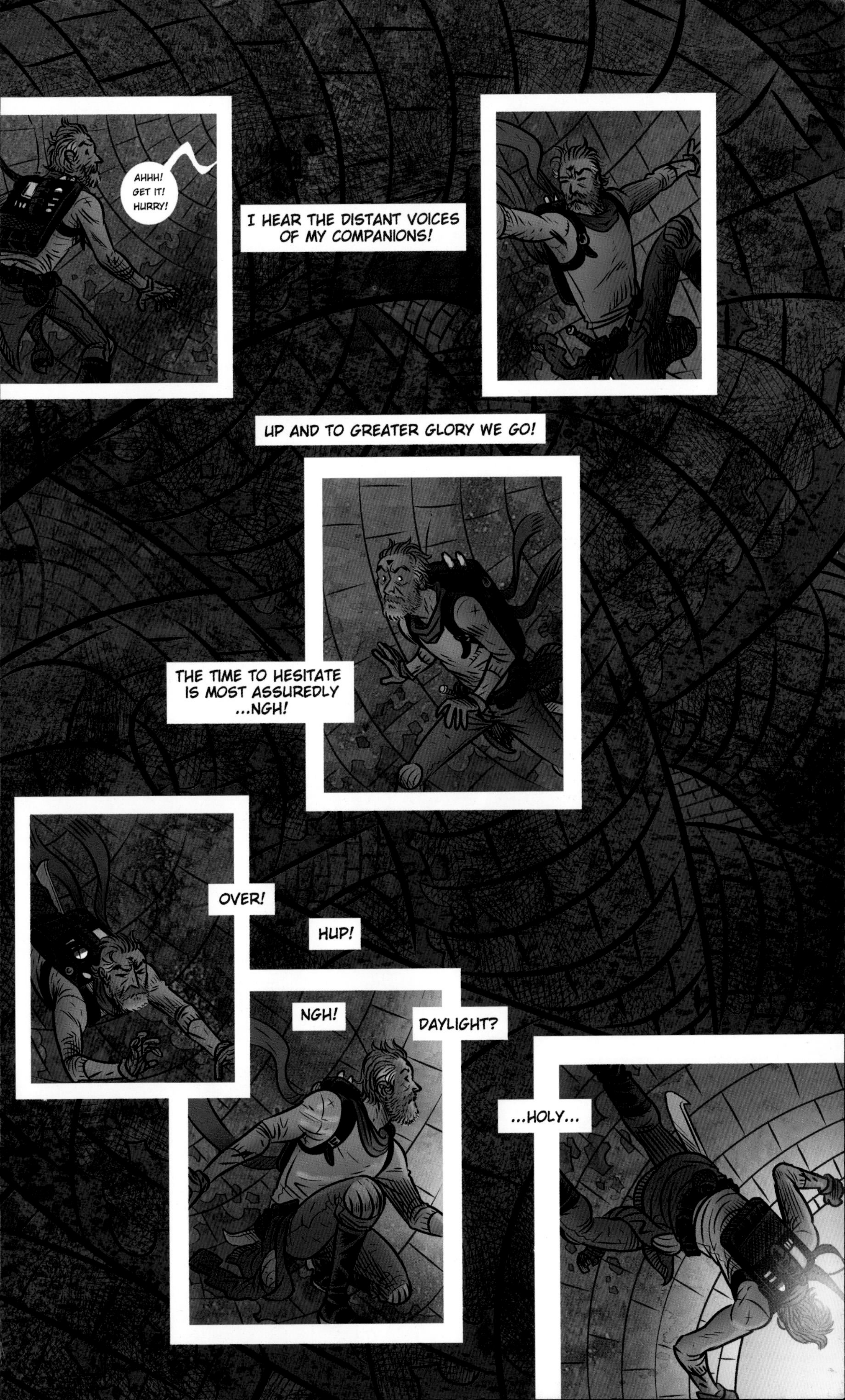
AHHH! GET IT! HURRY!
I HEAR THE DISTANT VOICES OF MY COMPANIONS!
UP AND TO GREATER GLORY WE GO!
THE TIME TO HESITATE IS MOST ASSUREDLY ...NGH!
OVER!
HUP!
NGH!
DAYLIGHT?
...HOLY...

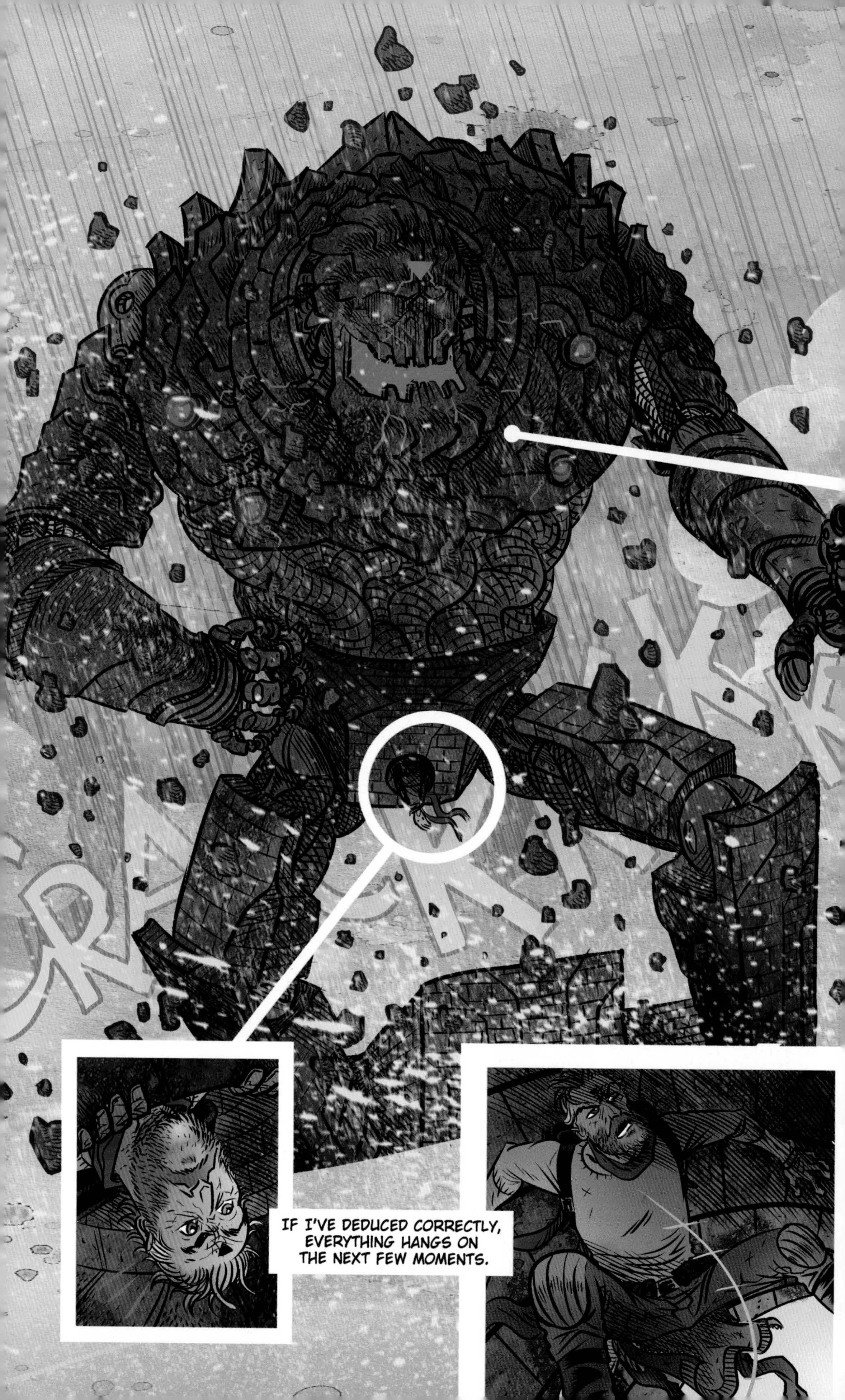
IF I'VE DEDUCED CORRECTLY, EVERYTHING HANGS ON THE NEXT FEW MOMENTS.

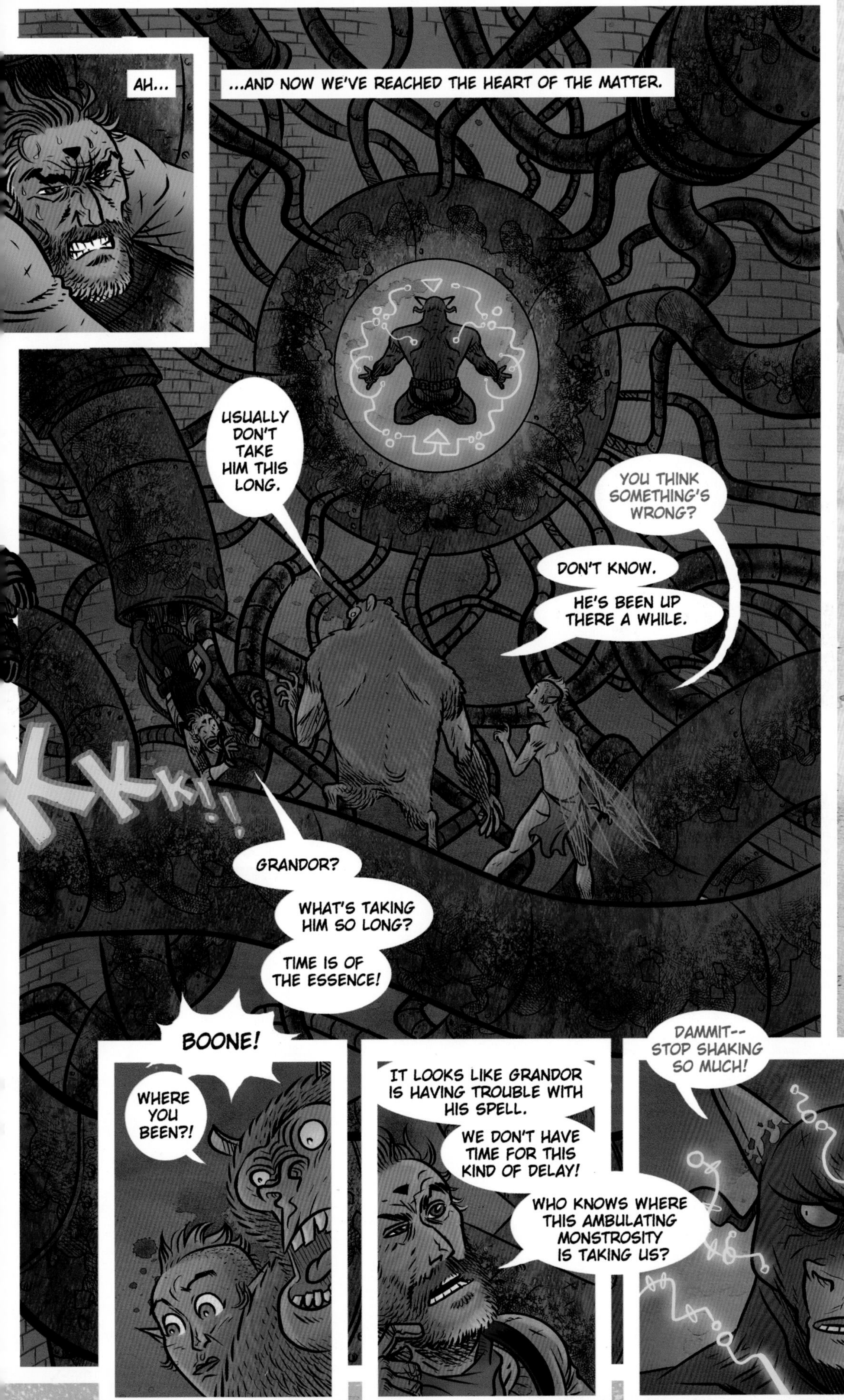
AH...
...AND NOW WE'VE REACHED THE HEART OF THE MATTER.
USUALLY DON'T TAKE HIM THIS LONG.
YOU THINK SOMETHING'S WRONG?
DON'T KNOW.
HE'S BEEN UP THERE A WHILE.
KKK!!
GRANDOR?
WHAT'S TAKING HIM SO LONG?
TIME IS OF THE ESSENCE!
BOONE!
WHERE YOU BEEN?!
IT LOOKS LIKE GRANDOR IS HAVING TROUBLE WITH HIS SPELL.
WE DON'T HAVE TIME FOR THIS KIND OF DELAY!
WHO KNOWS WHERE THIS AMBULATING MONSTROSITY IS TAKING US?
DAMMIT-- STOP SHAKING SO MUCH!

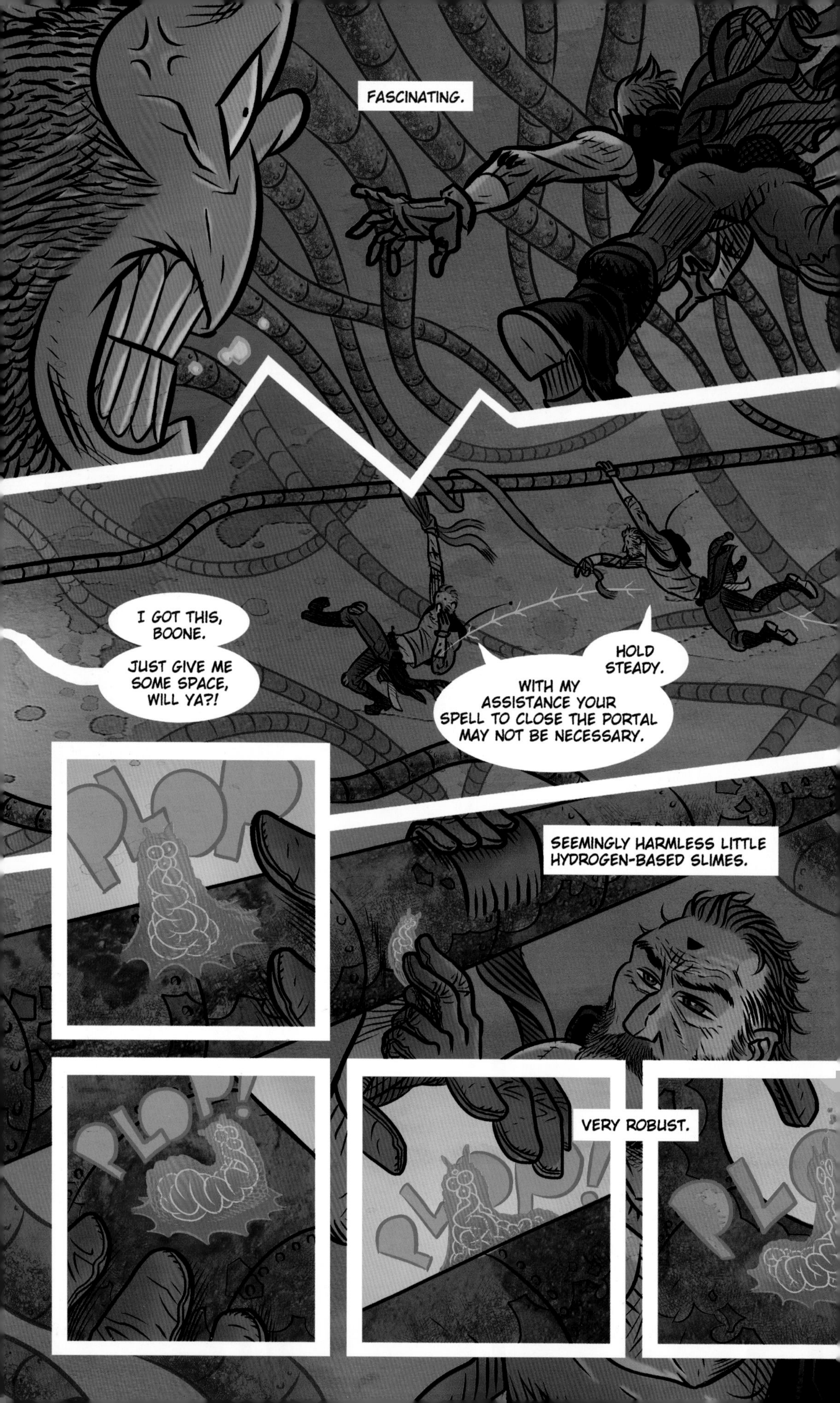
FASCINATING.
I GOT THIS, BOONE.
JUST GIVE ME SOME SPACE, WILL YA?!
HOLD STEADY.
WITH MY ASSISTANCE YOUR SPELL TO CLOSE THE PORTAL MAY NOT BE NECESSARY.
PLOP
SEEMINGLY HARMLESS LITTLE HYDROGEN-BASED SLIMES.
PLOP!
VERY ROBUST.
PLOP!
PLO

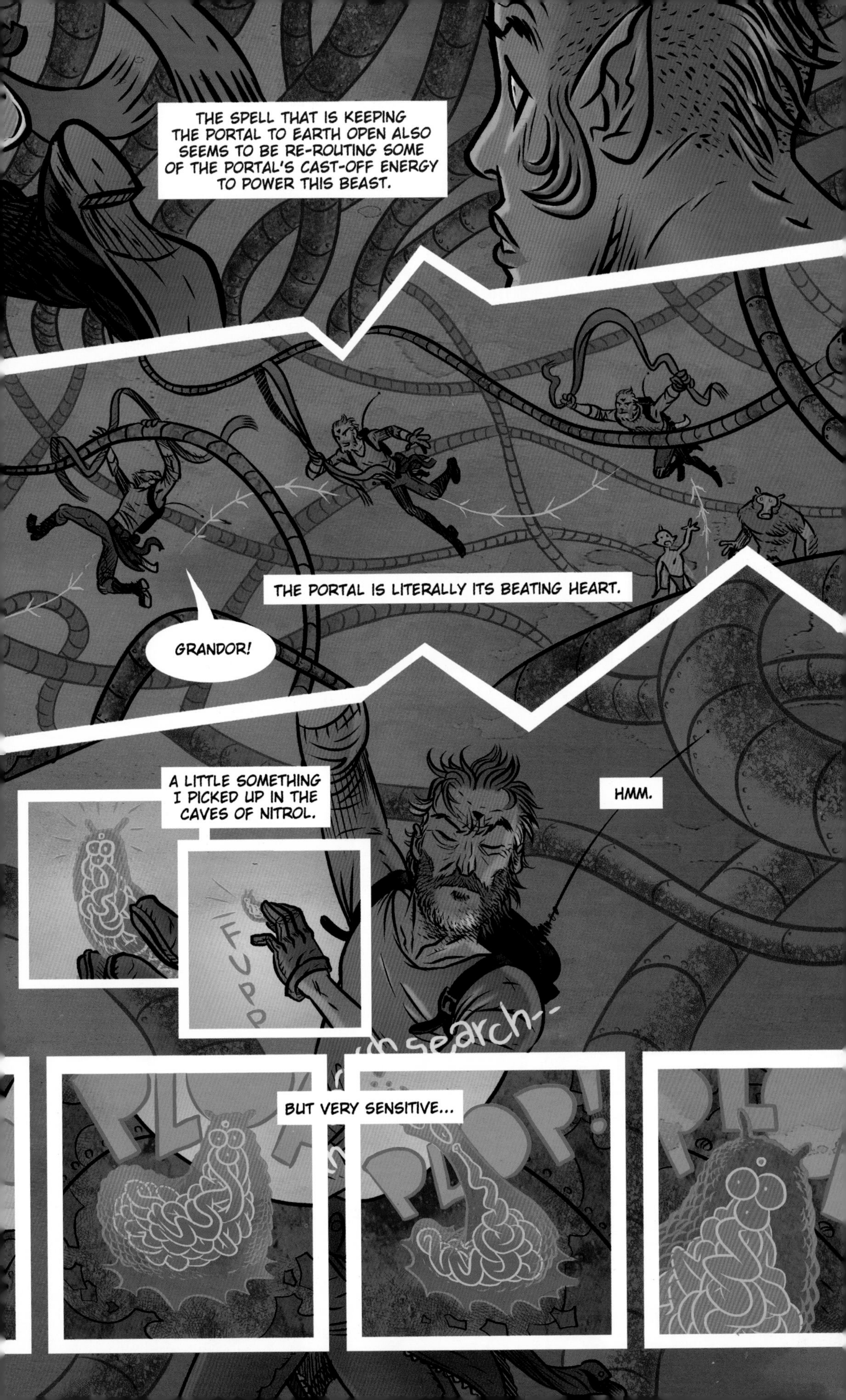
THE SPELL THAT IS KEEPING THE PORTAL TO EARTH OPEN ALSO SEEMS TO BE RE-ROUTING SOME OF THE PORTAL'S CAST-OFF ENERGY TO POWER THIS BEAST.
THE PORTAL IS LITERALLY ITS BEATING HEART.
GRANDOR!
A LITTLE SOMETHING I PICKED UP IN THE CAVES OF NITROL.
HMM.
FUPP
search--
BUT VERY SENSITIVE...
PLOOP!

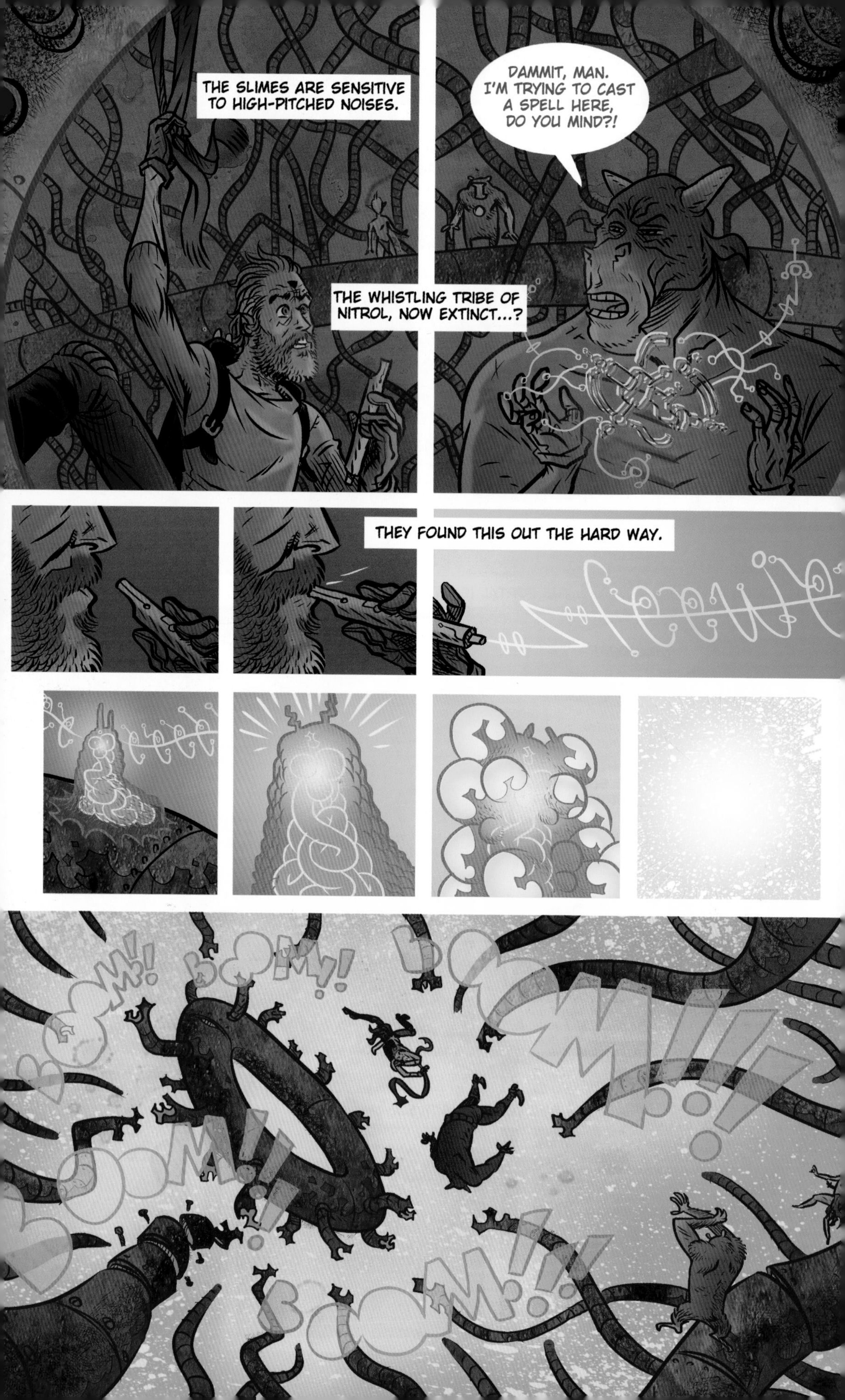
THE SLIMES ARE SENSITIVE TO HIGH-PITCHED NOISES.
DAMMIT, MAN. I'M TRYING TO CAST A SPELL HERE, DO YOU MIND?!
THE WHISTLING TRIBE OF NITROL, NOW EXTINCT...?
THEY FOUND THIS OUT THE HARD WAY.
BOOM!
BOOM!
BOOM!!
BOOM!!
BOOM!!!

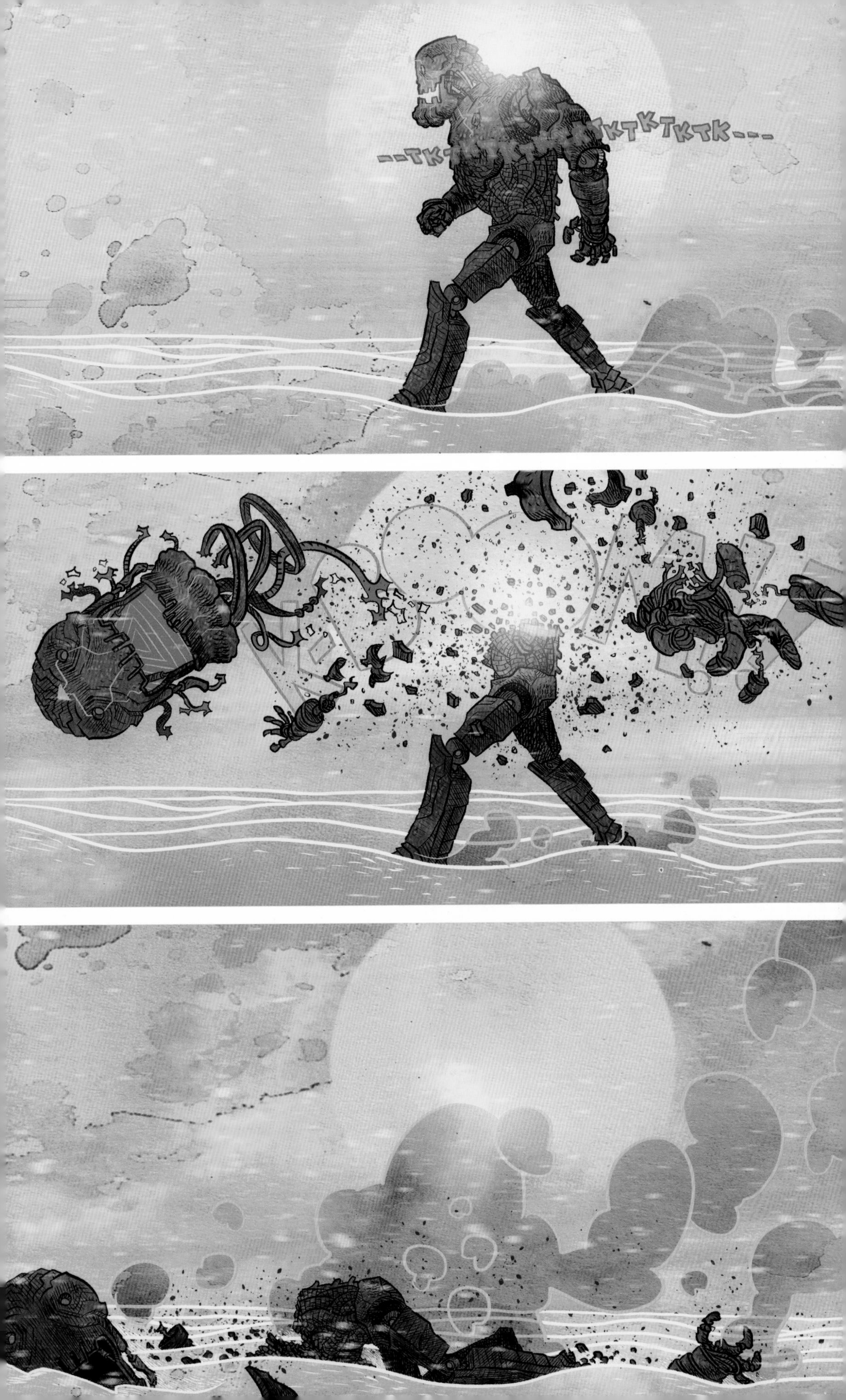
--TK- TKTKTKTK---

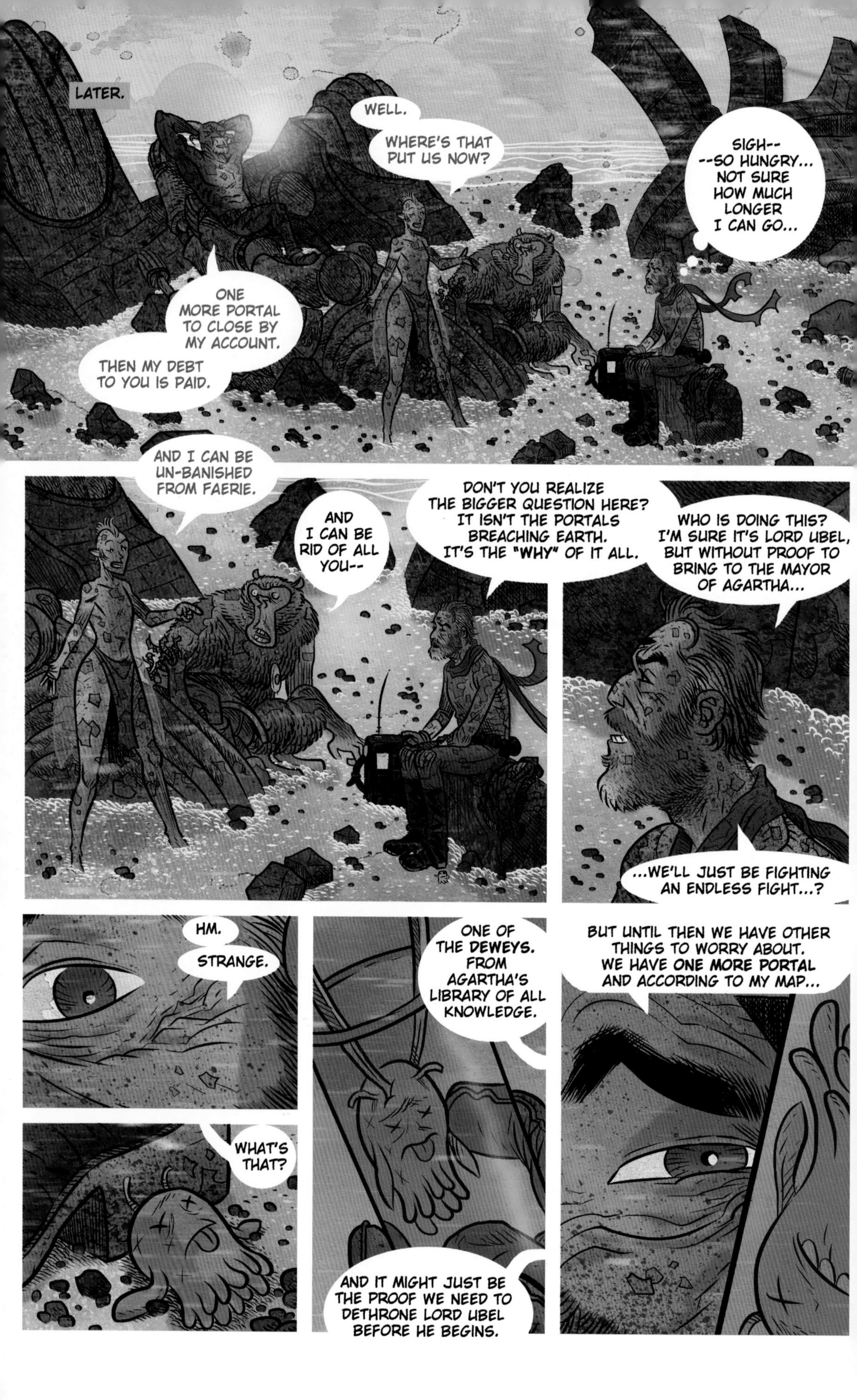
LATER.
WELL.
WHERE'S THAT PUT US NOW?
SIGH-- --SO HUNGRY... NOT SURE HOW MUCH LONGER I CAN GO...
ONE MORE PORTAL TO CLOSE BY MY ACCOUNT.
THEN MY DEBT TO YOU IS PAID.
AND I CAN BE UN-BANISHED FROM FAERIE.
AND I CAN BE RID OF ALL YOU--
DON'T YOU REALIZE THE BIGGER QUESTION HERE? IT ISN'T THE PORTALS BREACHING EARTH. IT'S THE "WHY" OF IT ALL.
WHO IS DOING THIS? I'M SURE IT'S LORD UBEL, BUT WITHOUT PROOF TO BRING TO THE MAYOR OF AGARTHA...
...WE'LL JUST BE FIGHTING AN ENDLESS FIGHT...?
HM.
STRANGE.
WHAT'S THAT?
ONE OF THE DEWEYS. FROM AGARTHA'S LIBRARY OF ALL KNOWLEDGE.
AND IT MIGHT JUST BE THE PROOF WE NEED TO DETHRONE LORD UBEL BEFORE HE BEGINS.
BUT UNTIL THEN WE HAVE OTHER THINGS TO WORRY ABOUT. WE HAVE ONE MORE PORTAL AND ACCORDING TO MY MAP...

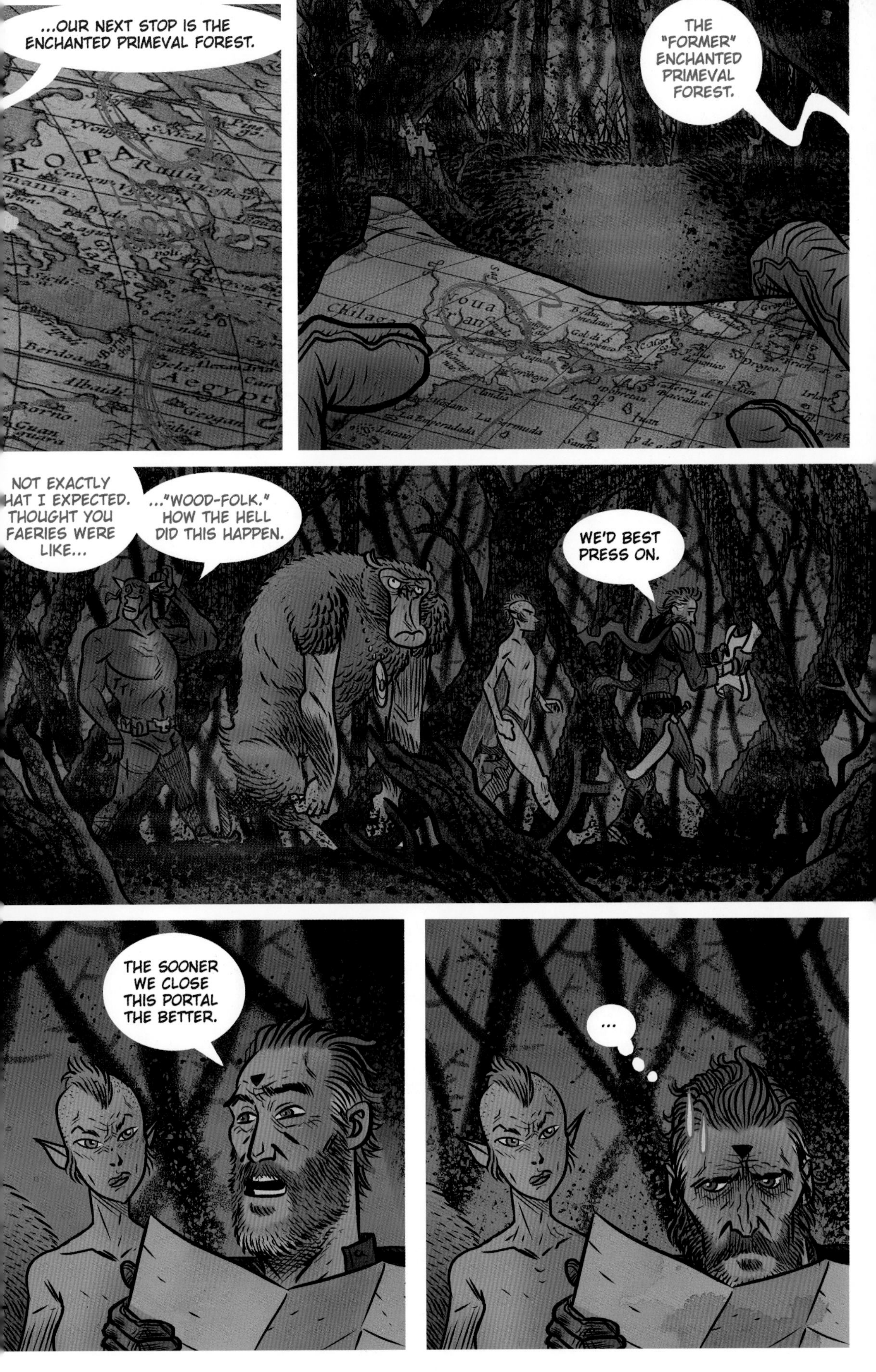
...OUR NEXT STOP IS THE ENCHANTED PRIMEVAL FOREST.
THE "FORMER" ENCHANTED PRIMEVAL FOREST.
NOT EXACTLY HAT I EXPECTED. THOUGHT YOU FAERIES WERE LIKE...
..."WOOD-FOLK." HOW THE HELL DID THIS HAPPEN.
WE'D BEST PRESS ON.
THE SOONER WE CLOSE THIS PORTAL THE BETTER.
...

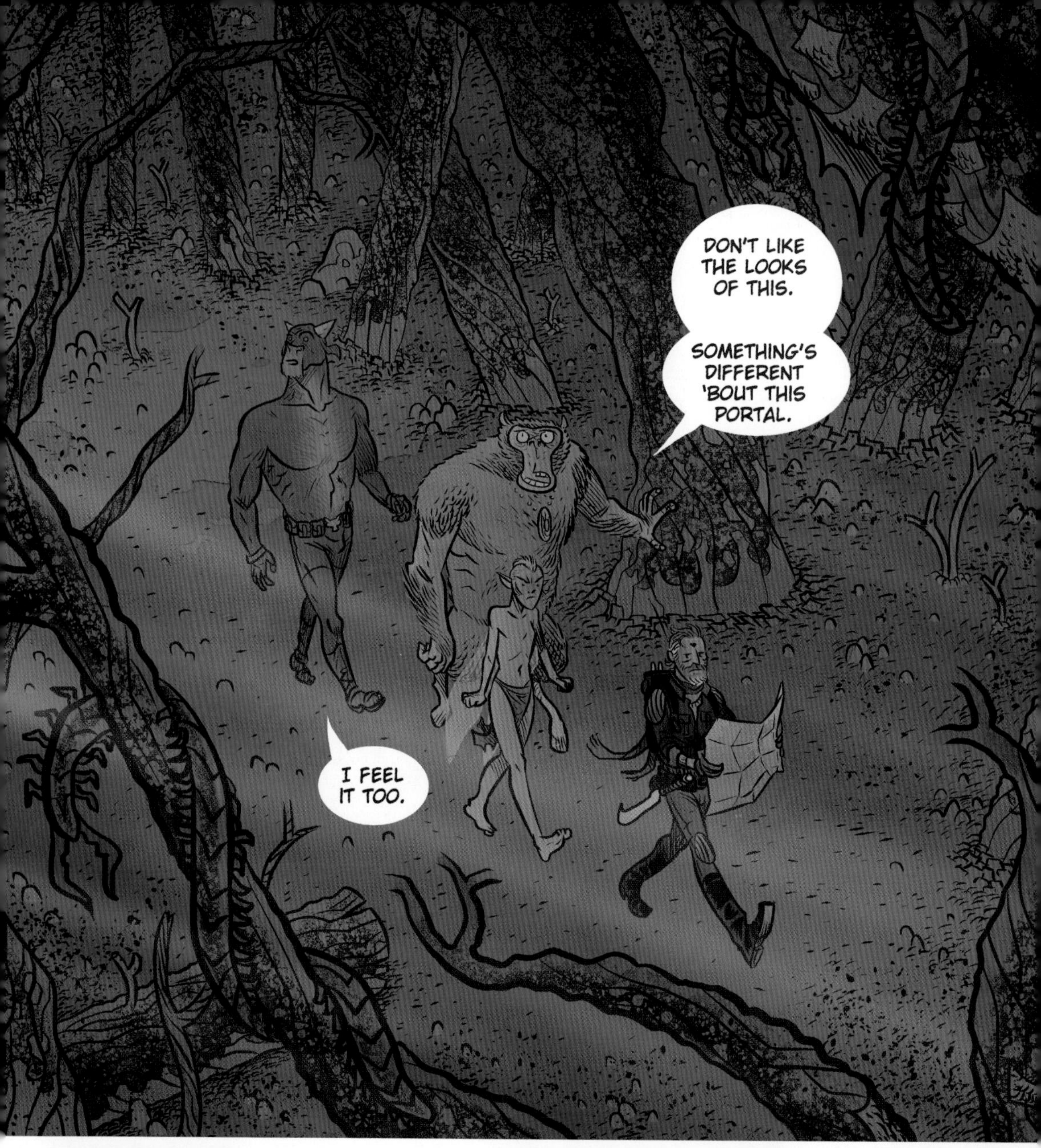
DON'T LIKE THE LOOKS OF THIS.
SOMETHING'S DIFFERENT 'BOUT THIS PORTAL.
I FEEL IT TOO.

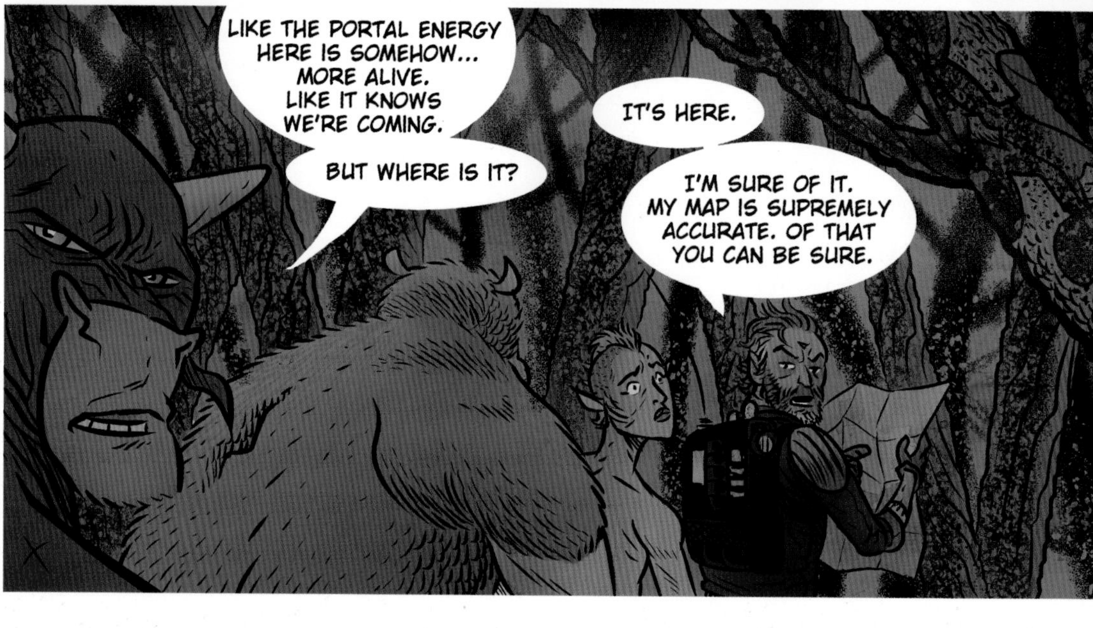
LIKE THE PORTAL ENERGY HERE IS SOMEHOW... MORE ALIVE. LIKE IT KNOWS WE'RE COMING.
BUT WHERE IS IT?
IT'S HERE.
I'M SURE OF IT. MY MAP IS SUPREMELY ACCURATE. OF THAT YOU CAN BE SURE.

GREETINGS, FELLOW TRAVELERS.

AND THE PORTAL YOU SHALL FIND.

BUT WITH THE PORTAL COMES A TALE.

A STORY WEAVED FOR YOU BY MYSELF. FOR I AM THE MASTER STORYTELLER.

THE GRAND ILLUSTRATOR OF NARRATIVE UNLIKE ANY YOU HAVE EVER--

WE'VE NOT TIME FOR TALES, LITTLE MAN.

LET US FINISH OUR BUSINESS AND THEN WE'LL BE ON OUR WAY. NO HARM, NO FOUL.

BUT YOU DO NOT UNDERSTAND. FOR I AM GALE ANIMIN. MASTER STORYTELLER.

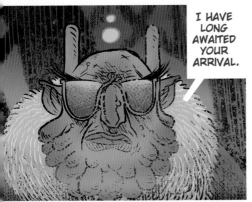

I HAVE LONG AWAITED YOUR ARRIVAL.

YOU'RE HERE FOR THE PORTAL.

AND MY FIRST TALE BEGINS THUS...

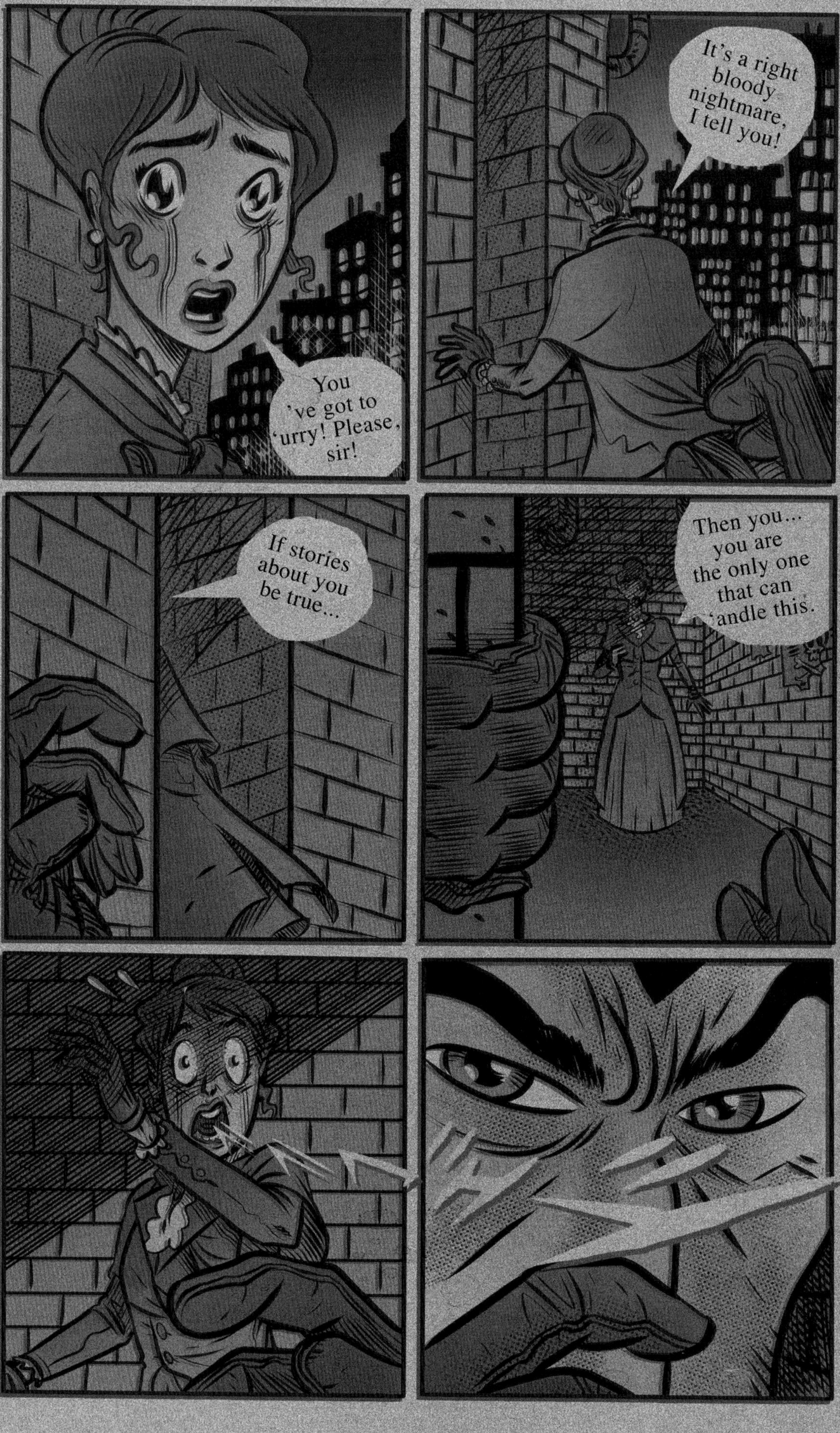
You 've got to 'urry! Please, sir!
It's a right bloody nightmare, I tell you!
If stories about you be true...
Then you... you are the only one that can 'andle this.

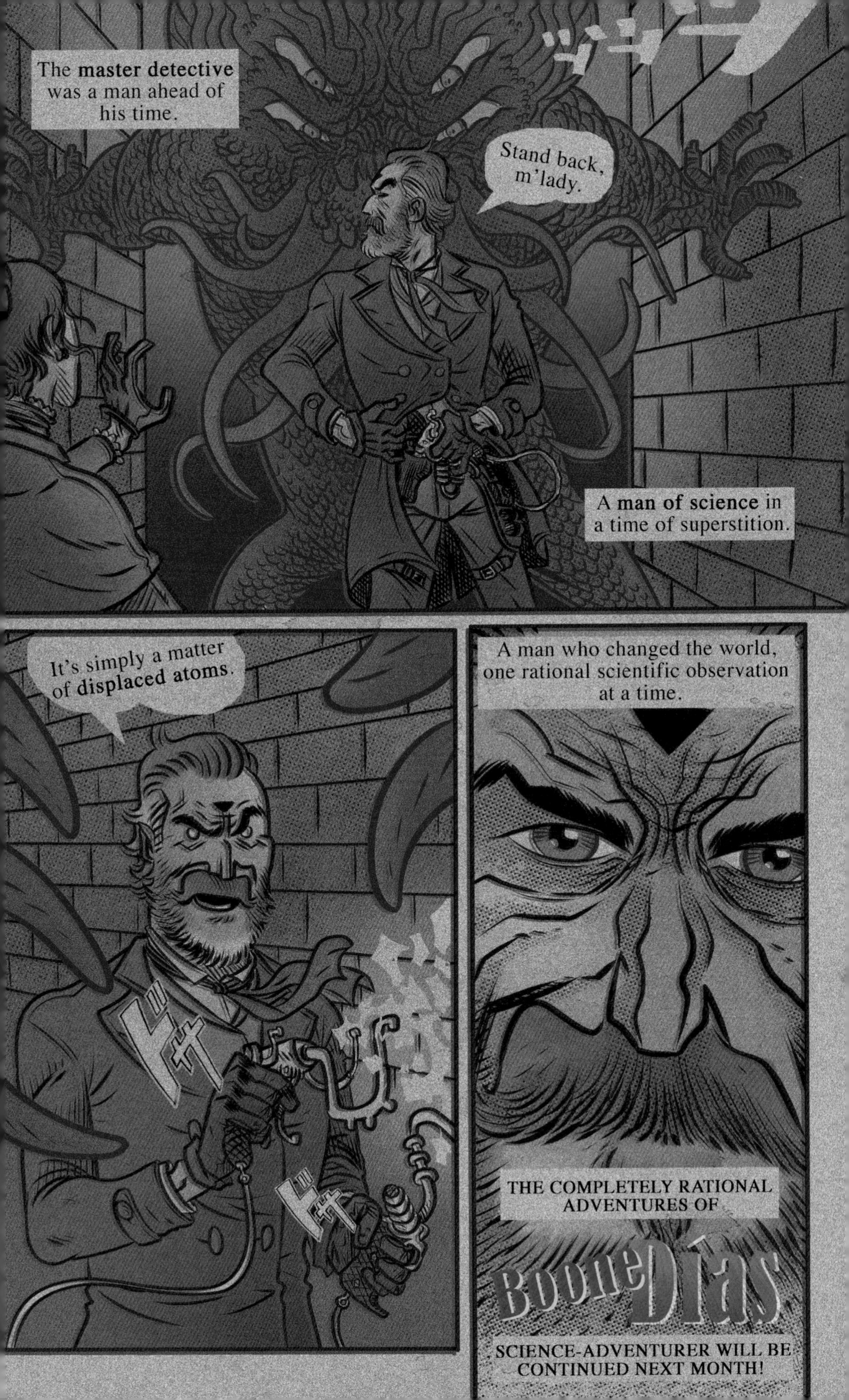

The **master detective** was a man ahead of his time.
Stand back, m'lady.
A **man of science** in a time of superstition.
It's simply a matter of **displaced atoms**.
A man who changed the world, one rational scientific observation at a time.
THE COMPLETELY RATIONAL ADVENTURES OF
Boone Días
SCIENCE-ADVENTURER WILL BE CONTINUED NEXT MONTH!

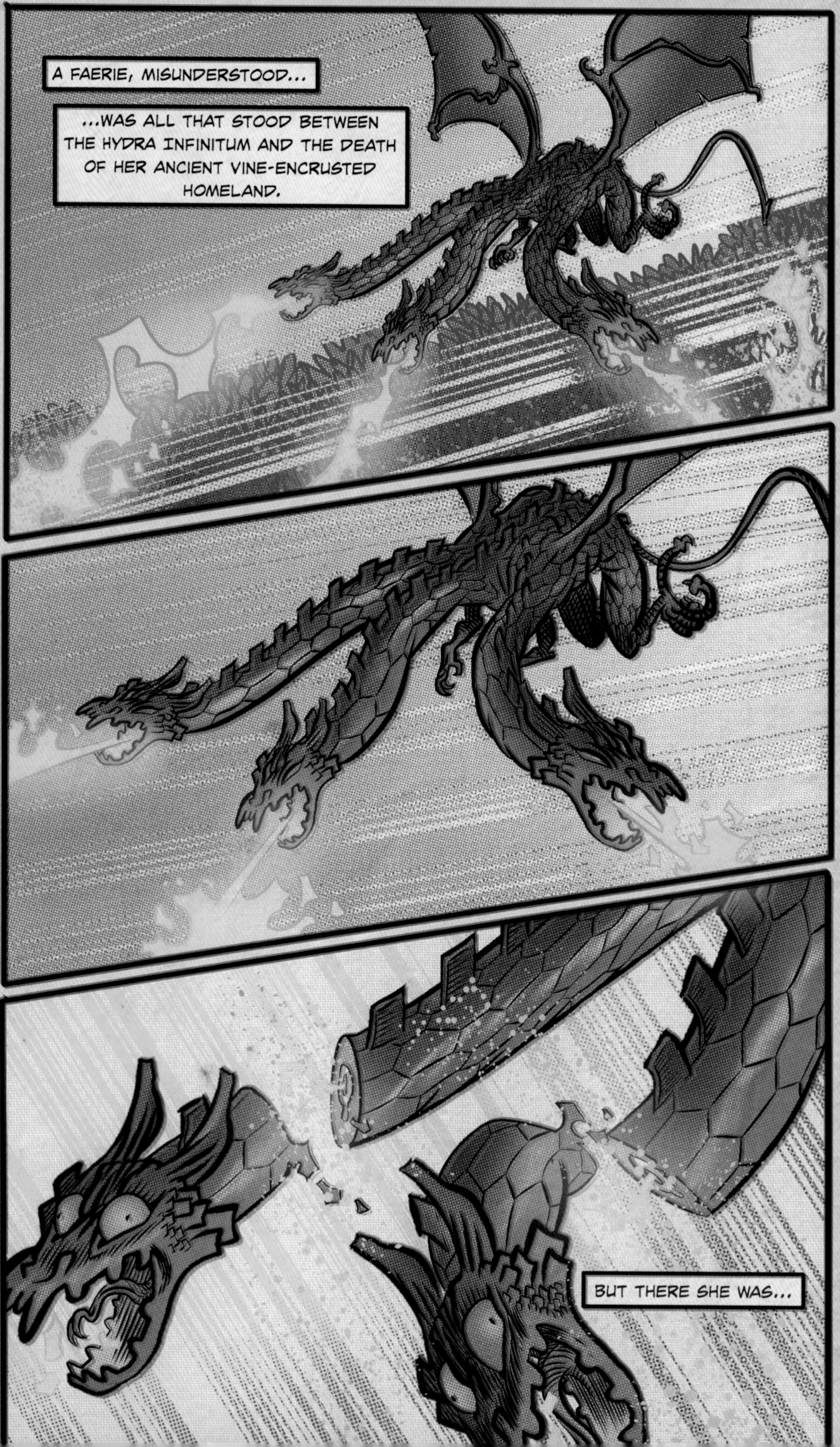
A FAERIE, MISUNDERSTOOD...
...WAS ALL THAT STOOD BETWEEN THE HYDRA INFINITUM AND THE DEATH OF HER ANCIENT VINE-ENCRUSTED HOMELAND.
BUT THERE SHE WAS...

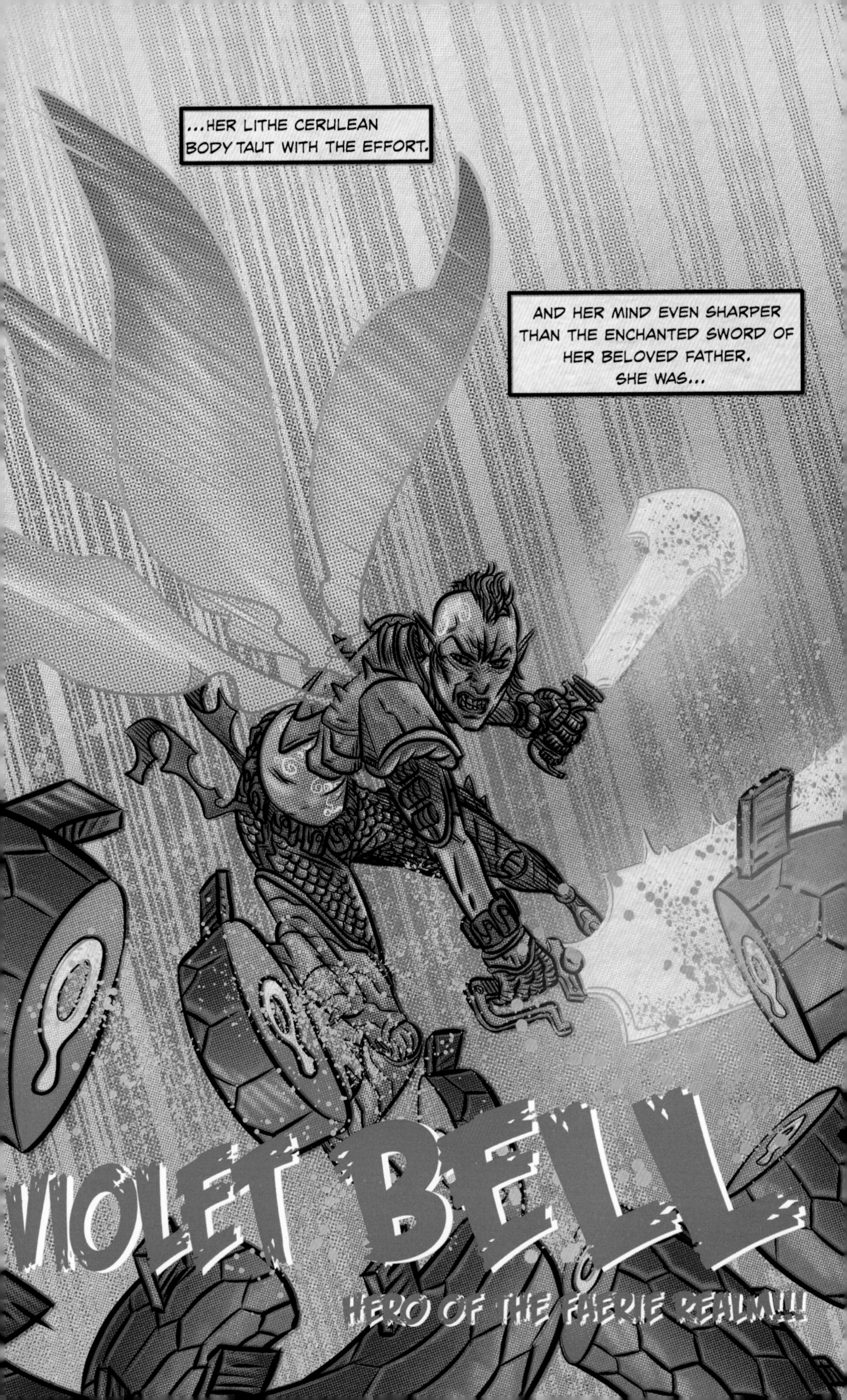
...HER LITHE CERULEAN BODY TAUT WITH THE EFFORT.
AND HER MIND EVEN SHARPER THAN THE ENCHANTED SWORD OF HER BELOVED FATHER. SHE WAS...
VIOLET BELL
HERO OF THE FAERIE REALM!!!

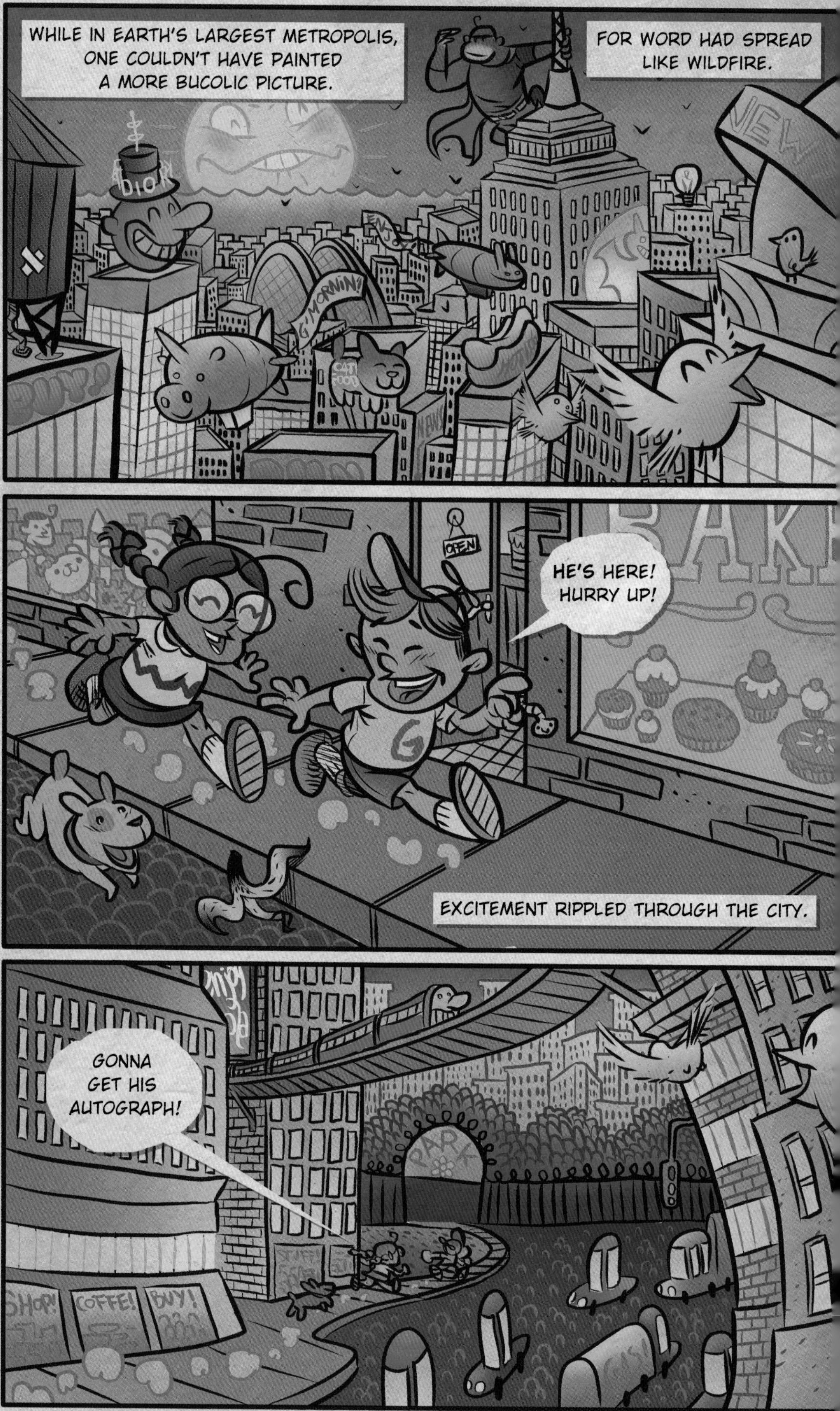
WHILE IN EARTH'S LARGEST METROPOLIS, ONE COULDN'T HAVE PAINTED A MORE BUCOLIC PICTURE.
FOR WORD HAD SPREAD LIKE WILDFIRE.
G'MORNIN'!
CAT FOOD
BUY!
HE'S HERE! HURRY UP!
OPEN
EXCITEMENT RIPPLED THROUGH THE CITY.
GONNA GET HIS AUTOGRAPH!
PARK
SHOP!
COFFE!
BUY!

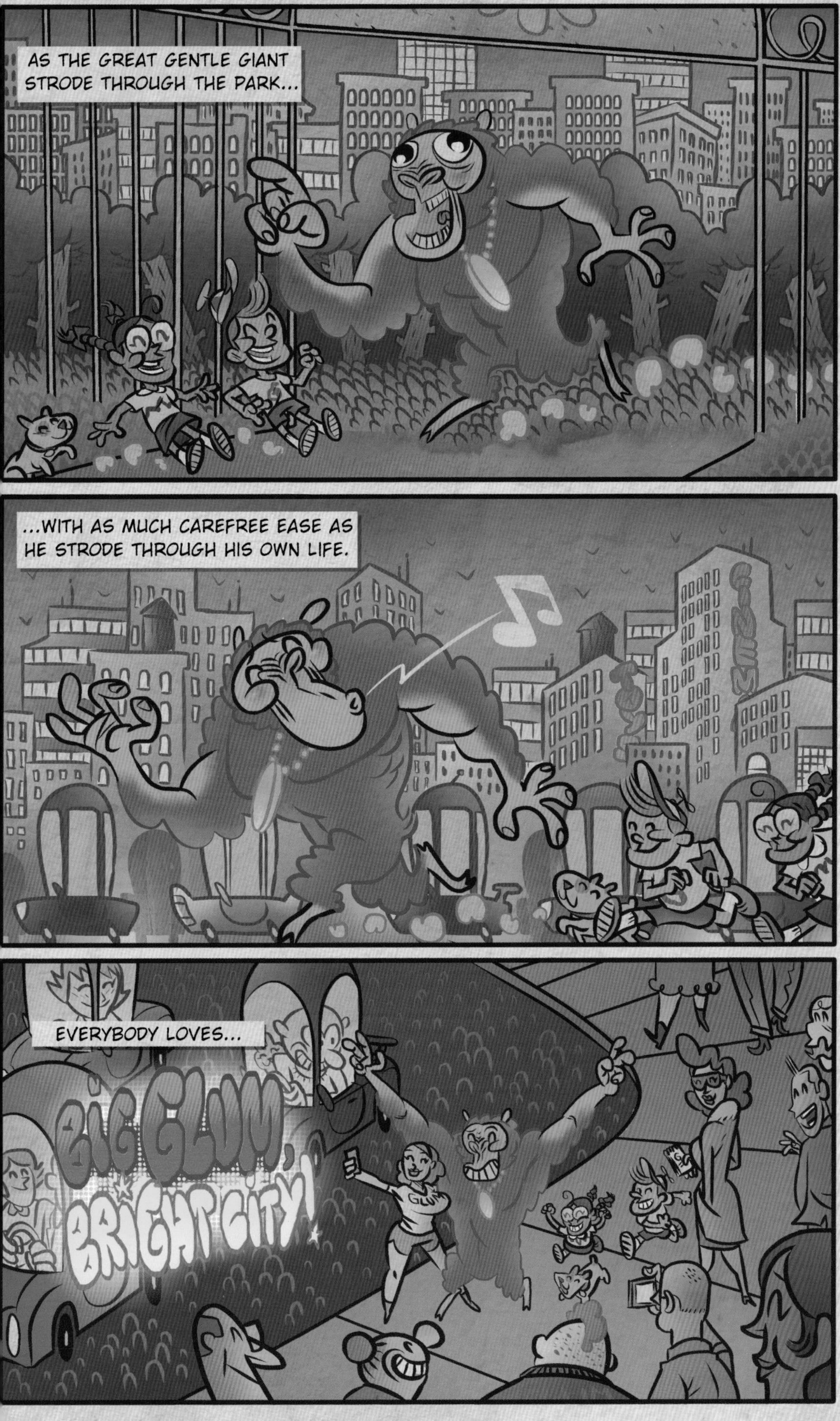
AS THE GREAT GENTLE GIANT STRODE THROUGH THE PARK...
...WITH AS MUCH CAREFREE EASE AS HE STRODE THROUGH HIS OWN LIFE.
EVERYBODY LOVES...
BIG GLUM, BRIGHT CITY!

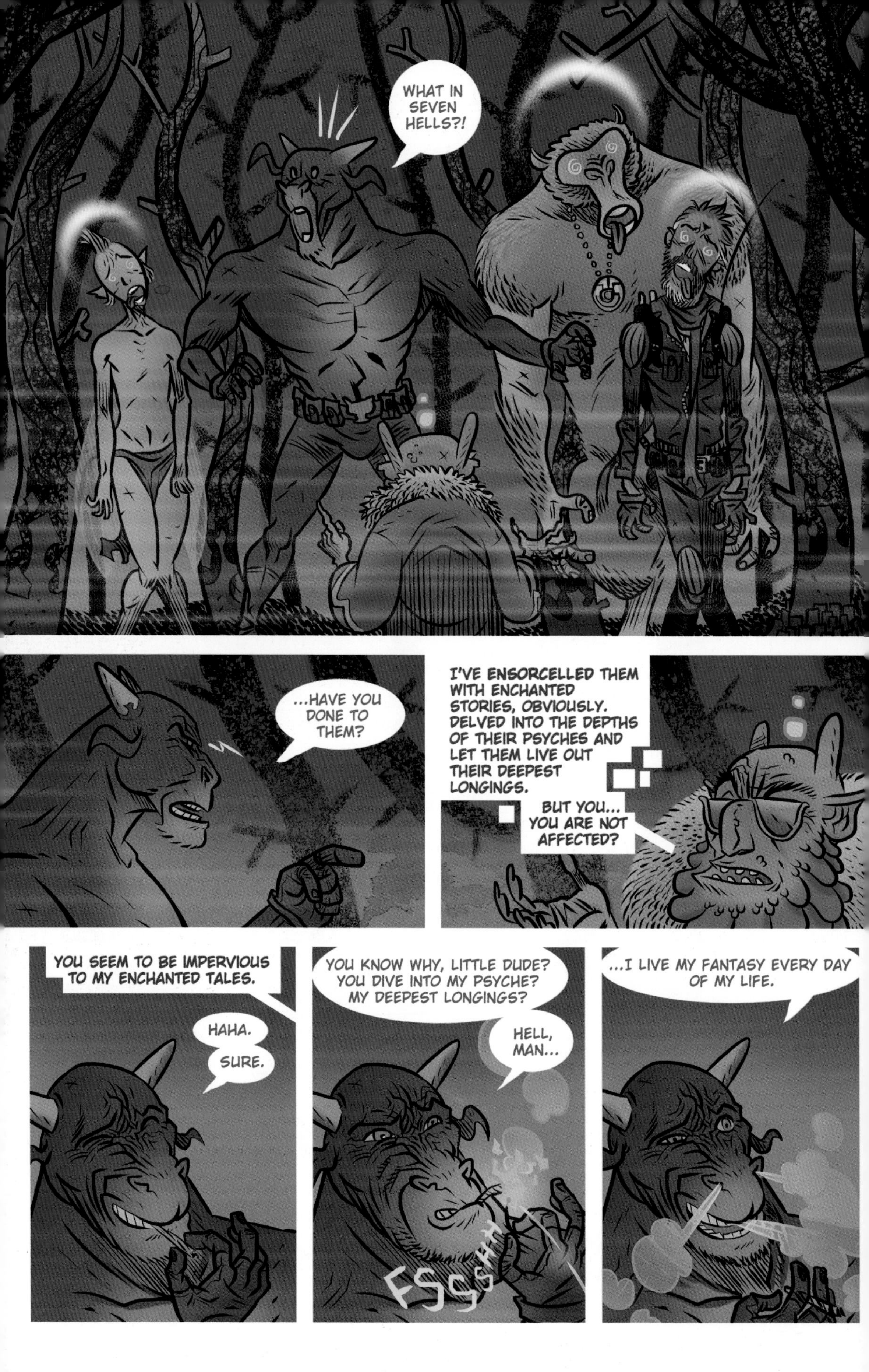
WHAT IN SEVEN HELLS?!
...HAVE YOU DONE TO THEM?
I'VE ENSORCELLED THEM WITH ENCHANTED STORIES, OBVIOUSLY. DELVED INTO THE DEPTHS OF THEIR PSYCHES AND LET THEM LIVE OUT THEIR DEEPEST LONGINGS.
BUT YOU... YOU ARE NOT AFFECTED?
YOU SEEM TO BE IMPERVIOUS TO MY ENCHANTED TALES.
HAHA.
SURE.
YOU KNOW WHY, LITTLE DUDE? YOU DIVE INTO MY PSYCHE? MY DEEPEST LONGINGS?
HELL, MAN...
FSSSSHH
...I LIVE MY FANTASY EVERY DAY OF MY LIFE.

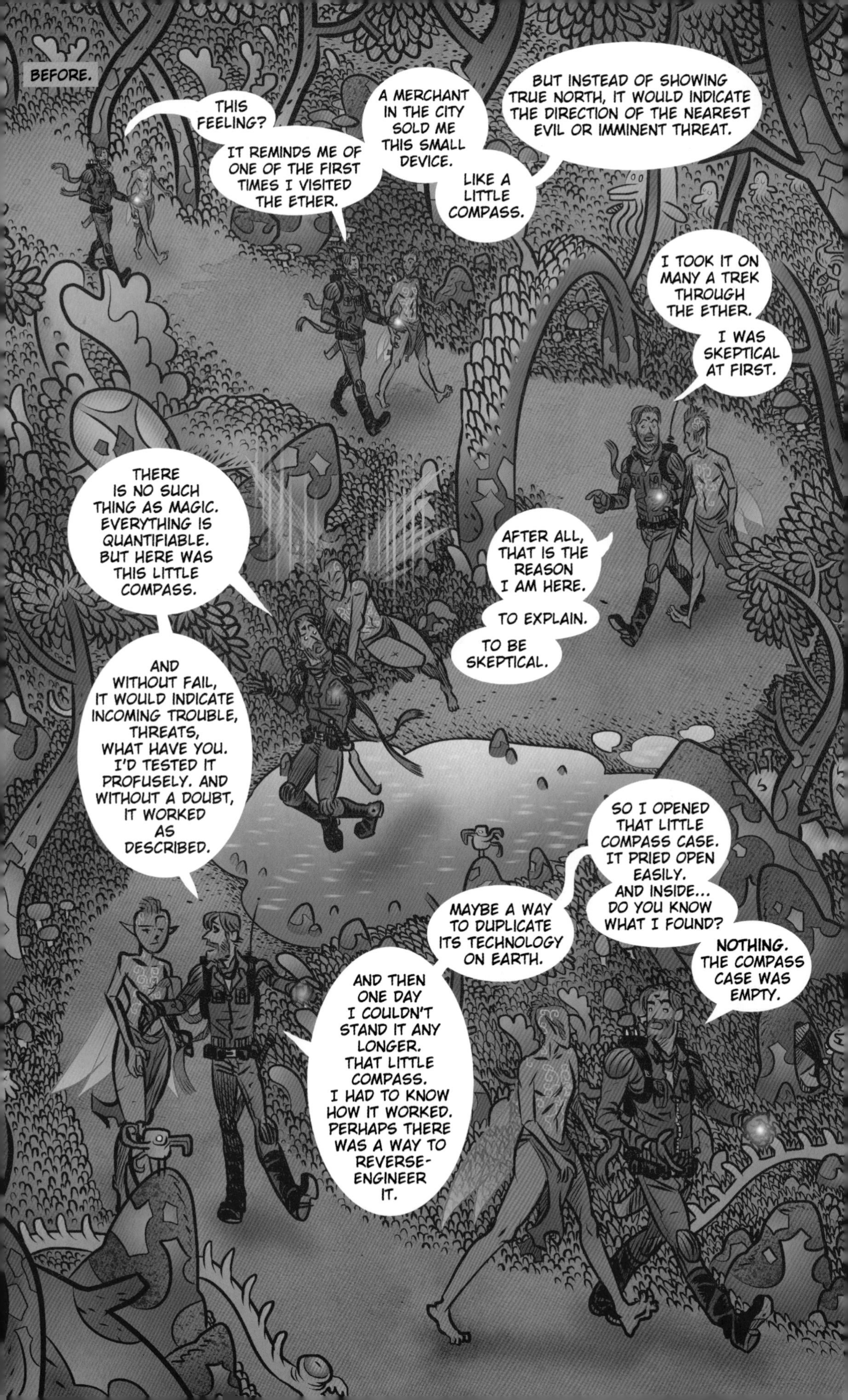
BEFORE.
THIS FEELING?
IT REMINDS ME OF ONE OF THE FIRST TIMES I VISITED THE ETHER.
A MERCHANT IN THE CITY SOLD ME THIS SMALL DEVICE.
LIKE A LITTLE COMPASS.
BUT INSTEAD OF SHOWING TRUE NORTH, IT WOULD INDICATE THE DIRECTION OF THE NEAREST EVIL OR IMMINENT THREAT.
I TOOK IT ON MANY A TREK THROUGH THE ETHER.
I WAS SKEPTICAL AT FIRST.
AFTER ALL, THAT IS THE REASON I AM HERE.
TO EXPLAIN.
TO BE SKEPTICAL.
THERE IS NO SUCH THING AS MAGIC. EVERYTHING IS QUANTIFIABLE. BUT HERE WAS THIS LITTLE COMPASS.
AND WITHOUT FAIL, IT WOULD INDICATE INCOMING TROUBLE, THREATS, WHAT HAVE YOU. I'D TESTED IT PROFUSELY. AND WITHOUT A DOUBT, IT WORKED AS DESCRIBED.
AND THEN ONE DAY I COULDN'T STAND IT ANY LONGER. THAT LITTLE COMPASS. I HAD TO KNOW HOW IT WORKED. PERHAPS THERE WAS A WAY TO REVERSE-ENGINEER IT.
MAYBE A WAY TO DUPLICATE ITS TECHNOLOGY ON EARTH.
SO I OPENED THAT LITTLE COMPASS CASE. IT PRIED OPEN EASILY. AND INSIDE... DO YOU KNOW WHAT I FOUND?
NOTHING. THE COMPASS CASE WAS EMPTY.

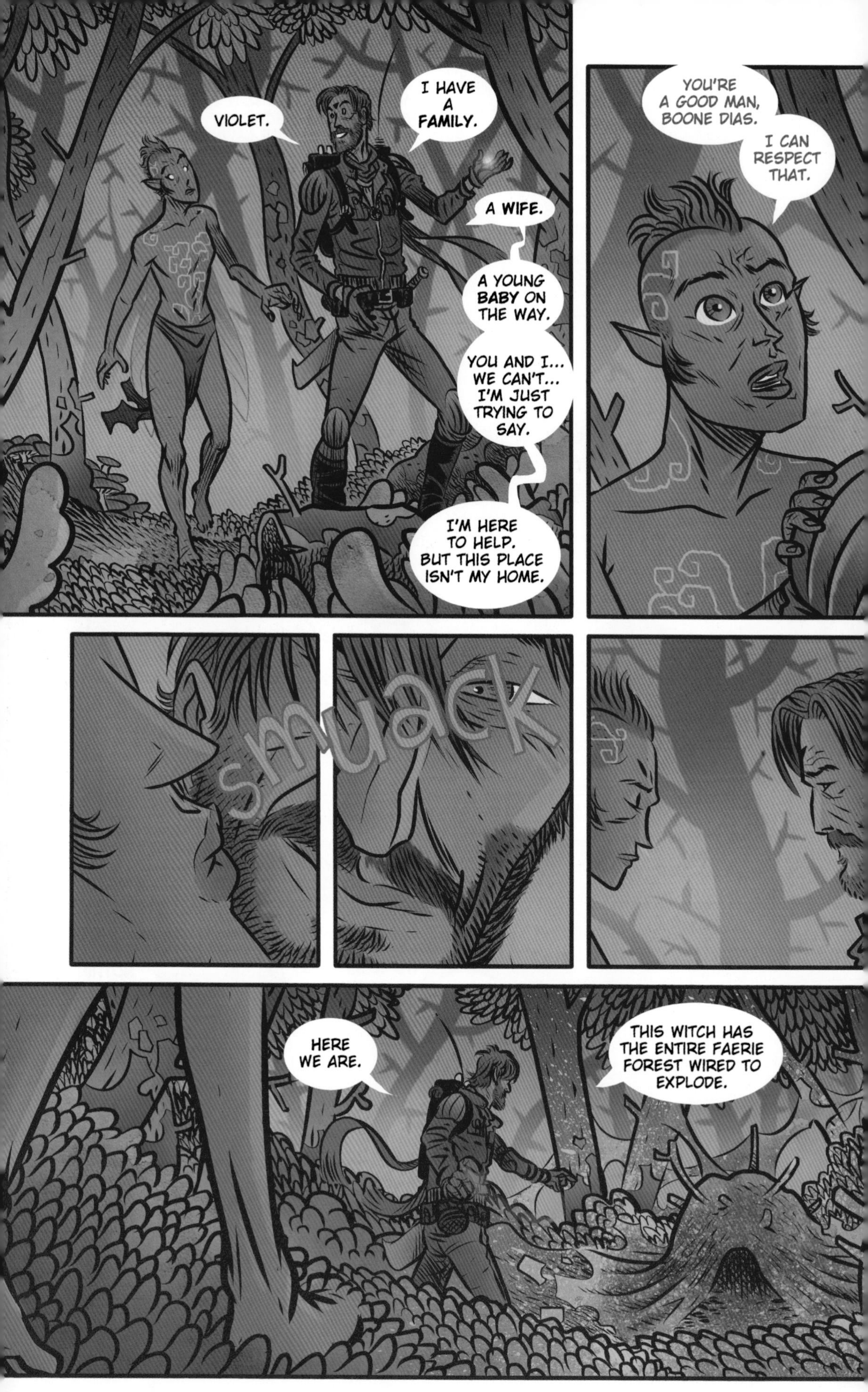
VIOLET.
I HAVE A FAMILY.
A WIFE.
A YOUNG BABY ON THE WAY.
YOU AND I... WE CAN'T... I'M JUST TRYING TO SAY.
I'M HERE TO HELP. BUT THIS PLACE ISN'T MY HOME.
YOU'RE A GOOD MAN, BOONE DIAS.
I CAN RESPECT THAT.
smuack
HERE WE ARE.
THIS WITCH HAS THE ENTIRE FAERIE FOREST WIRED TO EXPLODE.

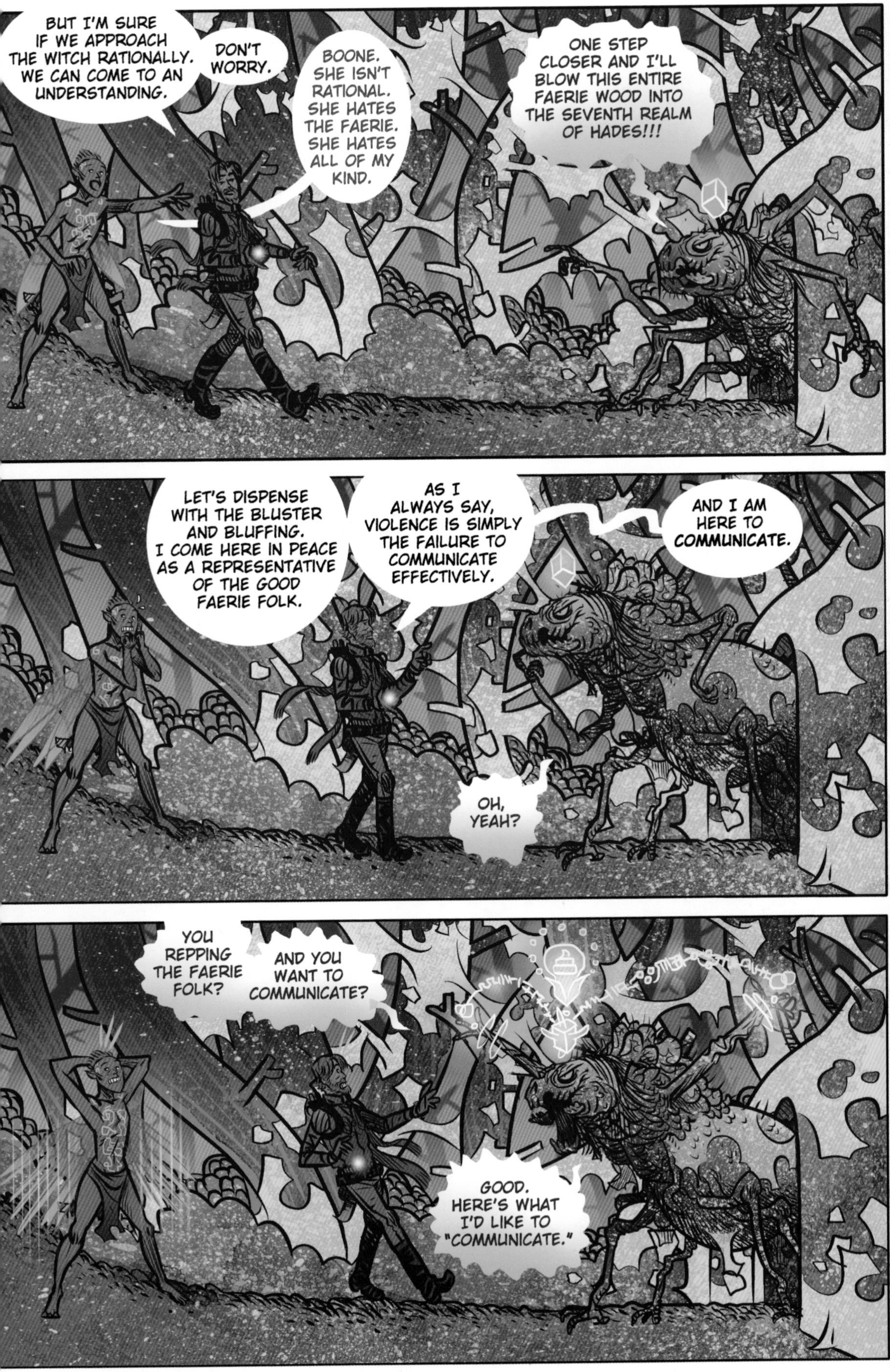
BUT I'M SURE IF WE APPROACH THE WITCH RATIONALLY. WE CAN COME TO AN UNDERSTANDING.
DON'T WORRY.
BOONE. SHE ISN'T RATIONAL. SHE HATES THE FAERIE. SHE HATES ALL OF MY KIND.
ONE STEP CLOSER AND I'LL BLOW THIS ENTIRE FAERIE WOOD INTO THE SEVENTH REALM OF HADES!!!
LET'S DISPENSE WITH THE BLUSTER AND BLUFFING. I COME HERE IN PEACE AS A REPRESENTATIVE OF THE GOOD FAERIE FOLK.
AS I ALWAYS SAY, VIOLENCE IS SIMPLY THE FAILURE TO COMMUNICATE EFFECTIVELY.
AND I AM HERE TO COMMUNICATE.
OH, YEAH?
YOU REPPING THE FAERIE FOLK?
AND YOU WANT TO COMMUNICATE?
GOOD. HERE'S WHAT I'D LIKE TO "COMMUNICATE."

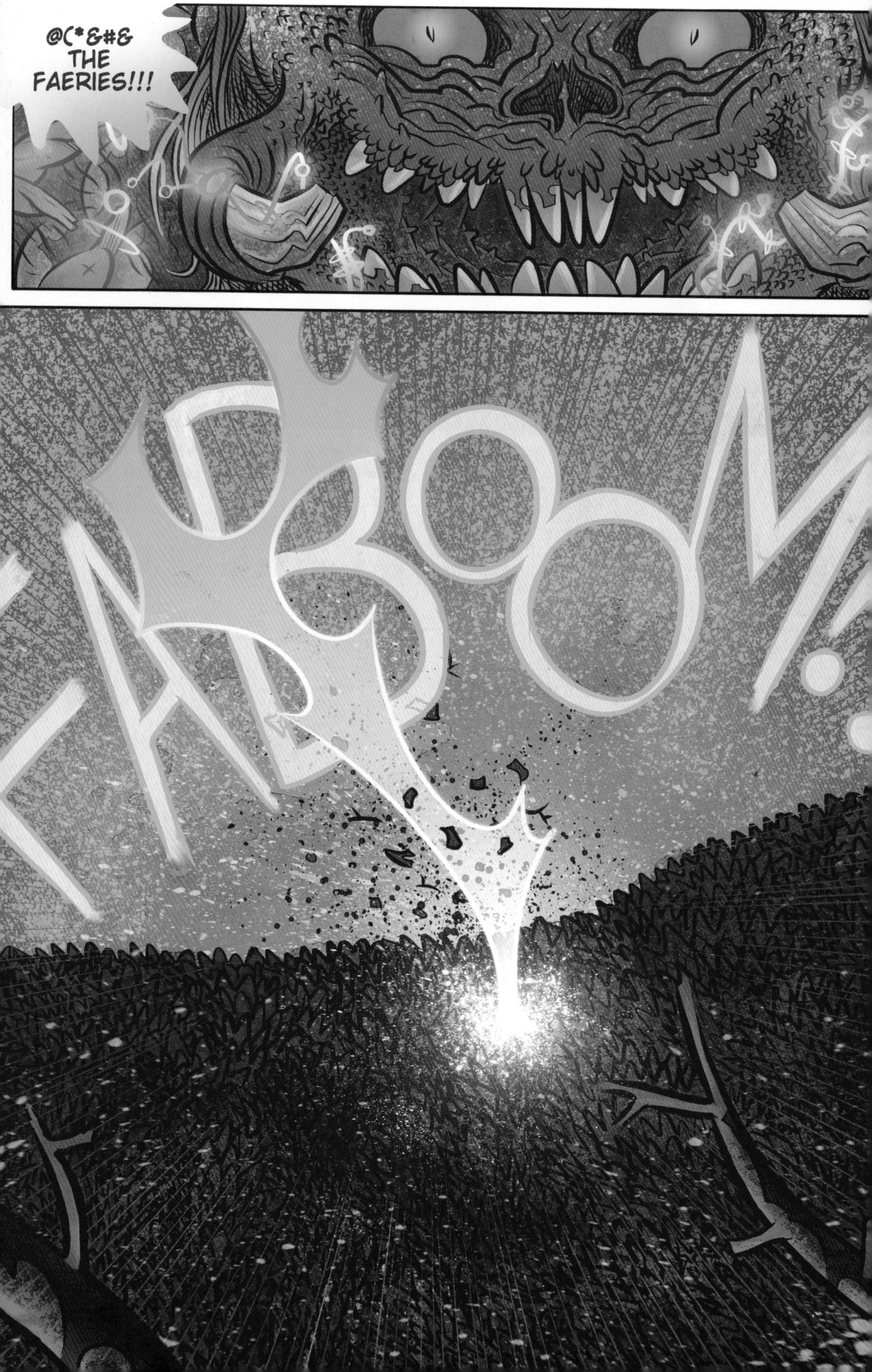
@(*&#& THE FAERIES!!!
KABOOM!!

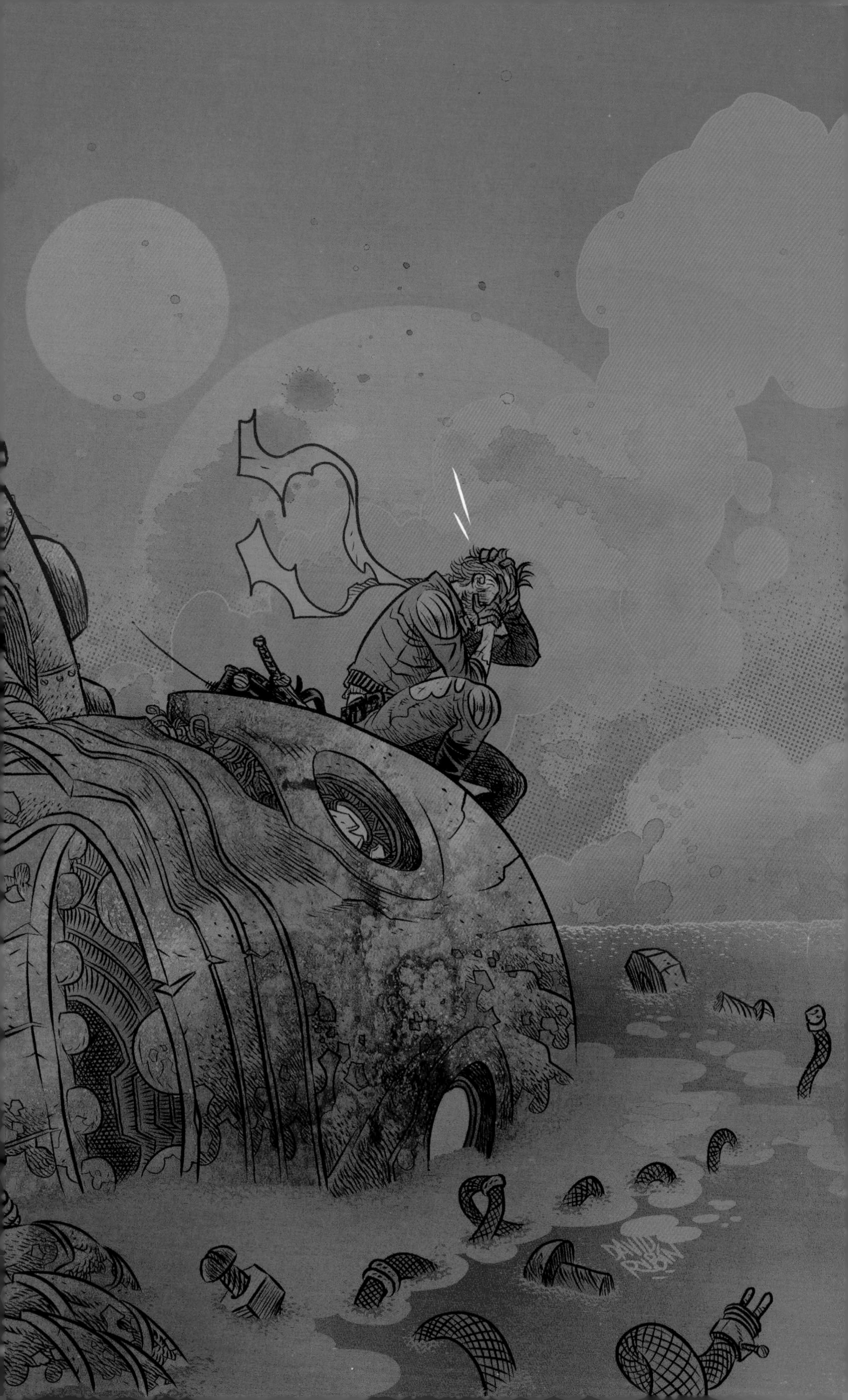

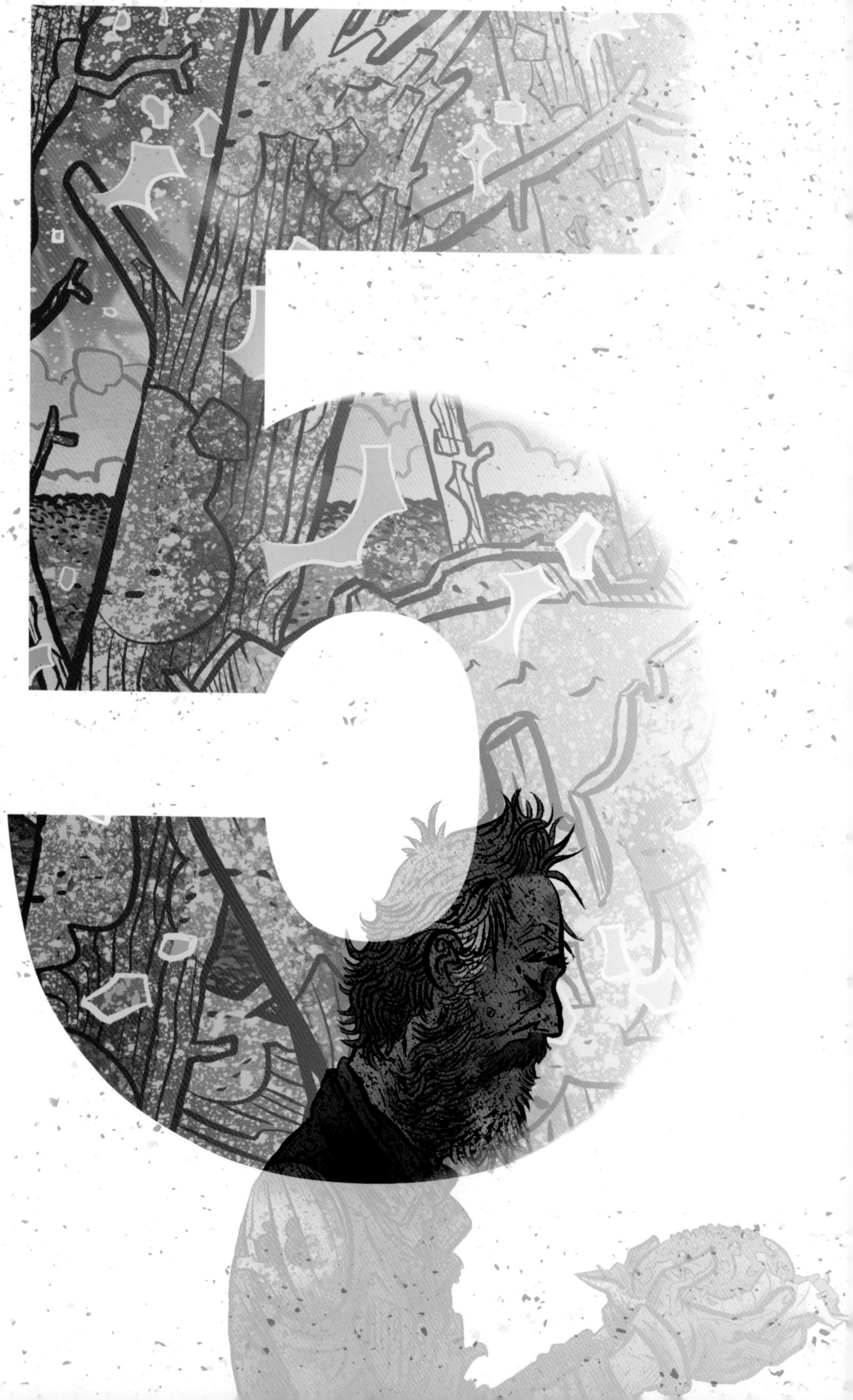
5

The hoary tentacles of the massive beast became engorged...

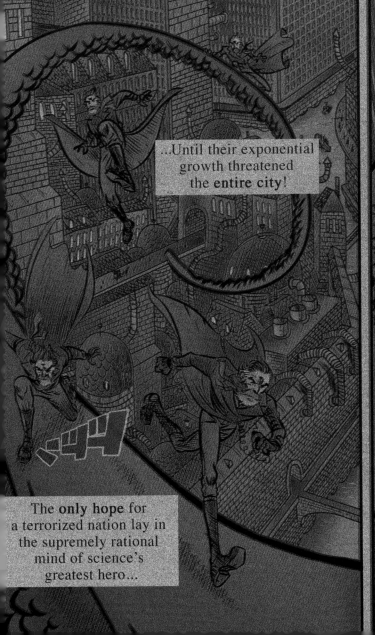

...Until their exponential growth threatened the entire city!

The **only hope** for a terrorized nation lay in the supremely rational mind of science's greatest hero...

Boone Días

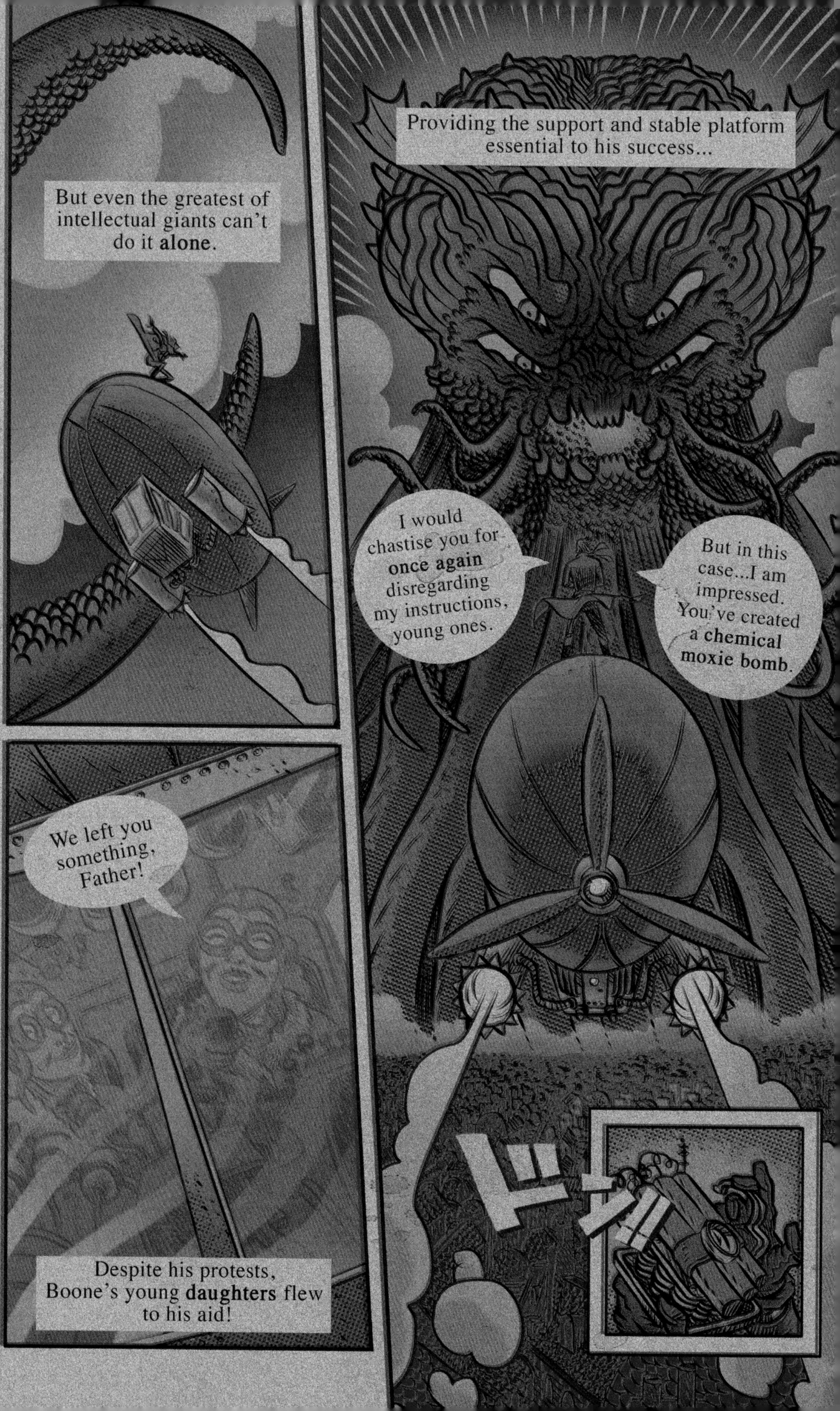

But even the greatest of intellectual giants can't do it **alone**.
We left you something, Father!
Despite his protests, Boone's young **daughters** flew to his aid!
Providing the support and stable platform essential to his success...
I would chastise you for **once again** disregarding my instructions, young ones.
But in this case...I am impressed. You've created a **chemical moxie bomb**.

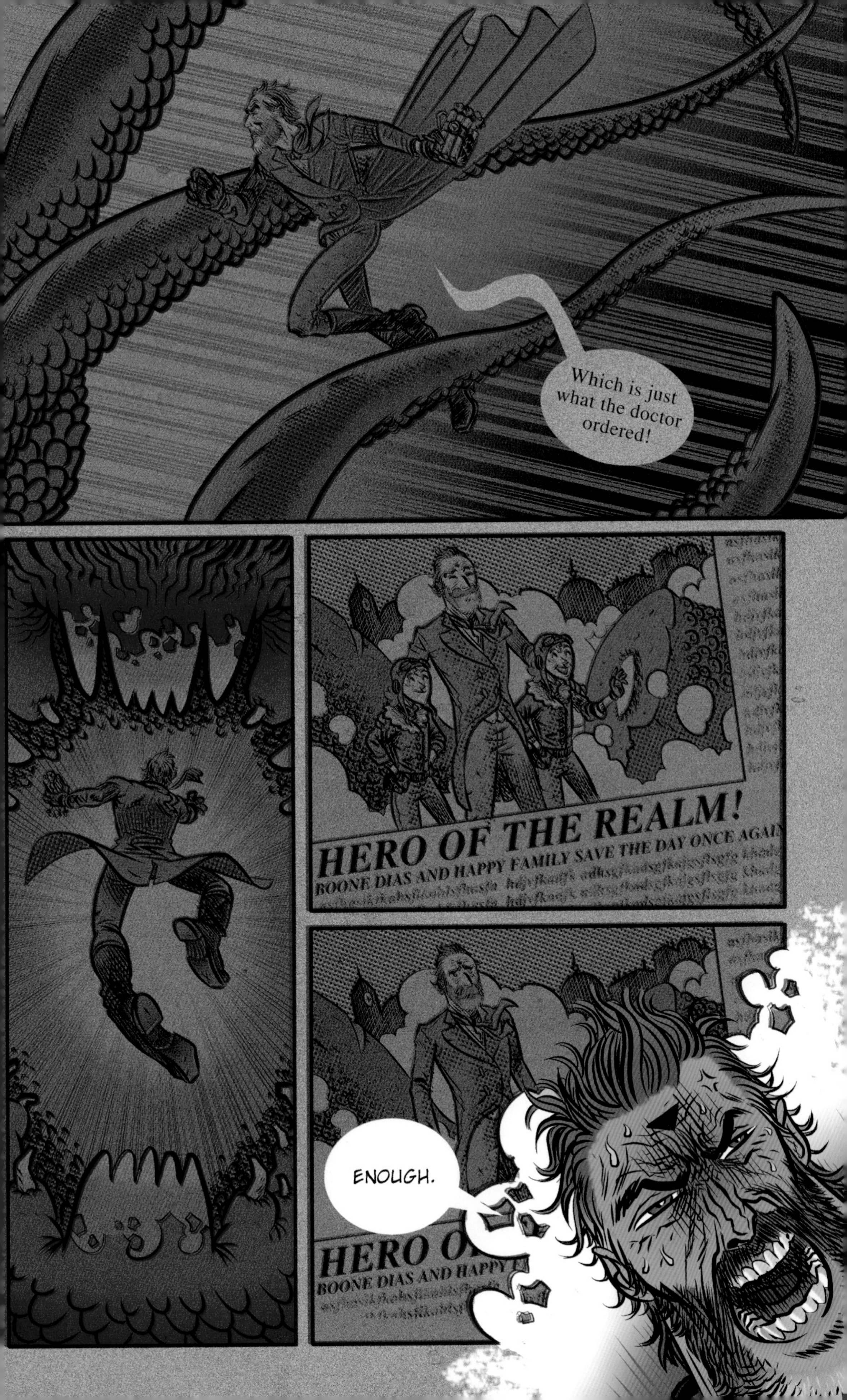
Which is just what the doctor ordered!
HERO OF THE REALM!
BOONE DIAS AND HAPPY FAMILY SAVE THE DAY ONCE AGAIN
ENOUGH.
HERO O
BOONE DIAS AND HAPPY

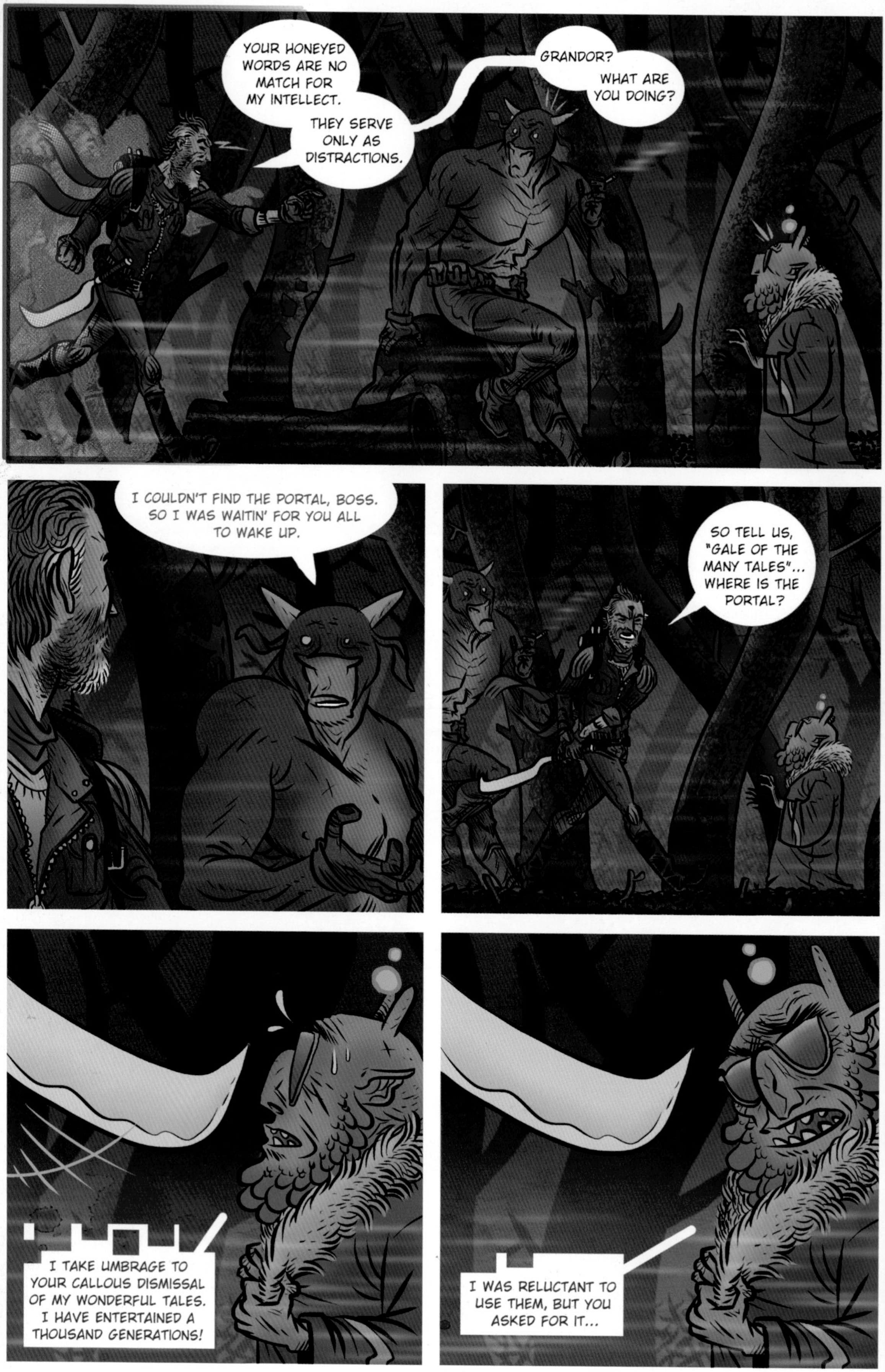
YOUR HONEYED WORDS ARE NO MATCH FOR MY INTELLECT.
THEY SERVE ONLY AS DISTRACTIONS.
GRANDOR?
WHAT ARE YOU DOING?
I COULDN'T FIND THE PORTAL, BOSS. SO I WAS WAITIN' FOR YOU ALL TO WAKE UP.
SO TELL US, "GALE OF THE MANY TALES"... WHERE IS THE PORTAL?
I TAKE UMBRAGE TO YOUR CALLOUS DISMISSAL OF MY WONDERFUL TALES. I HAVE ENTERTAINED A THOUSAND GENERATIONS!
I WAS RELUCTANT TO USE THEM, BUT YOU ASKED FOR IT...

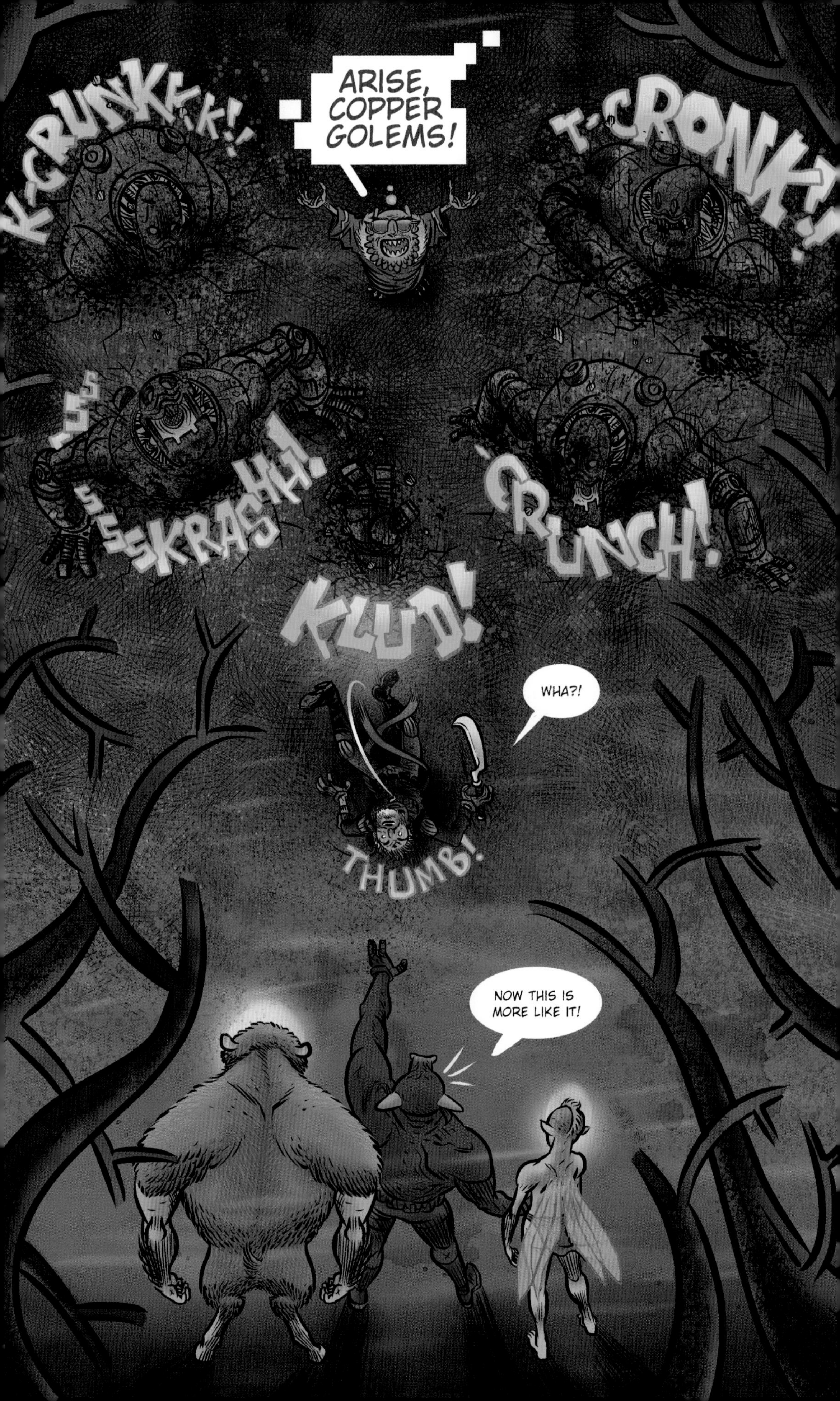
ARISE, COPPER GOLEMS!
K-CRUNKKK!!
T-CRONK!!
SSSSKRASHH!
CRUNCH!
KLUD!
WHA?!
THUMB!
NOW THIS IS MORE LIKE IT!

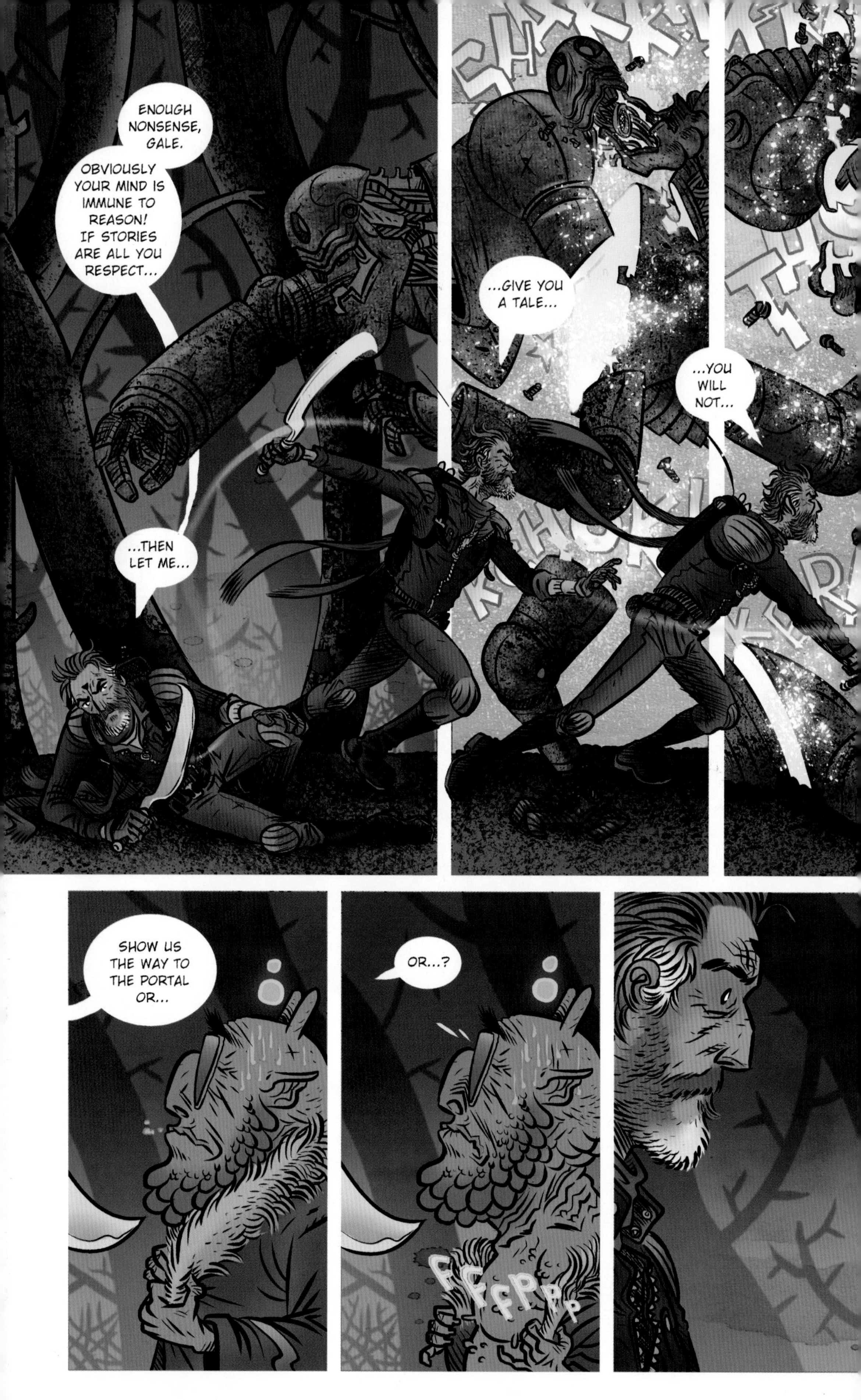
ENOUGH NONSENSE, GALE.
OBVIOUSLY YOUR MIND IS IMMUNE TO REASON! IF STORIES ARE ALL YOU RESPECT...
...THEN LET ME...
...GIVE YOU A TALE...
...YOU WILL NOT...
SHOW US THE WAY TO THE PORTAL OR...
OR...?
FFFPPP

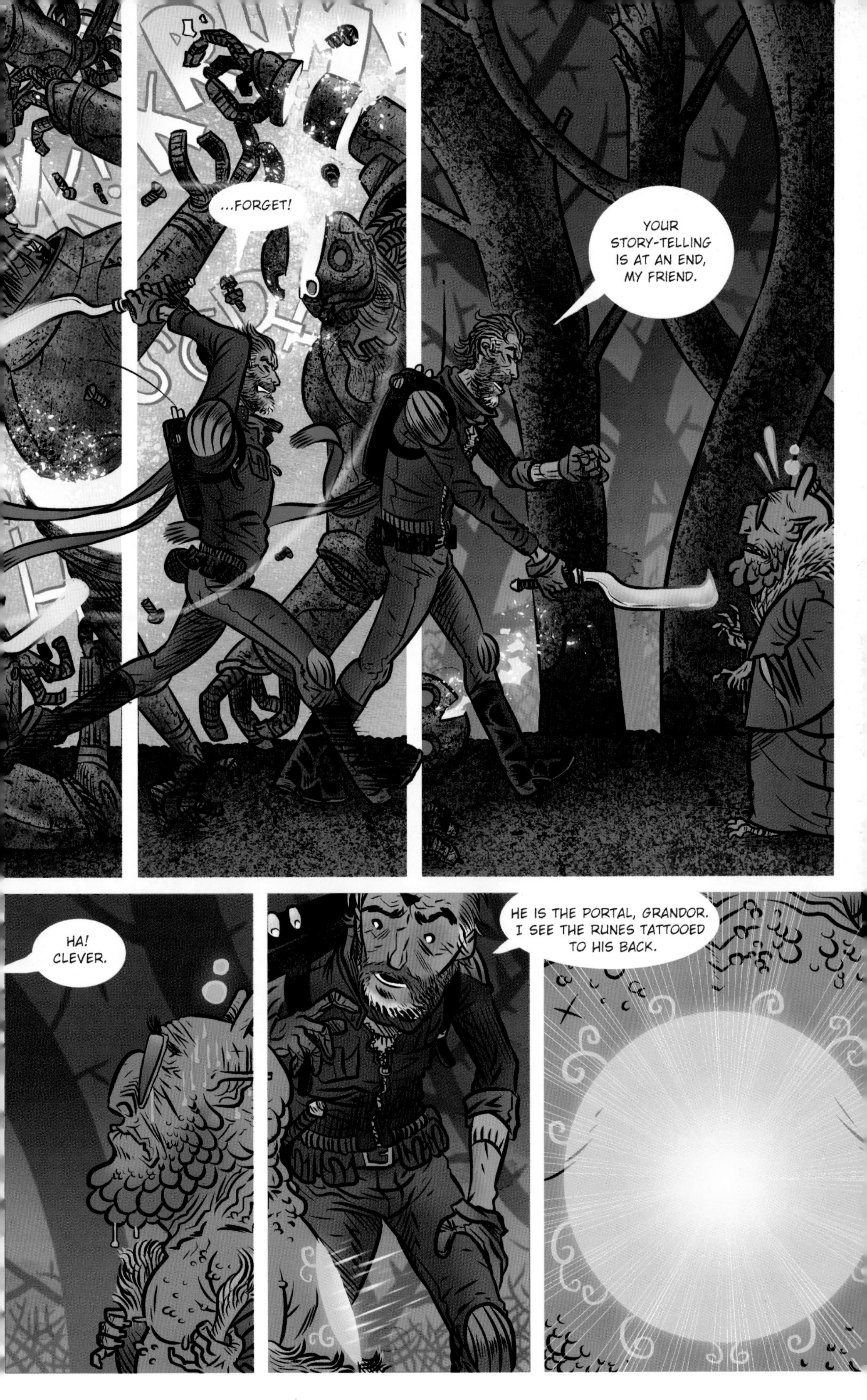
...FORGET!
YOUR STORY-TELLING IS AT AN END, MY FRIEND.
HA! CLEVER.
HE IS THE PORTAL, GRANDOR. I SEE THE RUNES TATTOOED TO HIS BACK.

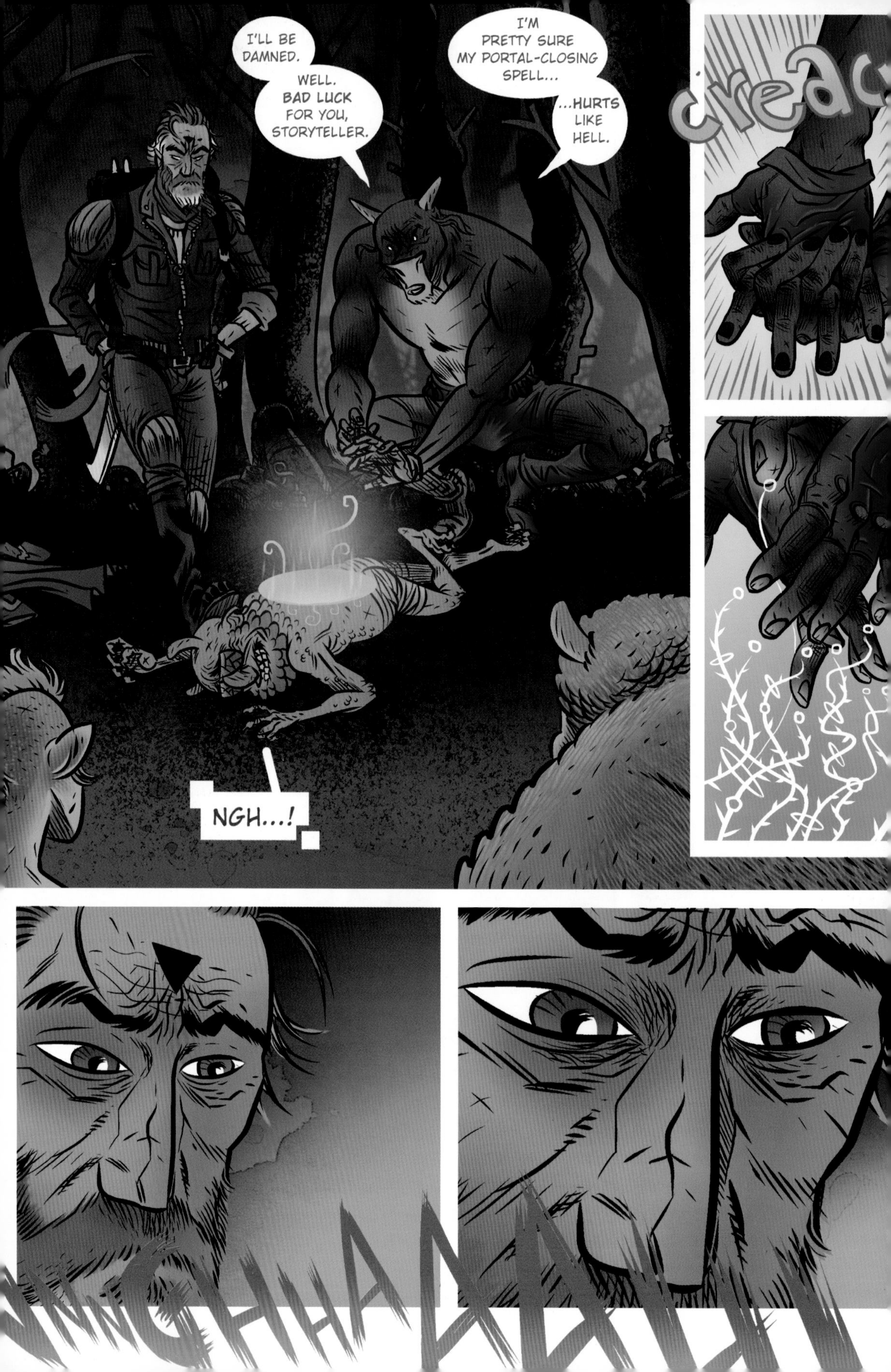
I'LL BE DAMNED.
WELL. BAD LUCK FOR YOU, STORYTELLER.
I'M PRETTY SURE MY PORTAL-CLOSING SPELL...
...HURTS LIKE HELL.
creac
NGH...!

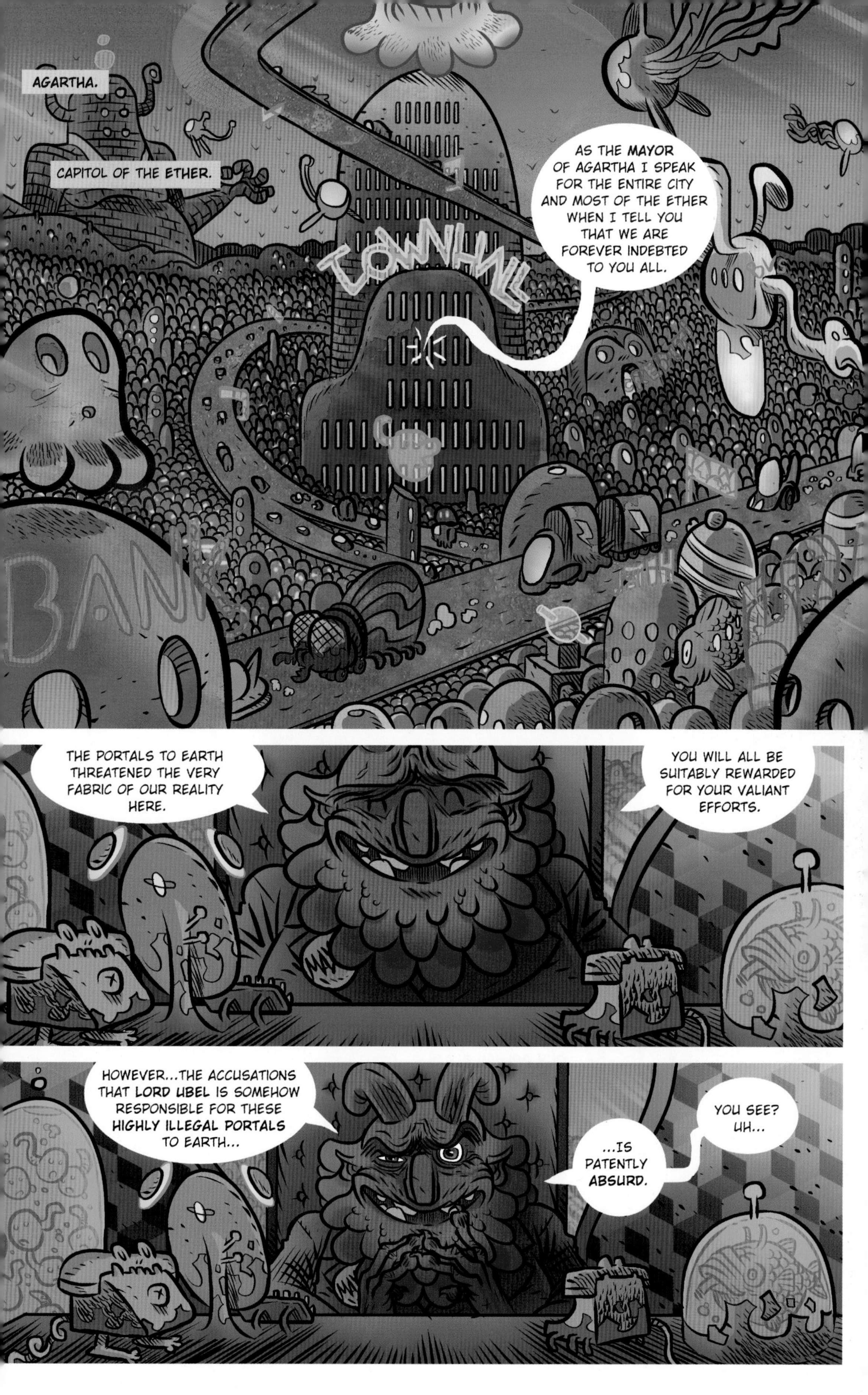
AGARTHA.
CAPITOL OF THE ETHER.
AS THE MAYOR OF AGARTHA I SPEAK FOR THE ENTIRE CITY AND MOST OF THE ETHER WHEN I TELL YOU THAT WE ARE FOREVER INDEBTED TO YOU ALL.
TOWNHALL
BANK
THE PORTALS TO EARTH THREATENED THE VERY FABRIC OF OUR REALITY HERE.
YOU WILL ALL BE SUITABLY REWARDED FOR YOUR VALIANT EFFORTS.
HOWEVER...THE ACCUSATIONS THAT LORD UBEL IS SOMEHOW RESPONSIBLE FOR THESE HIGHLY ILLEGAL PORTALS TO EARTH...
...IS PATENTLY ABSURD.
YOU SEE? UH...

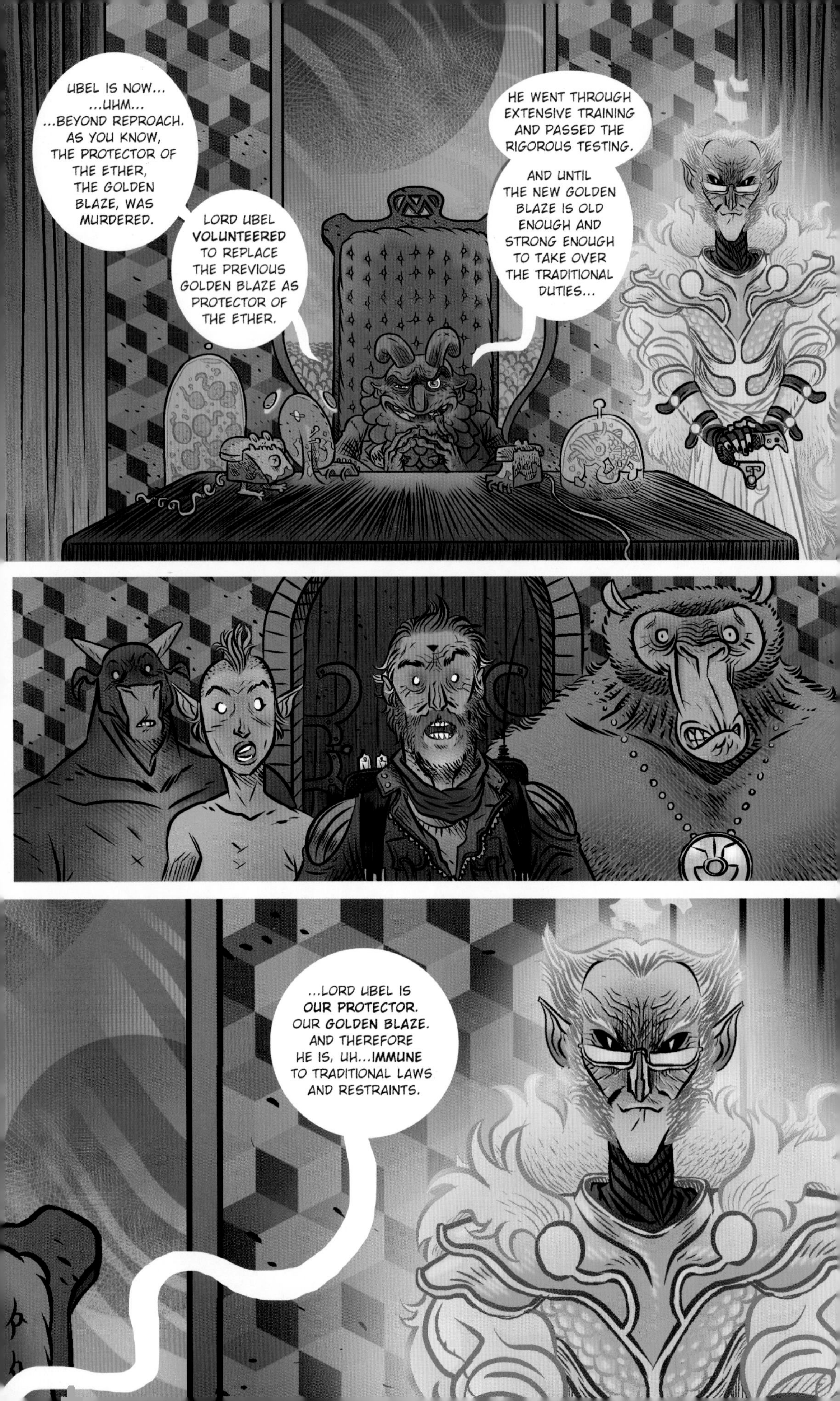
UBEL IS NOW... ...UHM... ...BEYOND REPROACH. AS YOU KNOW, THE PROTECTOR OF THE ETHER, THE GOLDEN BLAZE, WAS MURDERED.
LORD UBEL **VOLUNTEERED** TO REPLACE THE PREVIOUS GOLDEN BLAZE AS PROTECTOR OF THE ETHER.
HE WENT THROUGH EXTENSIVE TRAINING AND PASSED THE RIGOROUS TESTING.
AND UNTIL THE NEW GOLDEN BLAZE IS OLD ENOUGH AND STRONG ENOUGH TO TAKE OVER THE TRADITIONAL DUTIES...
...LORD UBEL IS **OUR PROTECTOR.** OUR **GOLDEN BLAZE.** AND THEREFORE HE IS, UH...**IMMUNE** TO TRADITIONAL LAWS AND RESTRAINTS.

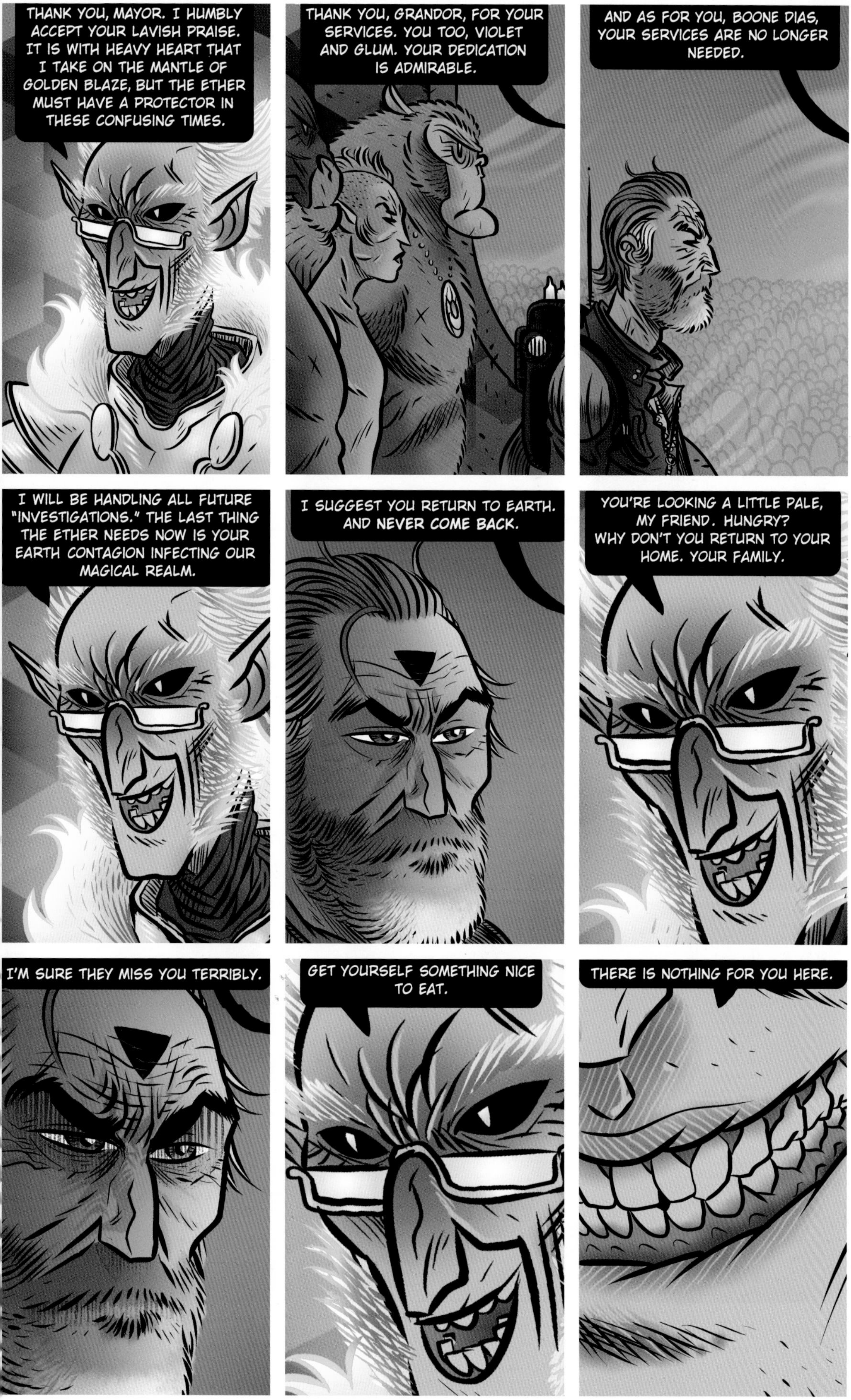
THANK YOU, MAYOR. I HUMBLY ACCEPT YOUR LAVISH PRAISE. IT IS WITH HEAVY HEART THAT I TAKE ON THE MANTLE OF GOLDEN BLAZE, BUT THE ETHER MUST HAVE A PROTECTOR IN THESE CONFUSING TIMES.
THANK YOU, GRANDOR, FOR YOUR SERVICES. YOU TOO, VIOLET AND GLUM. YOUR DEDICATION IS ADMIRABLE.
AND AS FOR YOU, BOONE DIAS, YOUR SERVICES ARE NO LONGER NEEDED.
I WILL BE HANDLING ALL FUTURE "INVESTIGATIONS." THE LAST THING THE ETHER NEEDS NOW IS YOUR EARTH CONTAGION INFECTING OUR MAGICAL REALM.
I SUGGEST YOU RETURN TO EARTH. AND NEVER COME BACK.
YOU'RE LOOKING A LITTLE PALE, MY FRIEND. HUNGRY? WHY DON'T YOU RETURN TO YOUR HOME. YOUR FAMILY.
I'M SURE THEY MISS YOU TERRIBLY.
GET YOURSELF SOMETHING NICE TO EAT.
THERE IS NOTHING FOR YOU HERE.

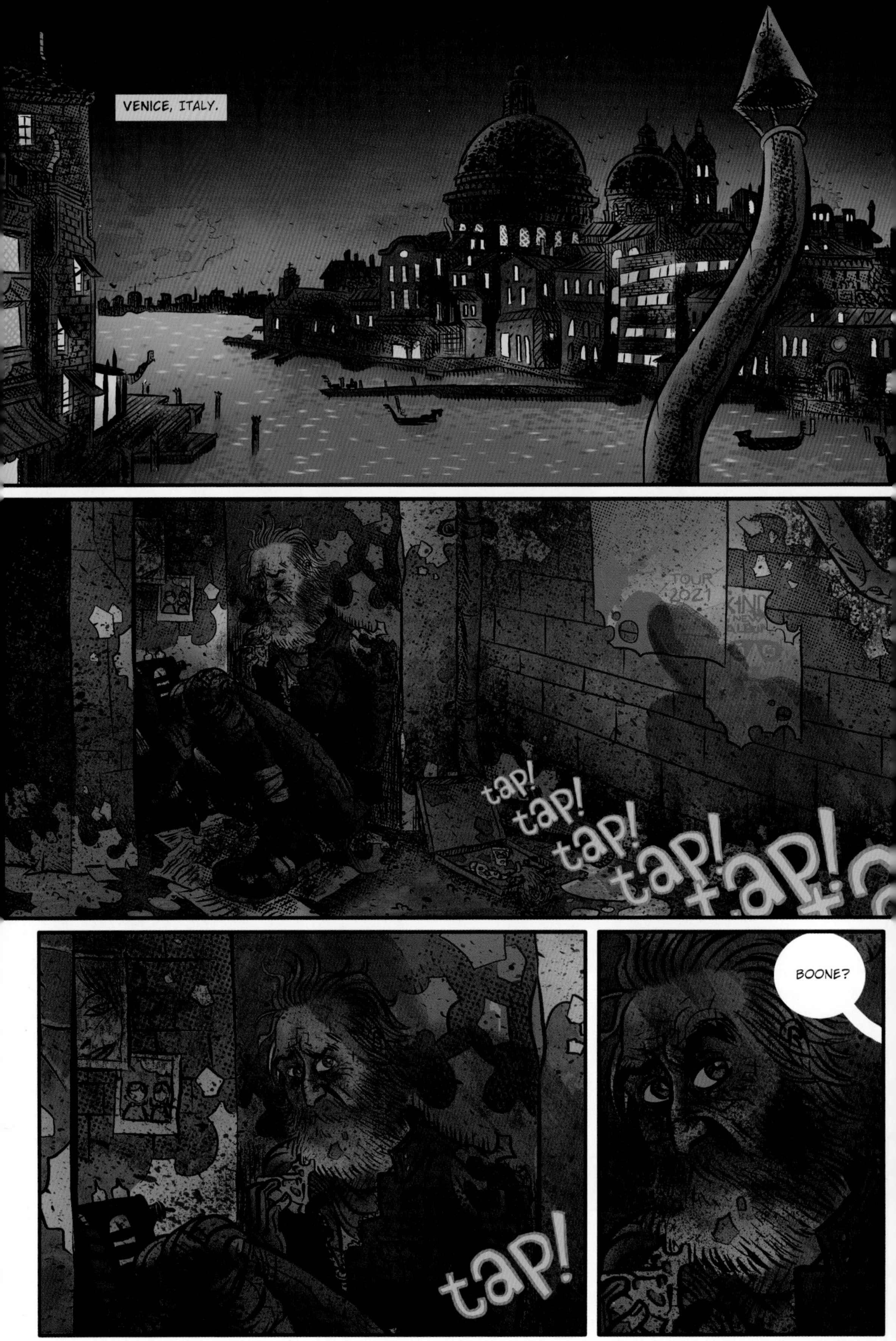
VENICE, ITALY.
TOUR 2021
tap!
tap!
tap!
tap!
tap!
tap!
BOONE?

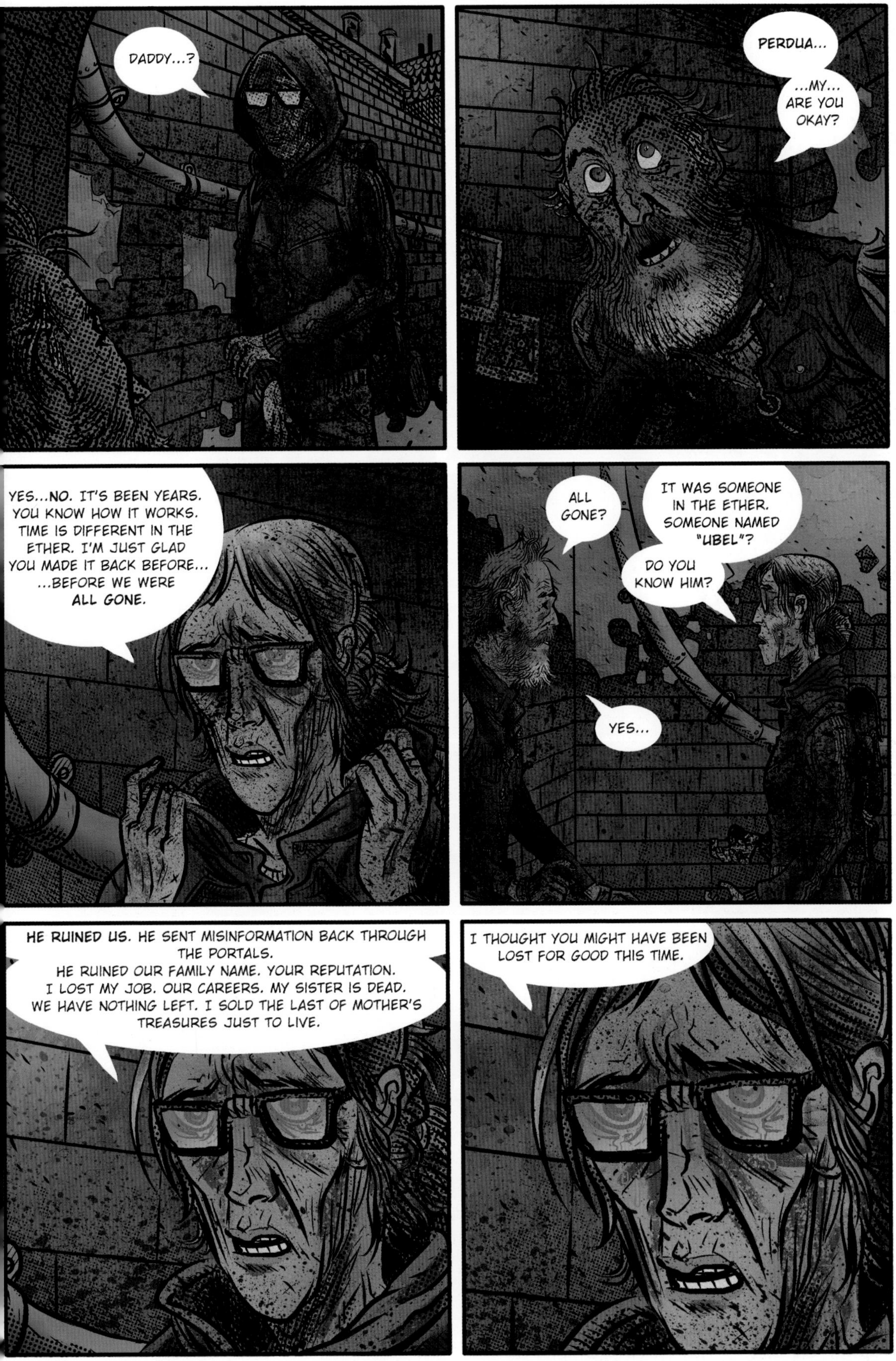
DADDY...?
PERDUA...
...MY... ARE YOU OKAY?
YES...NO. IT'S BEEN YEARS. YOU KNOW HOW IT WORKS. TIME IS DIFFERENT IN THE ETHER. I'M JUST GLAD YOU MADE IT BACK BEFORE... ...BEFORE WE WERE ALL GONE.
ALL GONE?
IT WAS SOMEONE IN THE ETHER. SOMEONE NAMED "UBEL"?
DO YOU KNOW HIM?
YES...
HE RUINED US. HE SENT MISINFORMATION BACK THROUGH THE PORTALS. HE RUINED OUR FAMILY NAME. YOUR REPUTATION. I LOST MY JOB. OUR CAREERS. MY SISTER IS DEAD. WE HAVE NOTHING LEFT. I SOLD THE LAST OF MOTHER'S TREASURES JUST TO LIVE.
I THOUGHT YOU MIGHT HAVE BEEN LOST FOR GOOD THIS TIME.

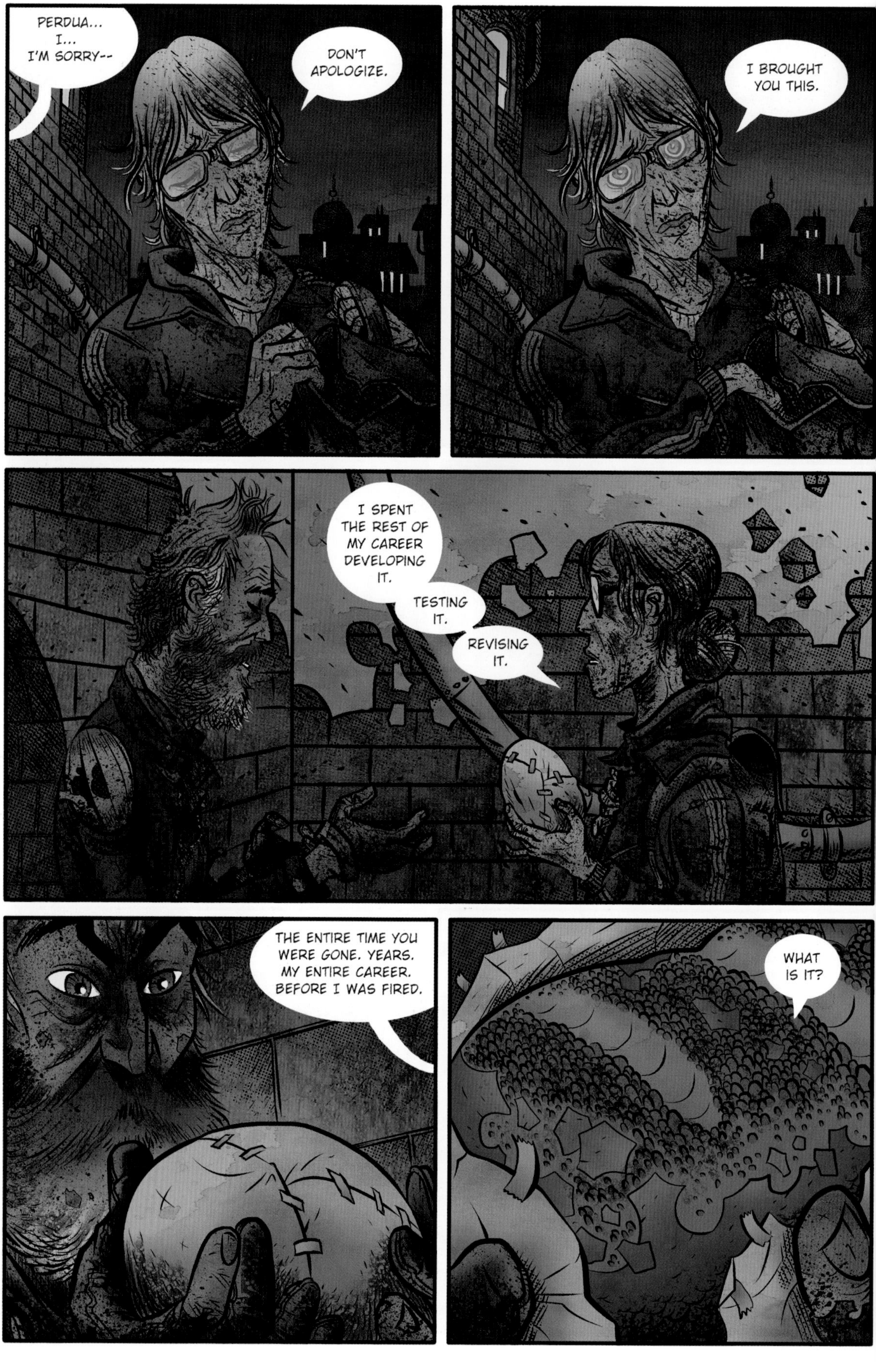
PERDUA...
I...
I'M SORRY--
DON'T APOLOGIZE.
I BROUGHT YOU THIS.
I SPENT THE REST OF MY CAREER DEVELOPING IT.
TESTING IT.
REVISING IT.
THE ENTIRE TIME YOU WERE GONE. YEARS. MY ENTIRE CAREER. BEFORE I WAS FIRED.
WHAT IS IT?

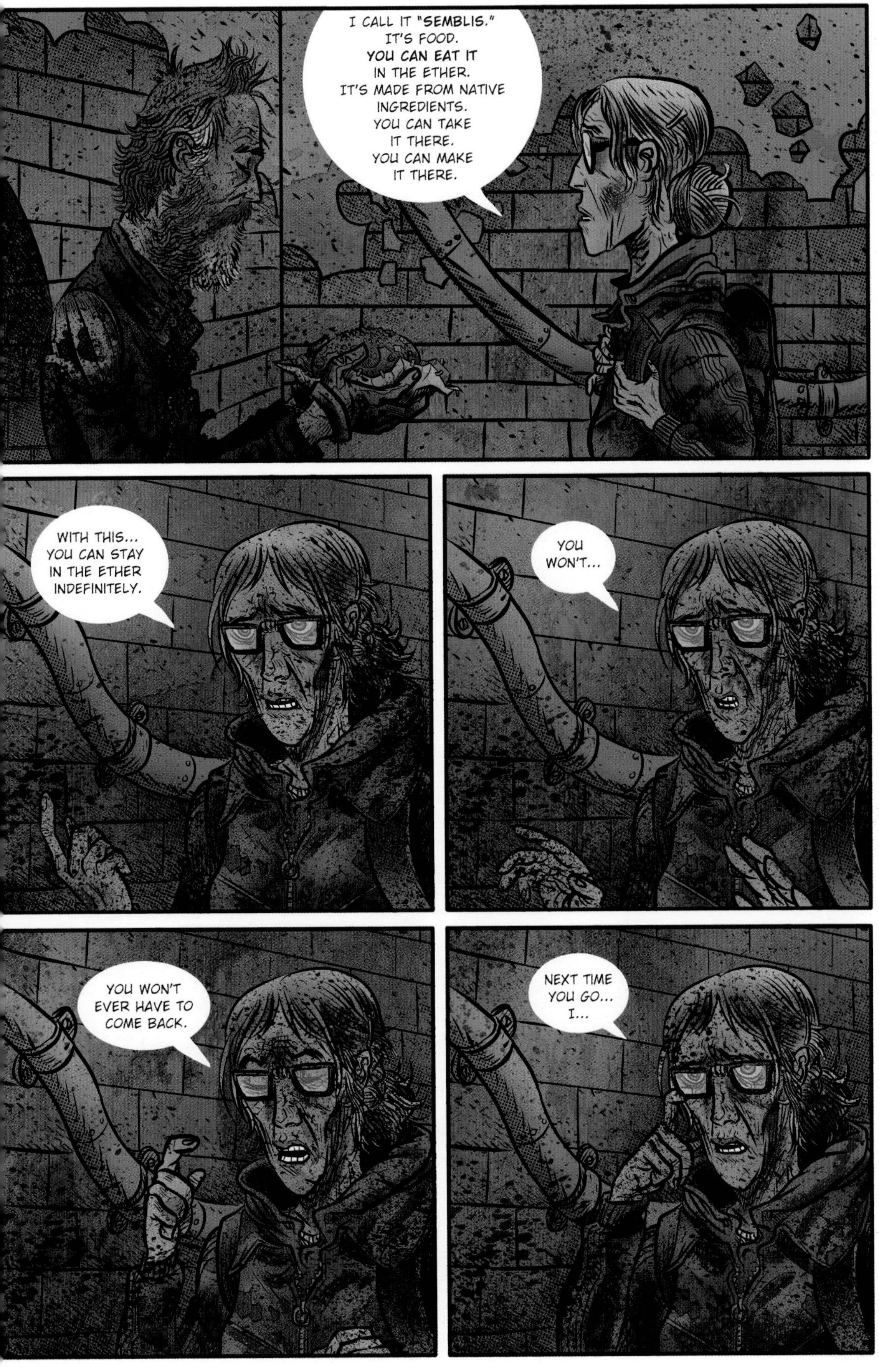
I CALL IT "SEMBLIS." IT'S FOOD. YOU CAN EAT IT IN THE ETHER. IT'S MADE FROM NATIVE INGREDIENTS. YOU CAN TAKE IT THERE. YOU CAN MAKE IT THERE.
WITH THIS... YOU CAN STAY IN THE ETHER INDEFINITELY.
YOU WON'T...
YOU WON'T EVER HAVE TO COME BACK.
NEXT TIME YOU GO... I...

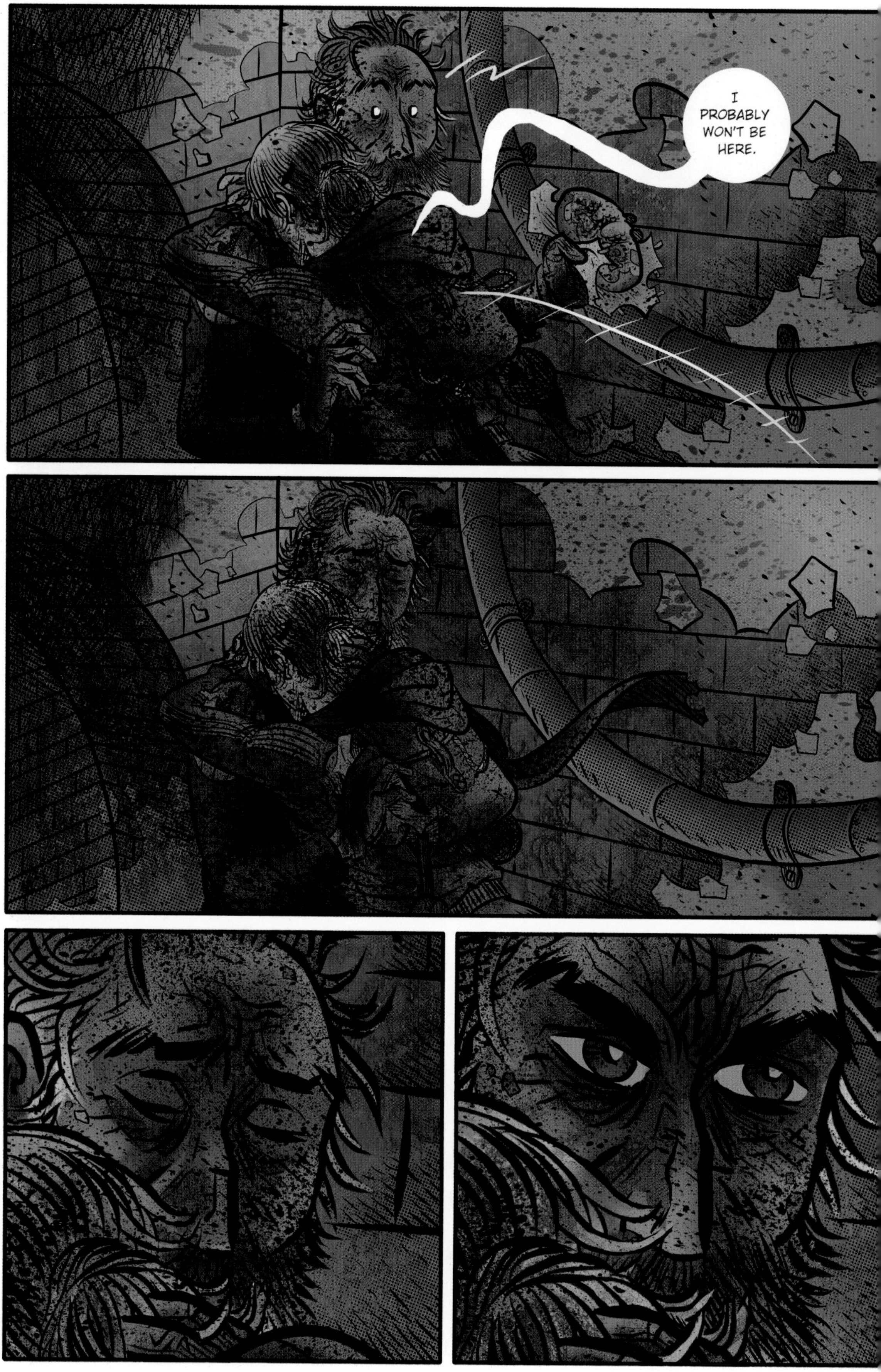
I PROBABLY WON'T BE HERE.

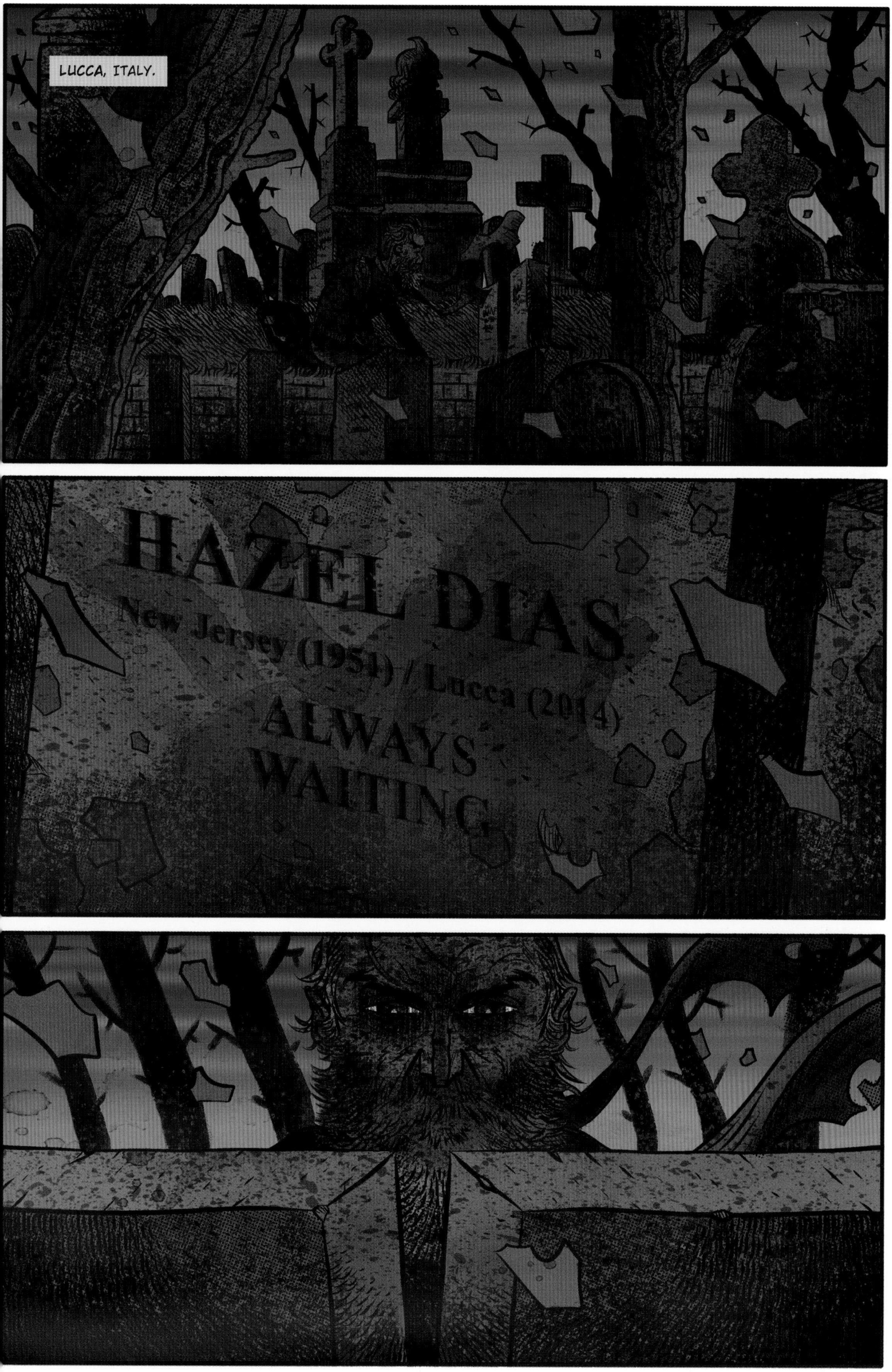
LUCCA, ITALY.
HAZEL DIAS
New Jersey (1951) / Lucca (2014)
ALWAYS WAITING

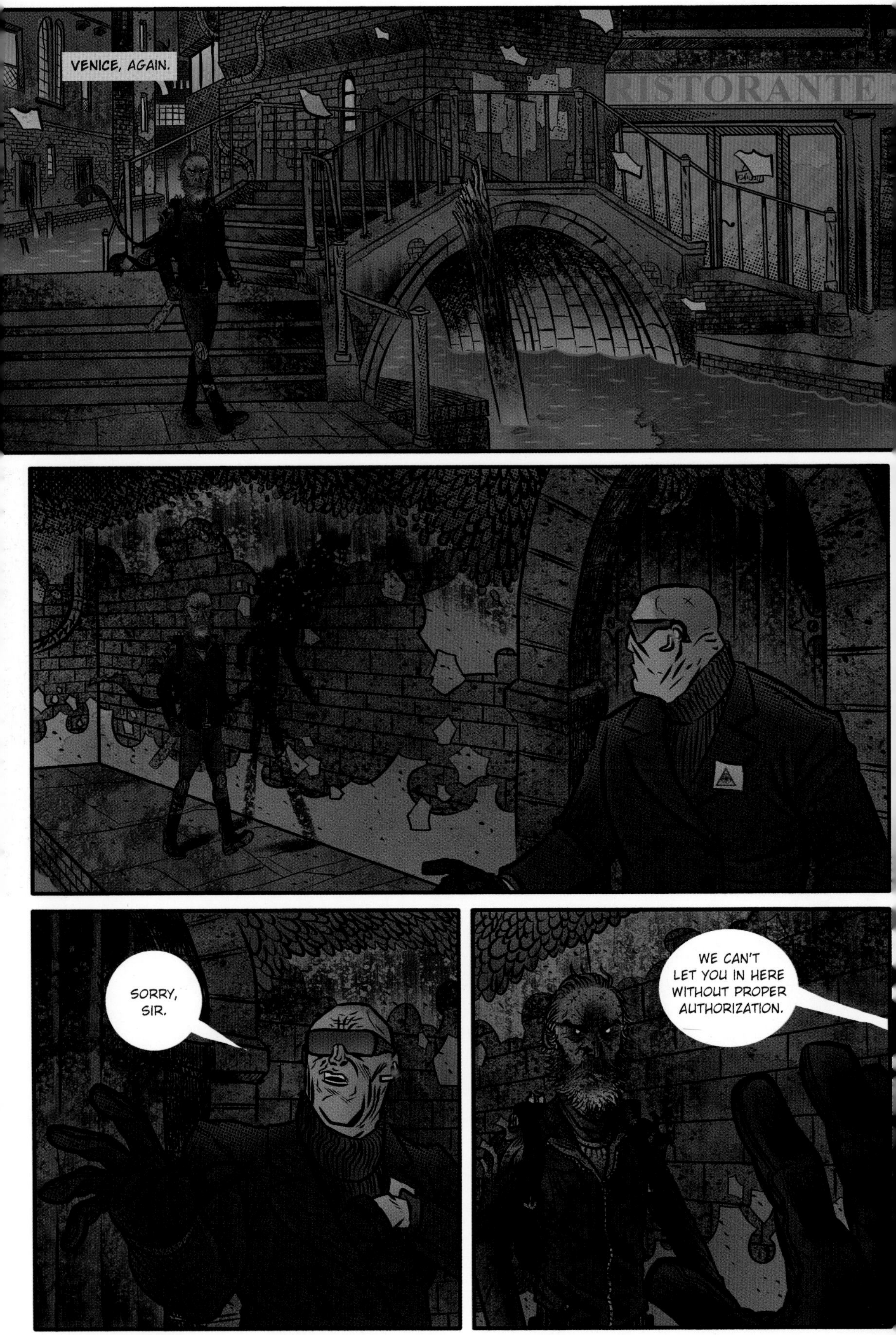
VENICE, AGAIN.
RISTORANTE
SORRY, SIR.
WE CAN'T LET YOU IN HERE WITHOUT PROPER AUTHORIZATION.

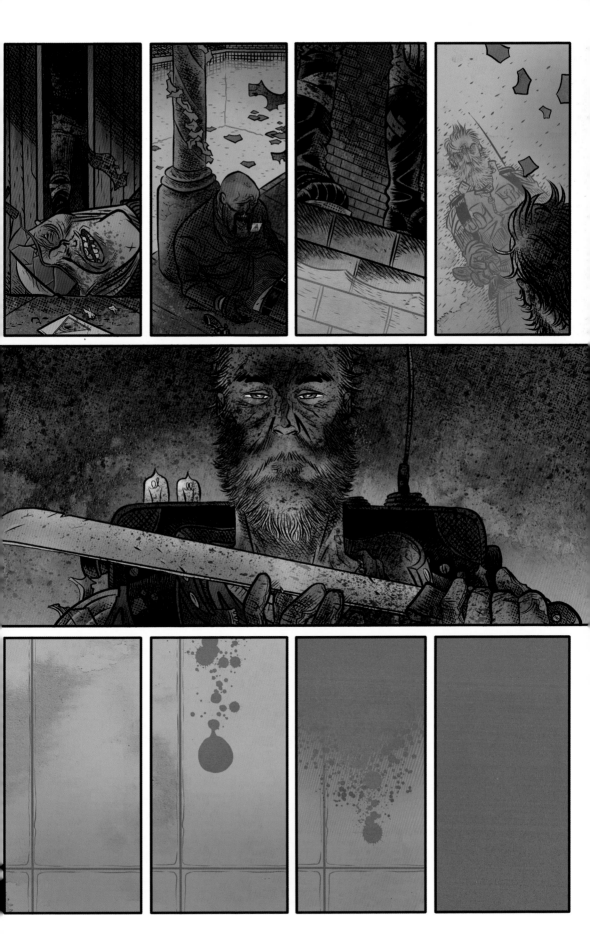

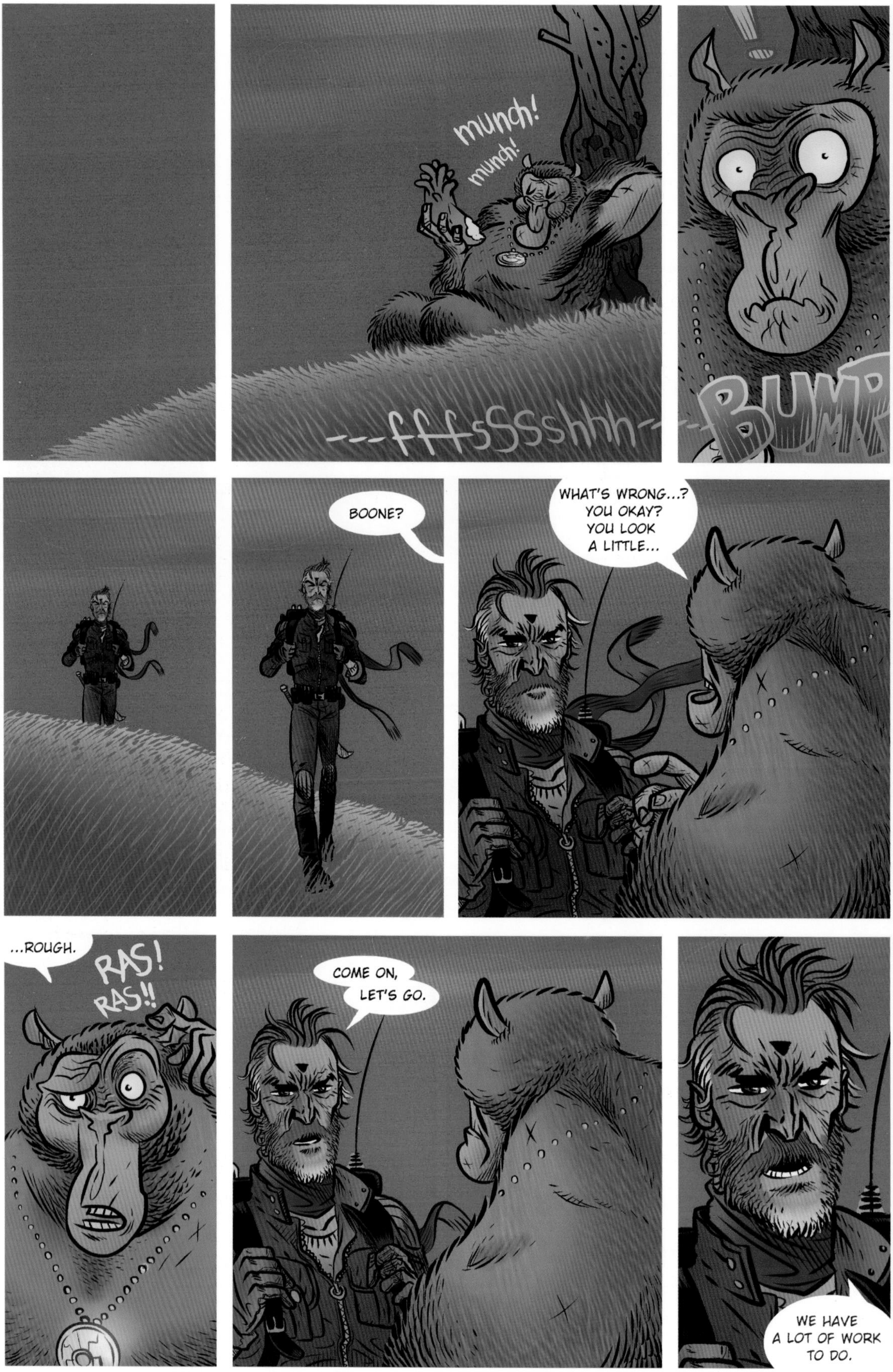
munch!
munch!
---fffsSSsshhh---
BUMP
BOONE?
WHAT'S WRONG...? YOU OKAY? YOU LOOK A LITTLE...
...ROUGH.
RAS!
RAS!!
COME ON, LET'S GO.
WE HAVE A LOT OF WORK TO DO.

THAT WITCH...
...BLEW IT
ALL UP!!

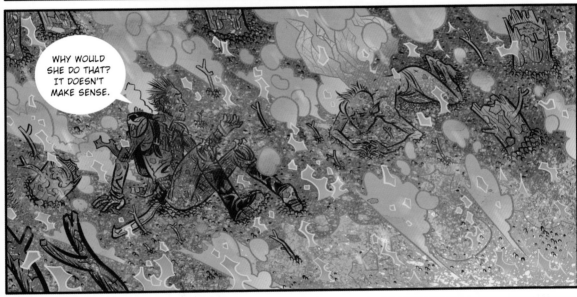

WHY WOULD
SHE DO THAT?
IT DOESN'T
MAKE SENSE.

THERE WAS
NO BENEFIT
TO HER.
NO RATIONAL
REASON...

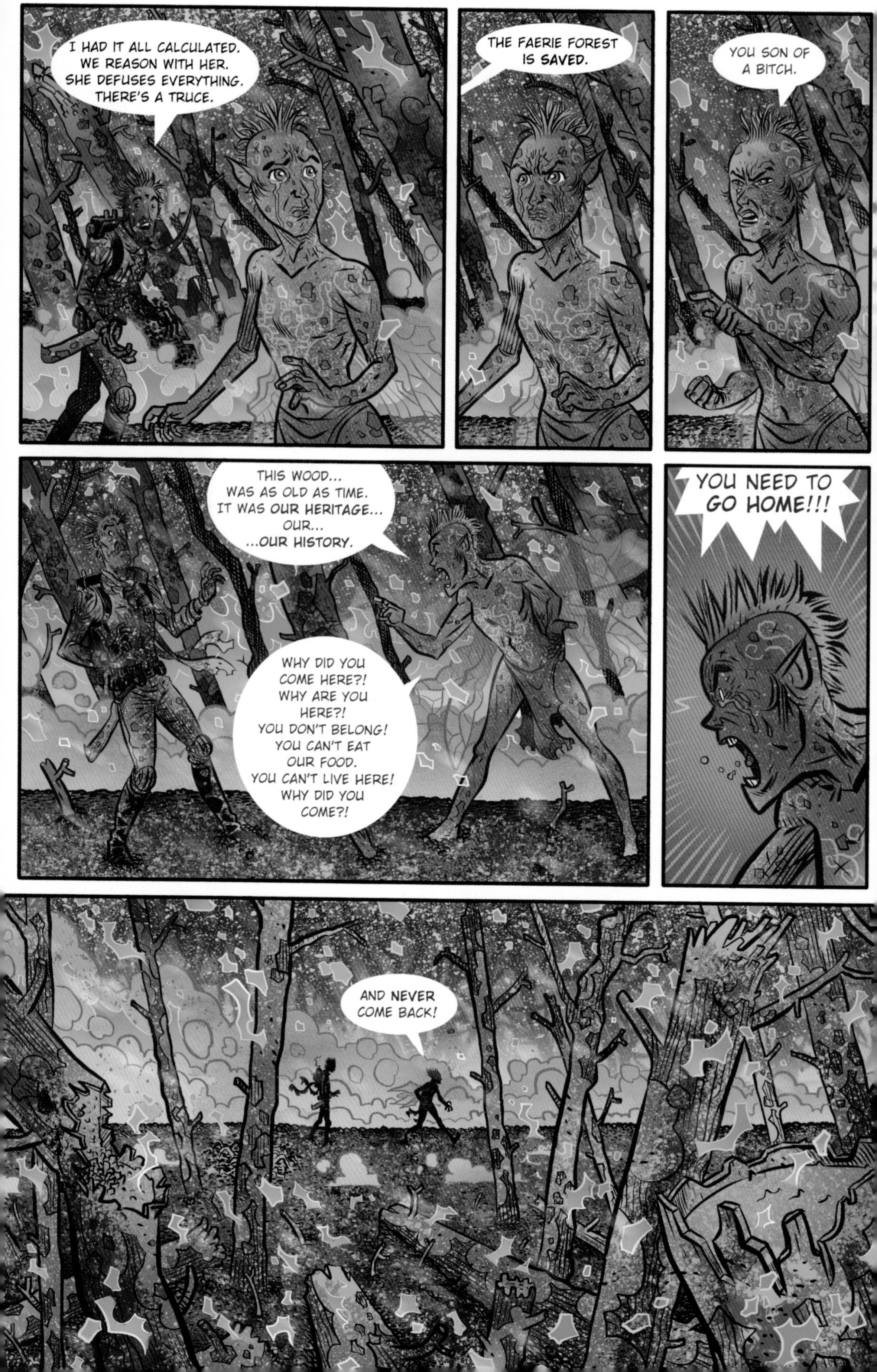
I HAD IT ALL CALCULATED. WE REASON WITH HER. SHE DEFUSES EVERYTHING. THERE'S A TRUCE.
THE FAERIE FOREST IS SAVED.
YOU SON OF A BITCH.
THIS WOOD... WAS AS OLD AS TIME. IT WAS OUR HERITAGE... OUR... ...OUR HISTORY.
WHY DID YOU COME HERE?! WHY ARE YOU HERE?! YOU DON'T BELONG! YOU CAN'T EAT OUR FOOD. YOU CAN'T LIVE HERE! WHY DID YOU COME?!
YOU NEED TO GO HOME!!!
AND NEVER COME BACK!

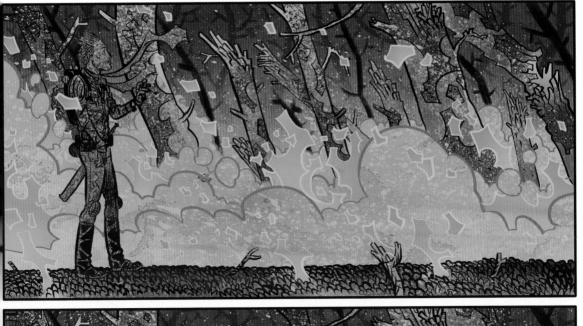

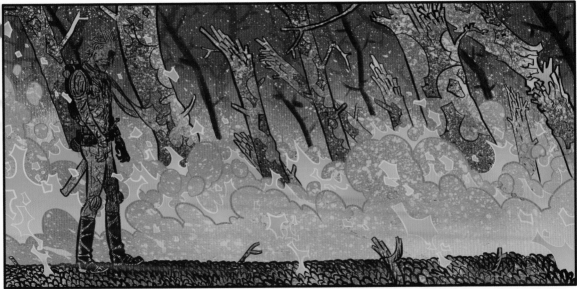

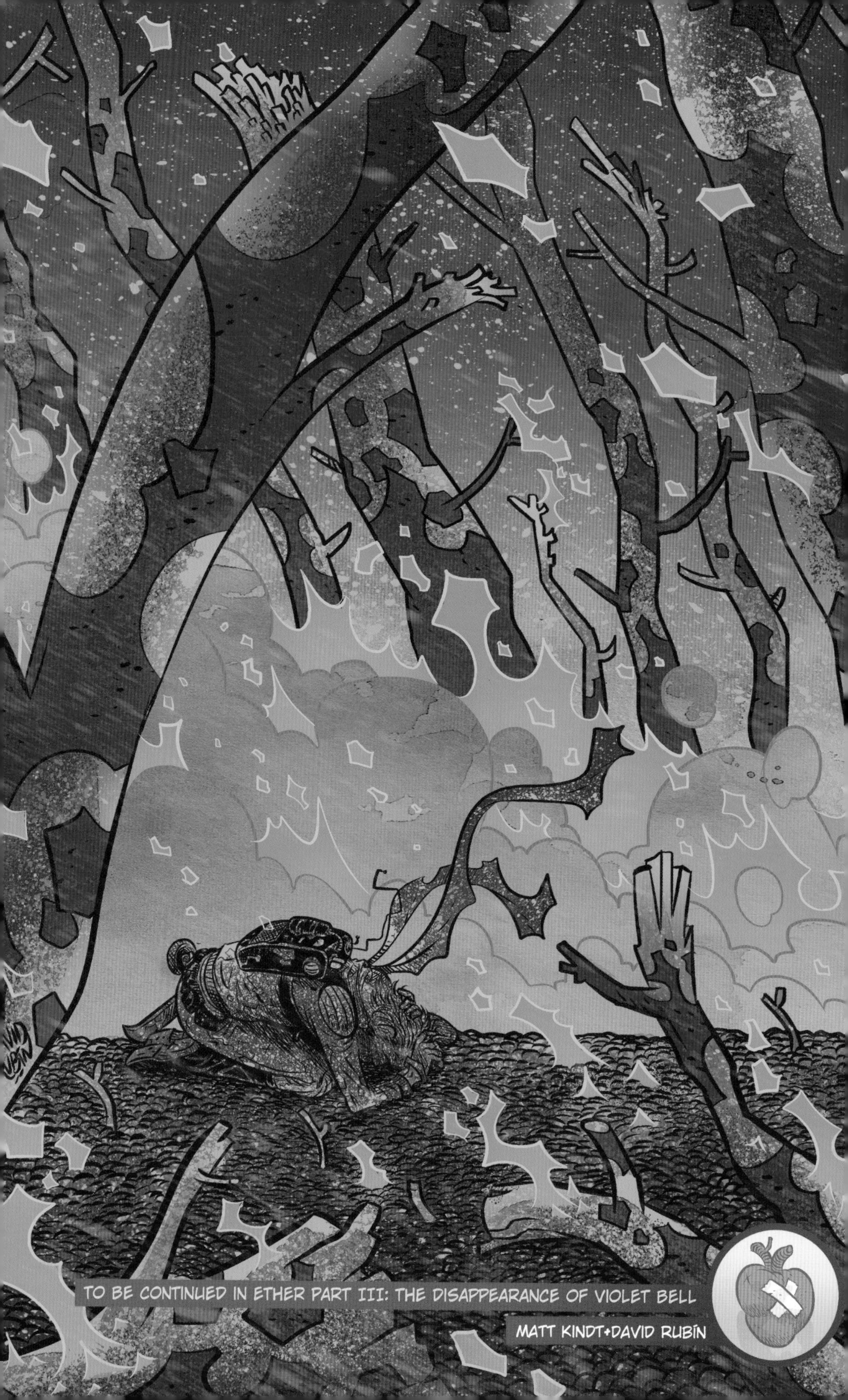
TO BE CONTINUED IN ETHER PART III: THE DISAPPEARANCE OF VIOLET BELL
MATT KINDT+DAVID RUBÍN

ETHER

SKETCHBOOK

notes by **DAVID RUBÍN**

GRANDOR
BOLDBODY
X D.RUBÍN

Matt said that Grandor was inspired by me, which made me worried what he thinks of me . . .

I think that Grandor is a force of nature, a character without fear.

I love drawing him! He's very fun because he always does a lot of crazy things, and I miss that pink fur cape. I can't understand why I did not include it in the series. Well, if Grandor appears in volume 3 I promise to draw him with that cool suit.

Oh, and take a look at his horns; in the comic they were shorter than in the preliminary sketch: ARTIST'S TRICK to draw less!

GALLIGA
✕ DAVIDRVBIN ✕

- GALLIGA, THE WIZARD GIANT, IS AN ABSTRACT TITAN MADE OF A STRANGE VEGETABLE STONE MATERIAL.
- IS FULL OF POWER.
- HIS TATTOOS AND MAGIC SPHERES ARE HIDDEN, AND GALLIGA SEEMS LIKE AN ANCIENT AND GIANT STONE. WHEN HE WAKES UP HE LOOKS LIKE THE IMAGE BELOW.

GALLIGA SLEEPING

BOONE

LATUM WOLVES ✕ D.RVBIN ✕

THAT MONSTER HORDE ARE COMPOSED BY A SKIN ARMOR MADE BY VOLCANIC ROCK. ITS BODY IS FLESH & FIRE!!

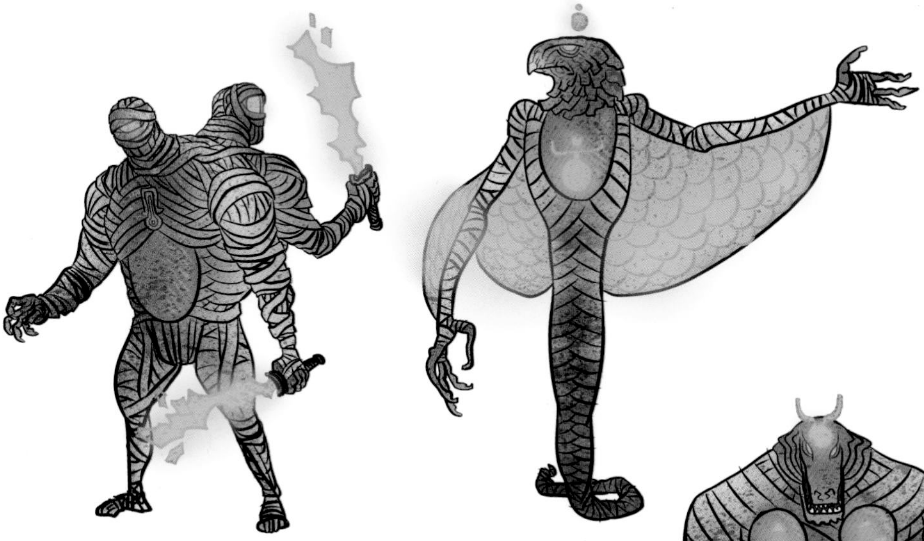

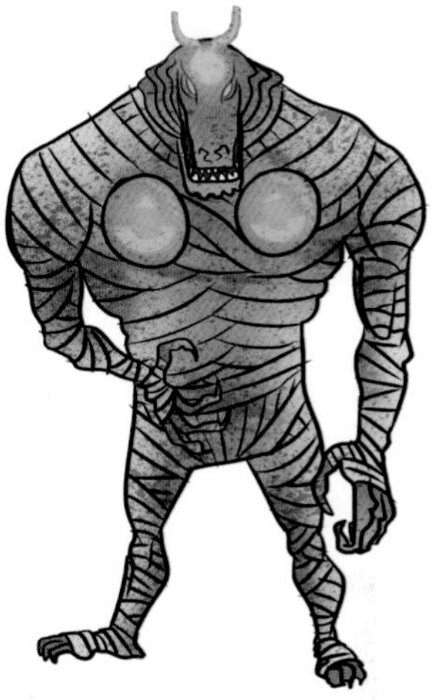

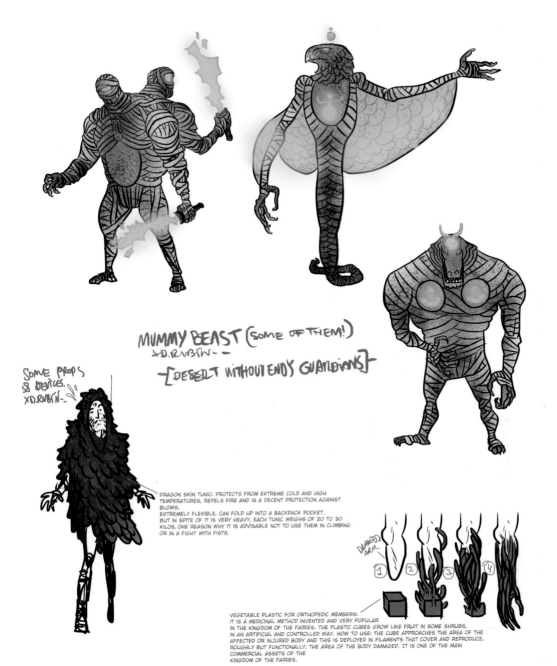

MUMMY BEAST (SOME OF THEM!)
XD.RUBIN-_
[DESERT WITHOUT END'S GUARDIANS]

SOME PROPS & DEVICES.
XD.RUBIN-_

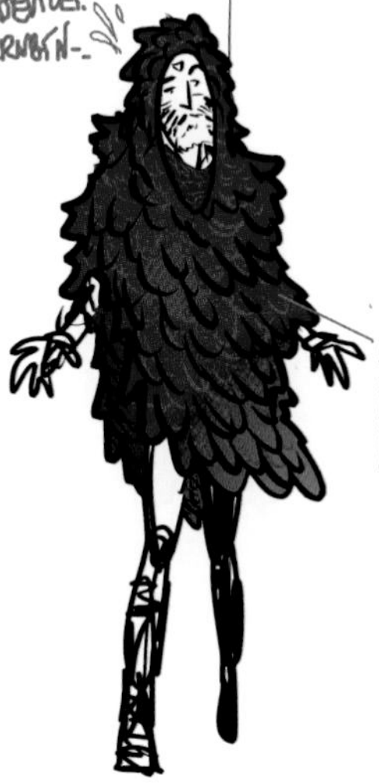

DRAGON SKIN TUNIC: PROTECTS FROM EXTREME COLD AND HIGH TEMPERATURES, REPELS FIRE AND IS A DECENT PROTECTION AGAINST BLOWS.
EXTREMELY FLEXIBLE, CAN FOLD UP INTO A BACKPACK POCKET.
BUT IN SPITE OF IT IS VERY HEAVY, EACH TUNIC WEIGHS OF 20 TO 30 KILOS, ONE REASON WHY IT IS ADVISABLE NOT TO USE THEM IN CLIMBING OR IN A FIGHT WITH FISTS.

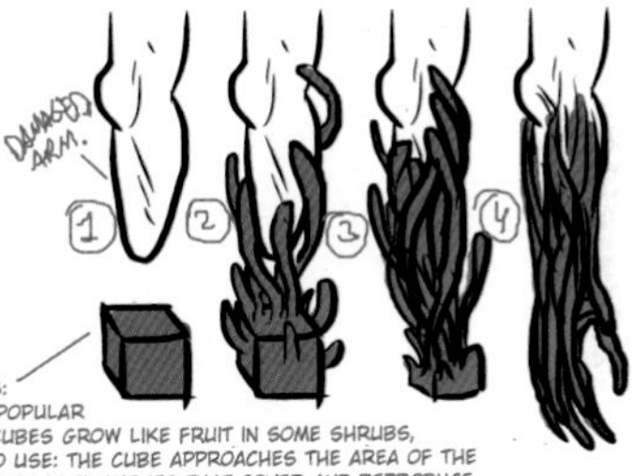
DAMAGED ARM.
1
2
3
4

VEGETABLE PLASTIC FOR ORTHOPEDIC MEMBERS:
IT IS A MEDICINAL METHOD INVENTED AND VERY POPULAR IN THE KINGDOM OF THE FAIRIES. THE PLASTIC CUBES GROW LIKE FRUIT IN SOME SHRUBS, IN AN ARTIFICIAL AND CONTROLLED WAY. HOW TO USE: THE CUBE APPROACHES THE AREA OF THE AFFECTED OR INJURED BODY AND THIS IS DEPLOYED IN FILAMENTS THAT COVER AND REPRODUCE, ROUGHLY BUT FUNCTIONALLY, THE AREA OF THE BODY DAMAGED. IT IS ONE OF THE MAIN COMMERCIAL ASSETS OF THE KINGDOM OF THE FAIRIES.

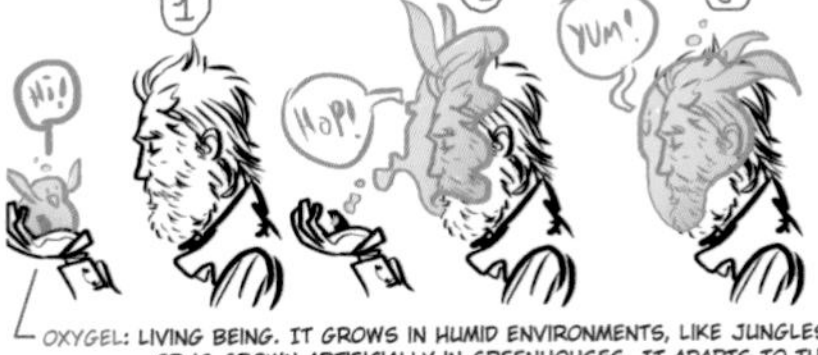
HI!
1
HOP!
2
YUM!
3

OXYGEL: LIVING BEING. IT GROWS IN HUMID ENVIRONMENTS, LIKE JUNGLES, OR IS GROWN ARTIFICIALLY IN GREENHOUSES. IT ADAPTS TO THE FACE PHYSIOGNOMY OF THE PERSON USING IT, ALLOWING IT TO BREATHE UNDERWATER OR IN ENVIRONMENTS WITH LITTLE OXYGEN OR TOXIC. IT FEEDS ON THE CARBON DIOXIDE EXHALED BY THE USERS AND THEIR DEAD SKIN PARTICLES.

MATT, WE MUST USE THE BIO-MOTORCYCLE ON THAT ARC!!!

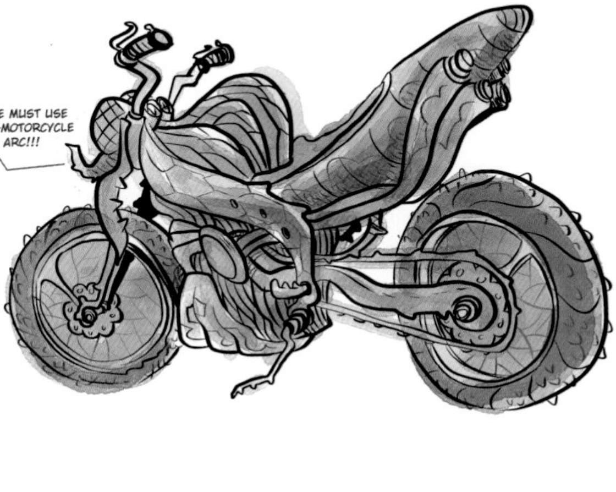

SPIDER-COPPER GOLEM × DAVID RUBÍN

—ALL ON HIS BODY IS MOVILE, THE GOLEM
COULD CHANGES HIS SHAPE AND ADD A
LOT OF ARMS, WEAPONS & DEVICES.

-THEY'RE A HOMAGE TO OSAMU TEZUKA'S ASTRO BOY.

-BOONE AND CO. COULD FIND THEM IN THE COPPER MINES, WITH OTHER GOLEMS.

-SEEM LIKE NINE OR TEN YEAR OLD CHILDREN.

-THEY AREN'T EVIL, THINK BY THEMSELVES, THEY ARE NOT UBEL'S PUPPETS LIKE THE OTHER GOLEMS.

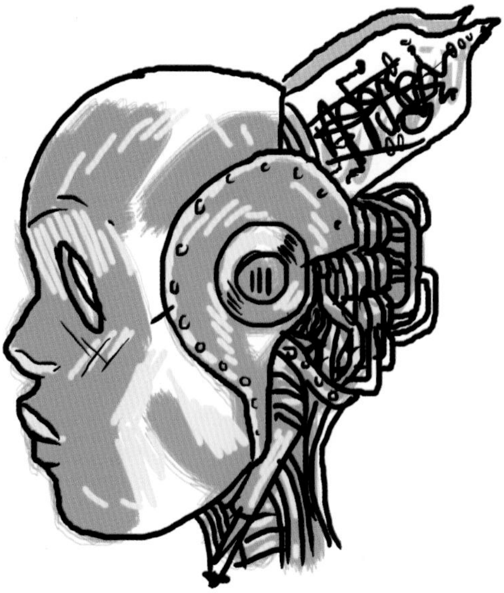

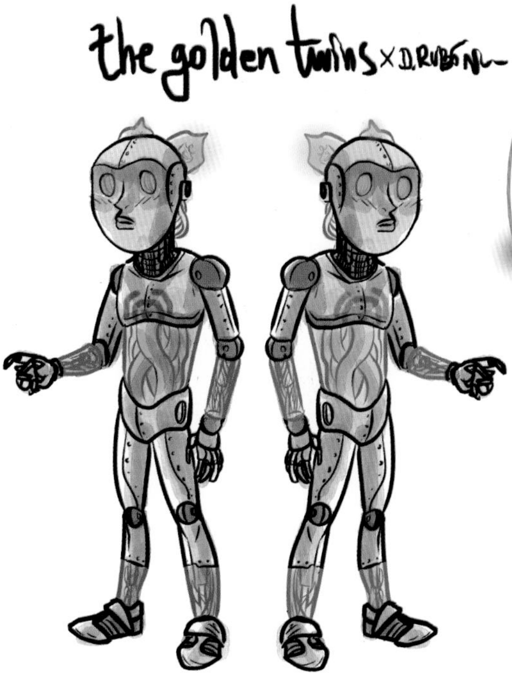
the golden twins

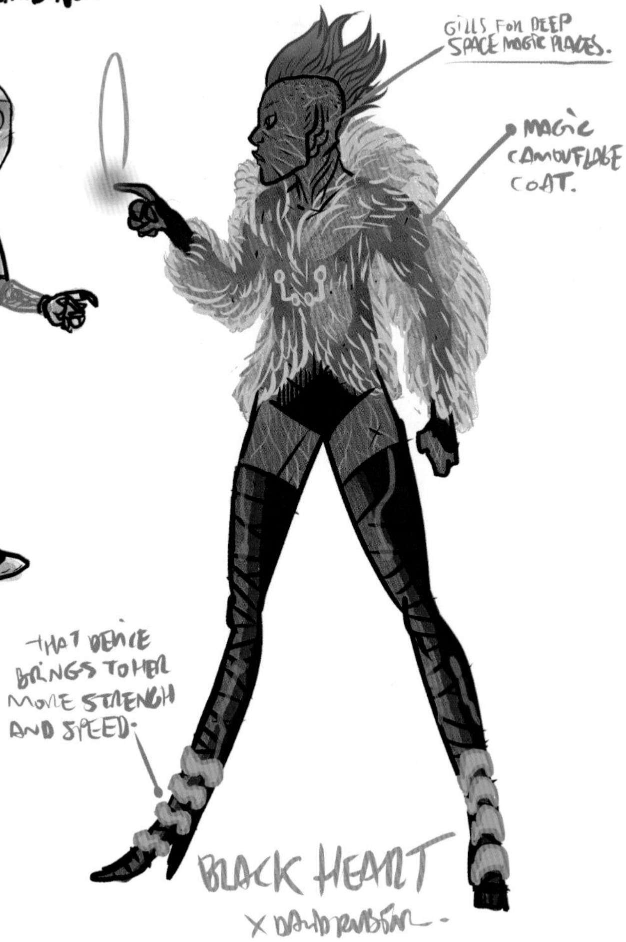
GILLS FOR DEEP SPACE MAGIC PLACES.
MAGIC CAMOUFLAGE COAT.
THAT DEVICE BRINGS TO HER MORE STRENGH AND SPEED.
BLACK HEART
× DAVID RUBÍN

THE CROWN IS AN EXTENSION OF HIS/HER HAIR, THE HAIR IS LIKE A HEAVY LIQUID, DENSE AND ALWAYS FLOATING AND CHANGING ITS SHAPE.

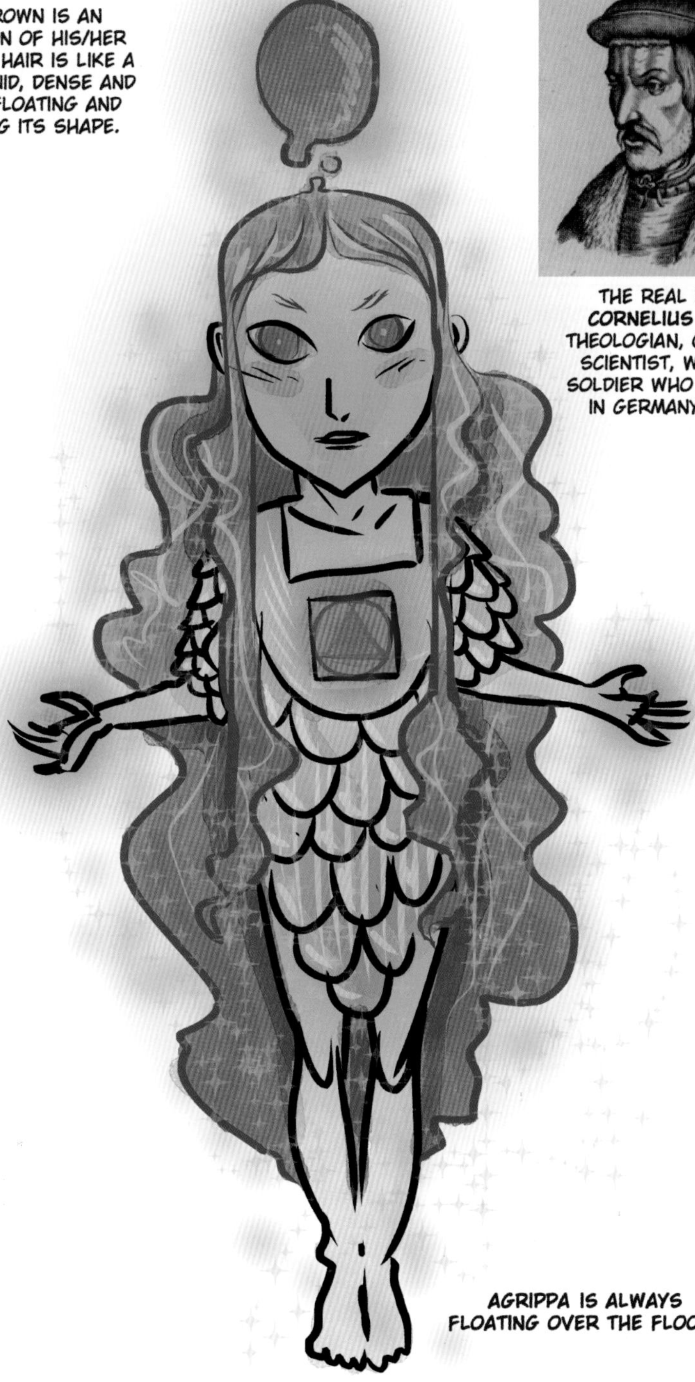

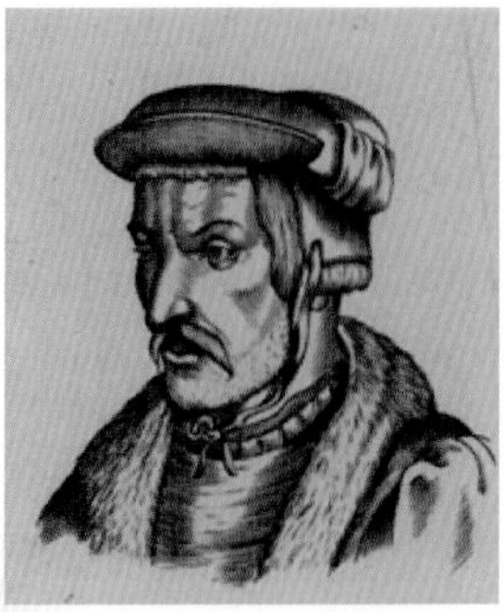

THE REAL HENRICH CORNELIUS AGRIPPA: THEOLOGIAN, OCCULTIST, SCIENTIST, WRITER, AND SOLDIER WHO WAS BORN IN GERMANY, IN 1486.

AGRIPPA IS ALWAYS FLOATING OVER THE FLOOR.

I imagined Agrippa like a female child with an old man soul inside her tiny body, but in the final script of that issue Matt describes her like a teenager. It worked better than in my preliminary sketch and gave me a chance to include in the series a t-shirt of one of my favourite musicians: Morrissey!

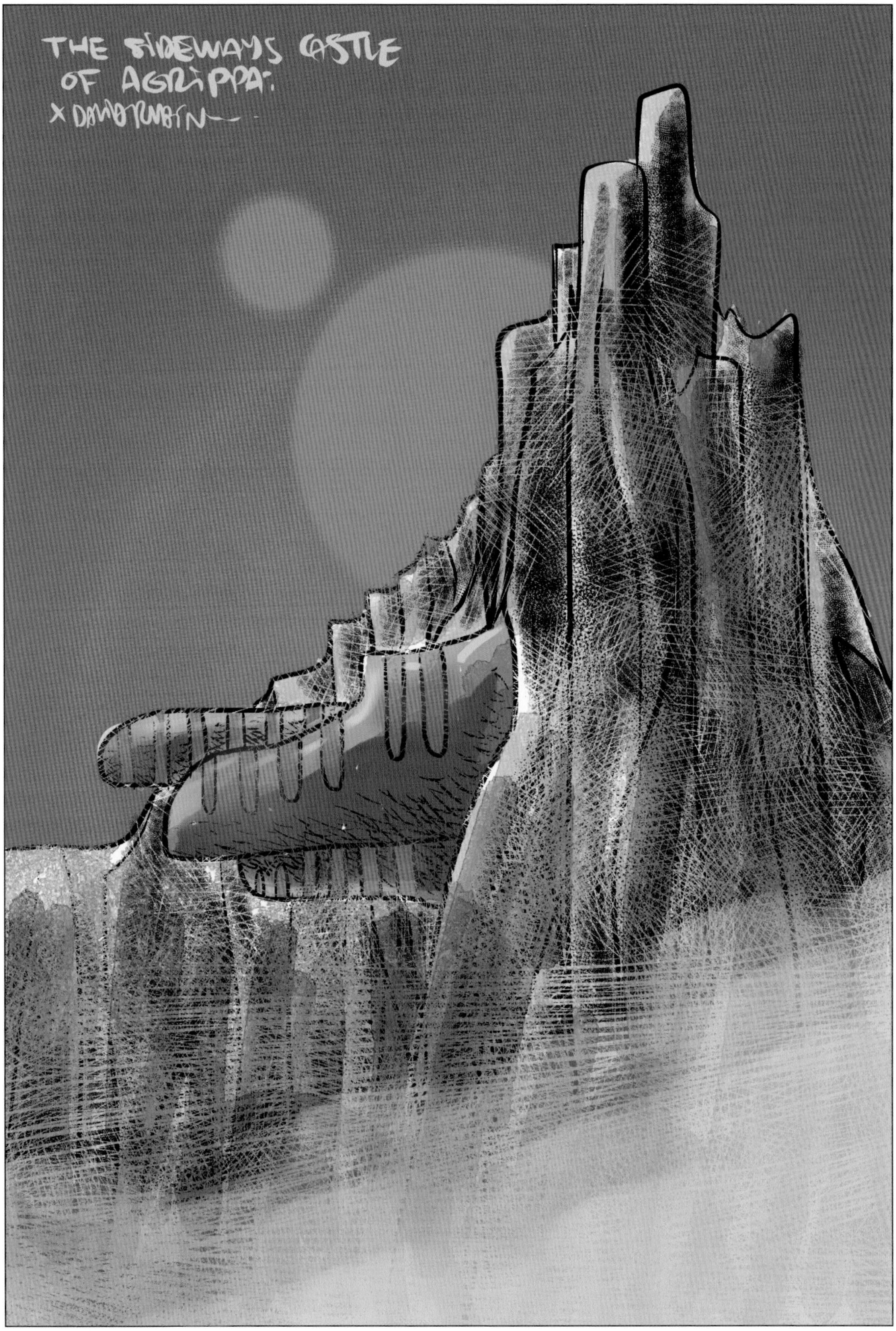
THE SIDEWAYS CASTLE
OF AGRIPPA:
x DAVID RUBIN

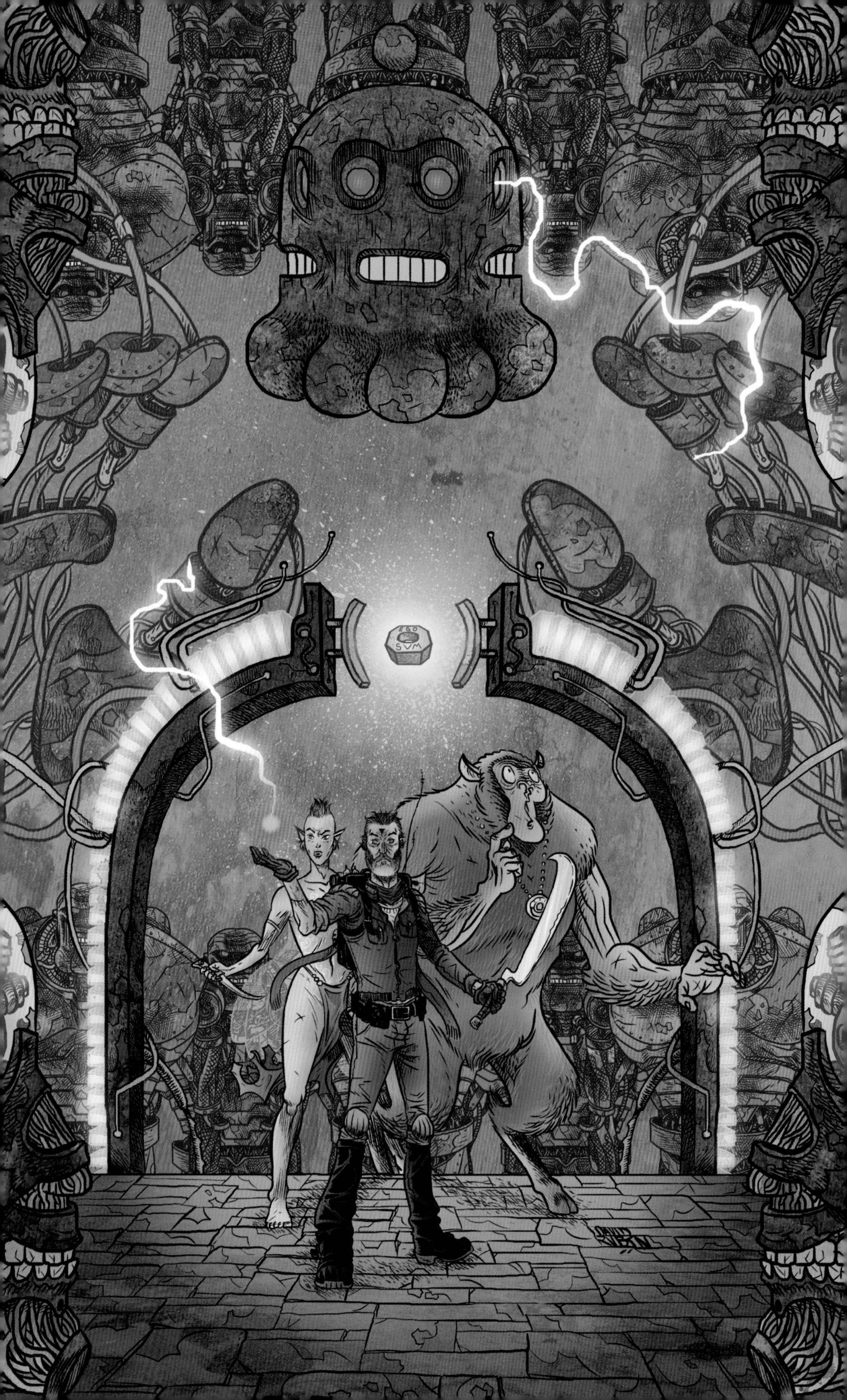
EGO
SVM

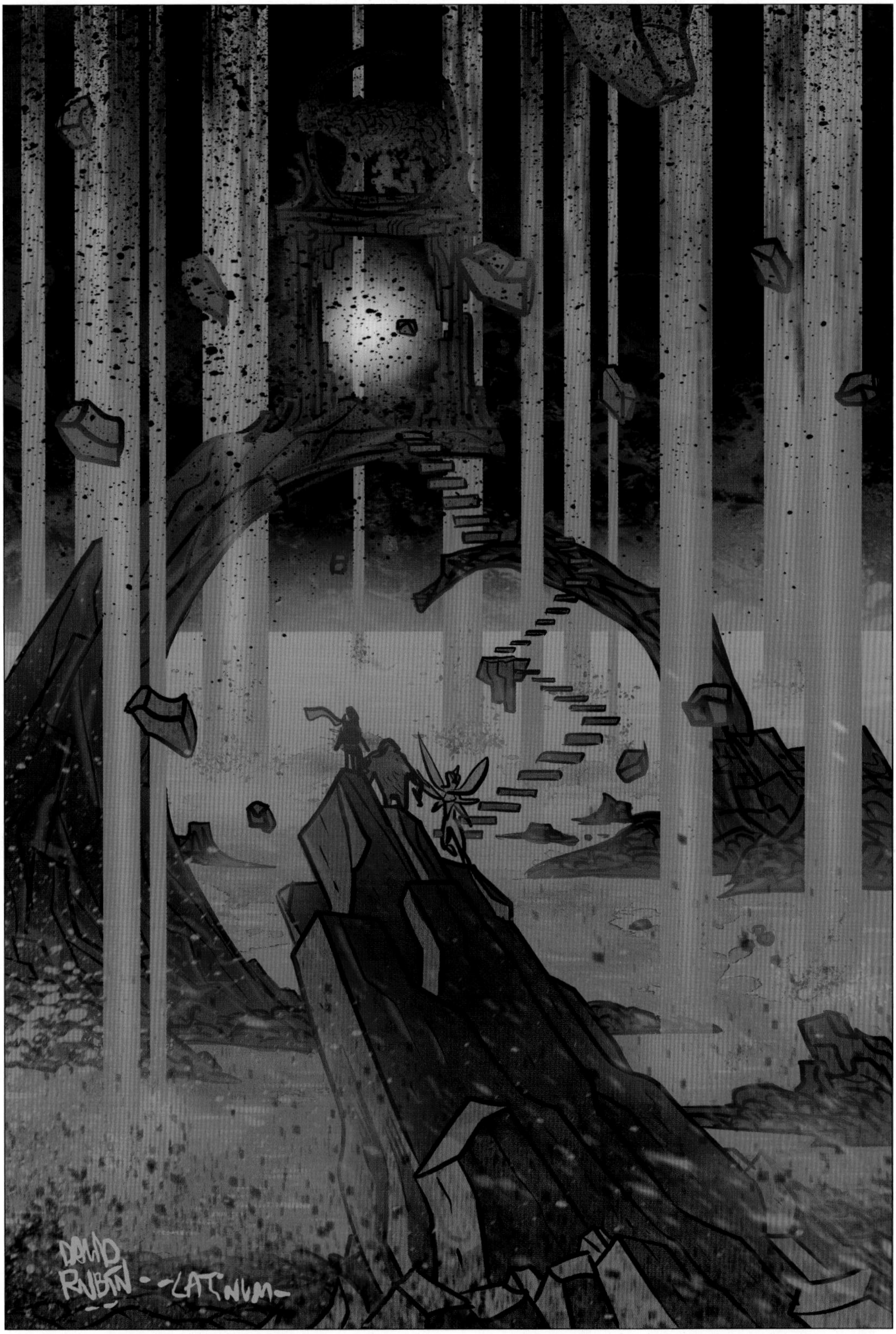

Left: On this page you can see the original illustration I did for the front cover of this trade. I decided to change it to the current wraparound cover because I think the old one was too busy and confusing for a trade cover. The current one is more simple and clear, and, at the same time, more powerful. It works much better for me as the cover for this volume. It's always hard to throw away the work you do, but I think it was worth it in this case, and well . . . we have this sketchbook section to show you, hope that you like it!

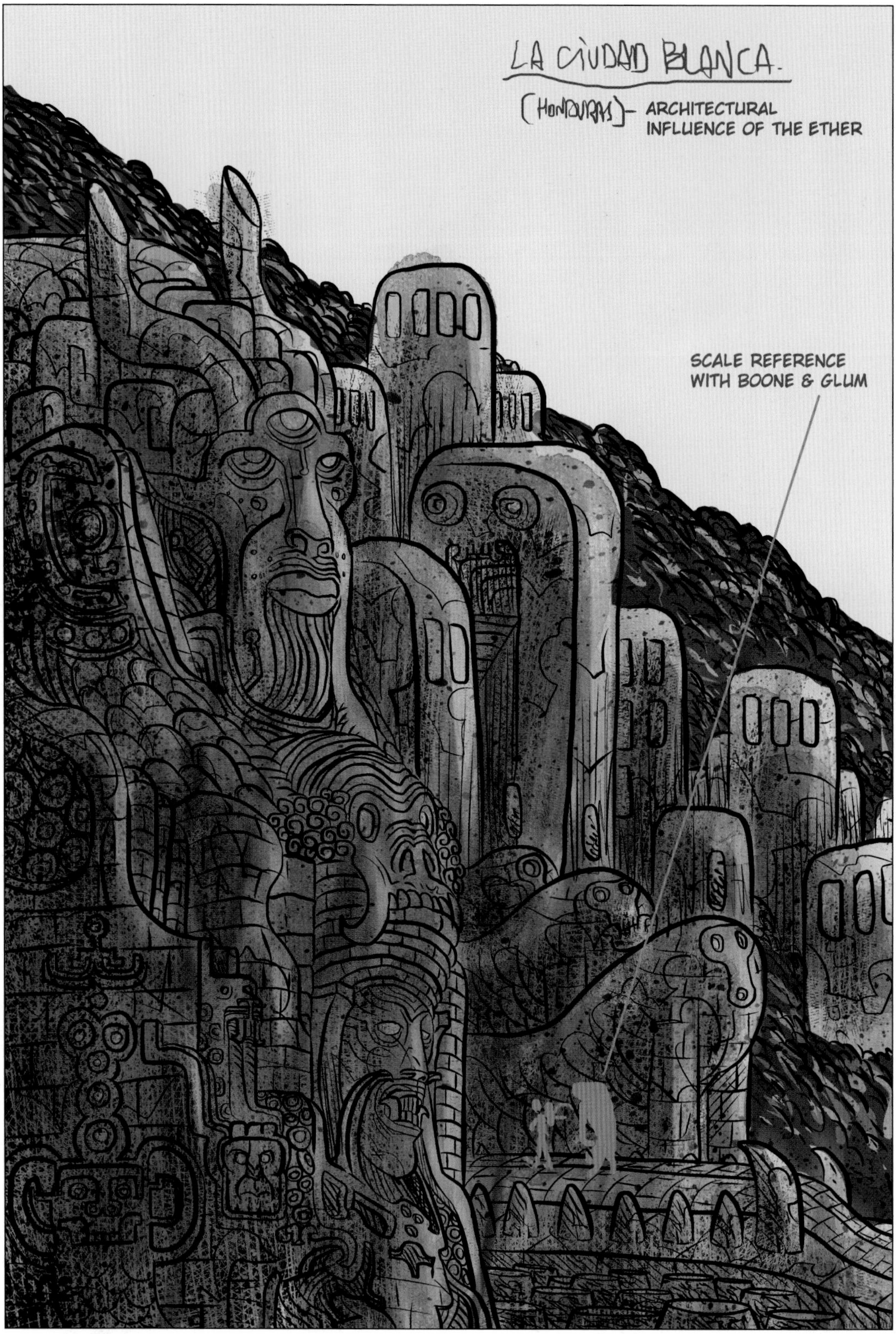

LA CIUDAD BLANCA.
(HONDURAS) - ARCHITECTURAL INFLUENCE OF THE ETHER
SCALE REFERENCE WITH BOONE & GLUM

Ether 2 #1 variant cover by **PAUL POPE**

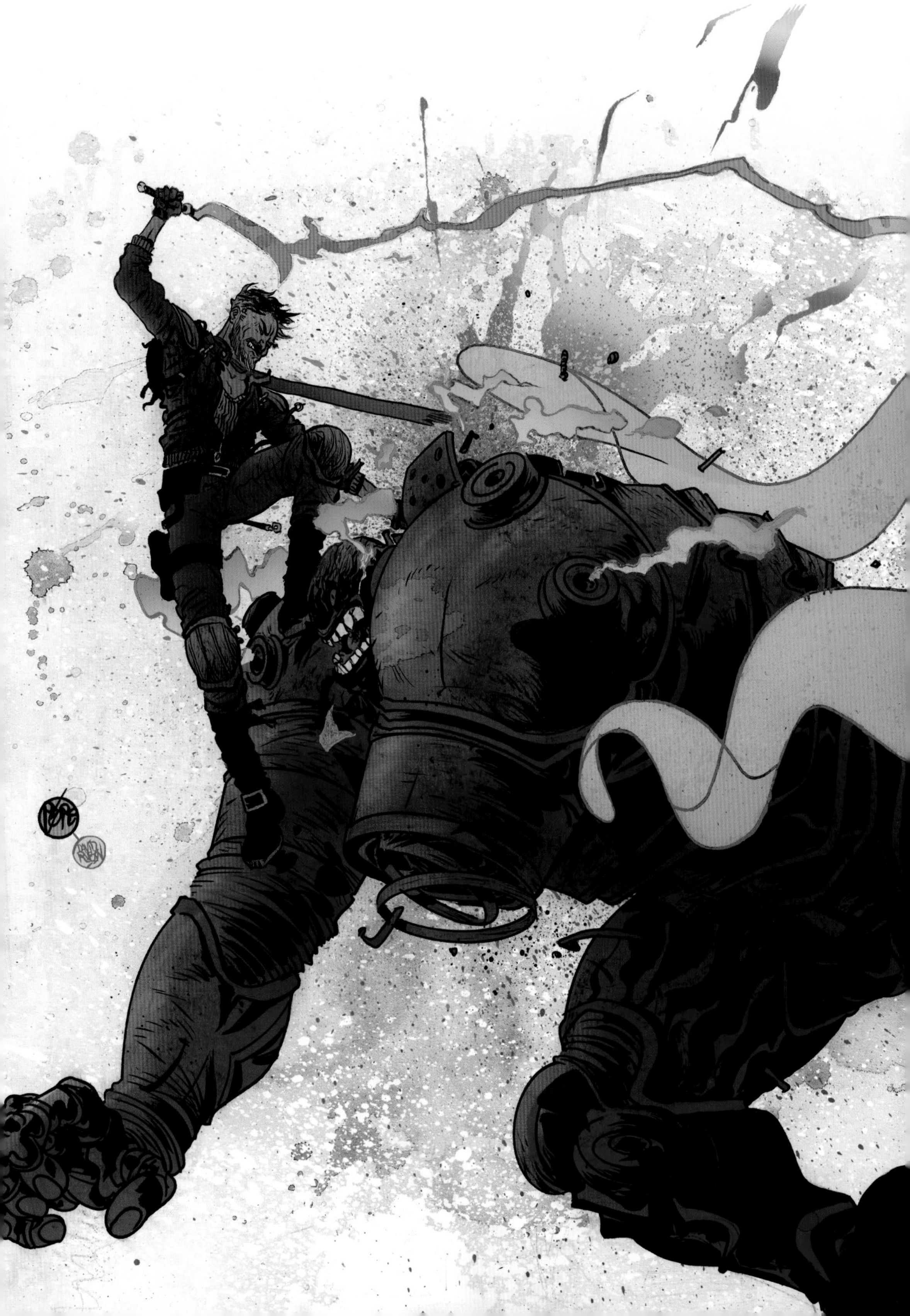

Ether 2 #2 variant cover by **BILL SIENKIEWICZ**

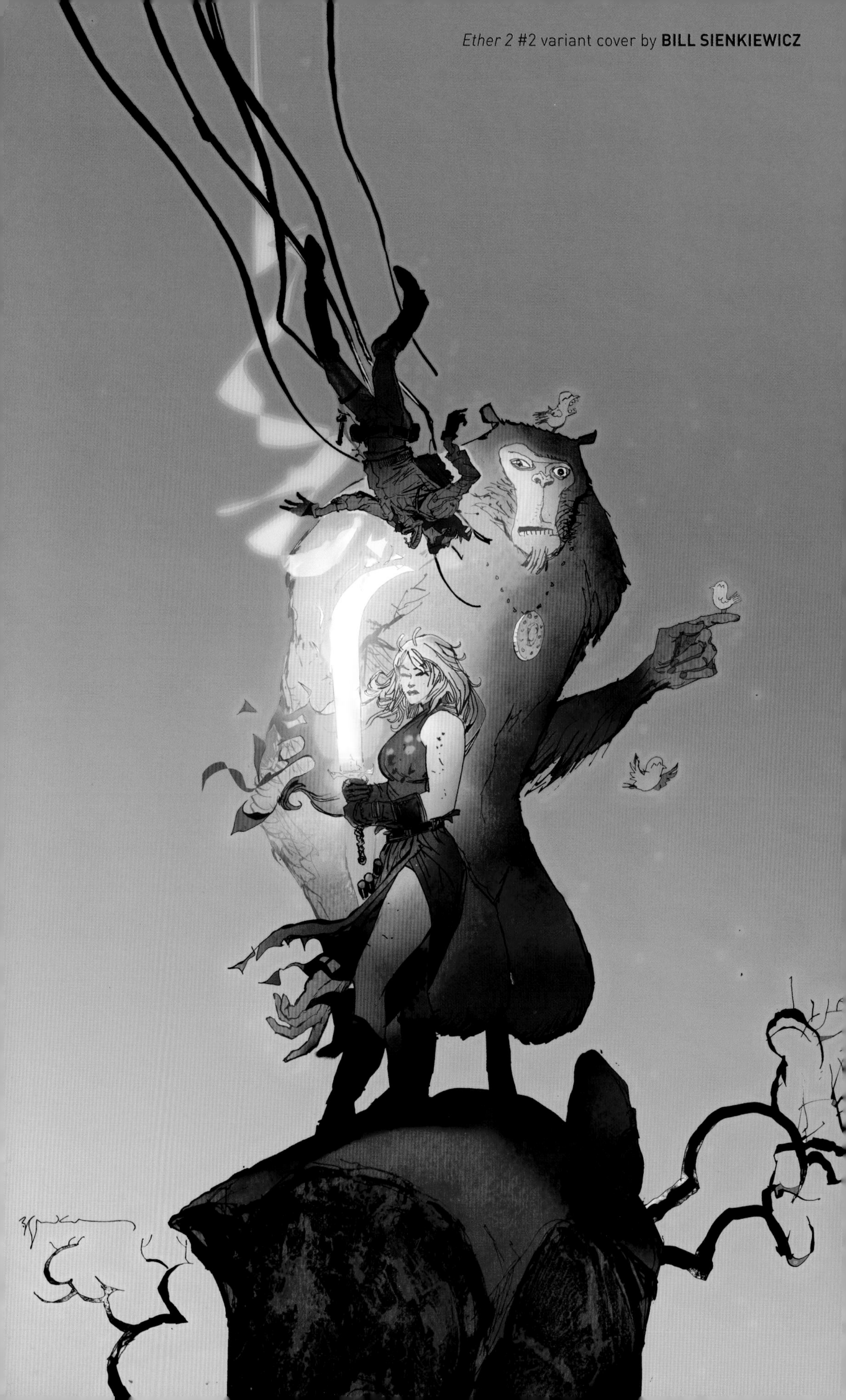

Ether 2 #3 variant cover by **MARCOS MARTIN**

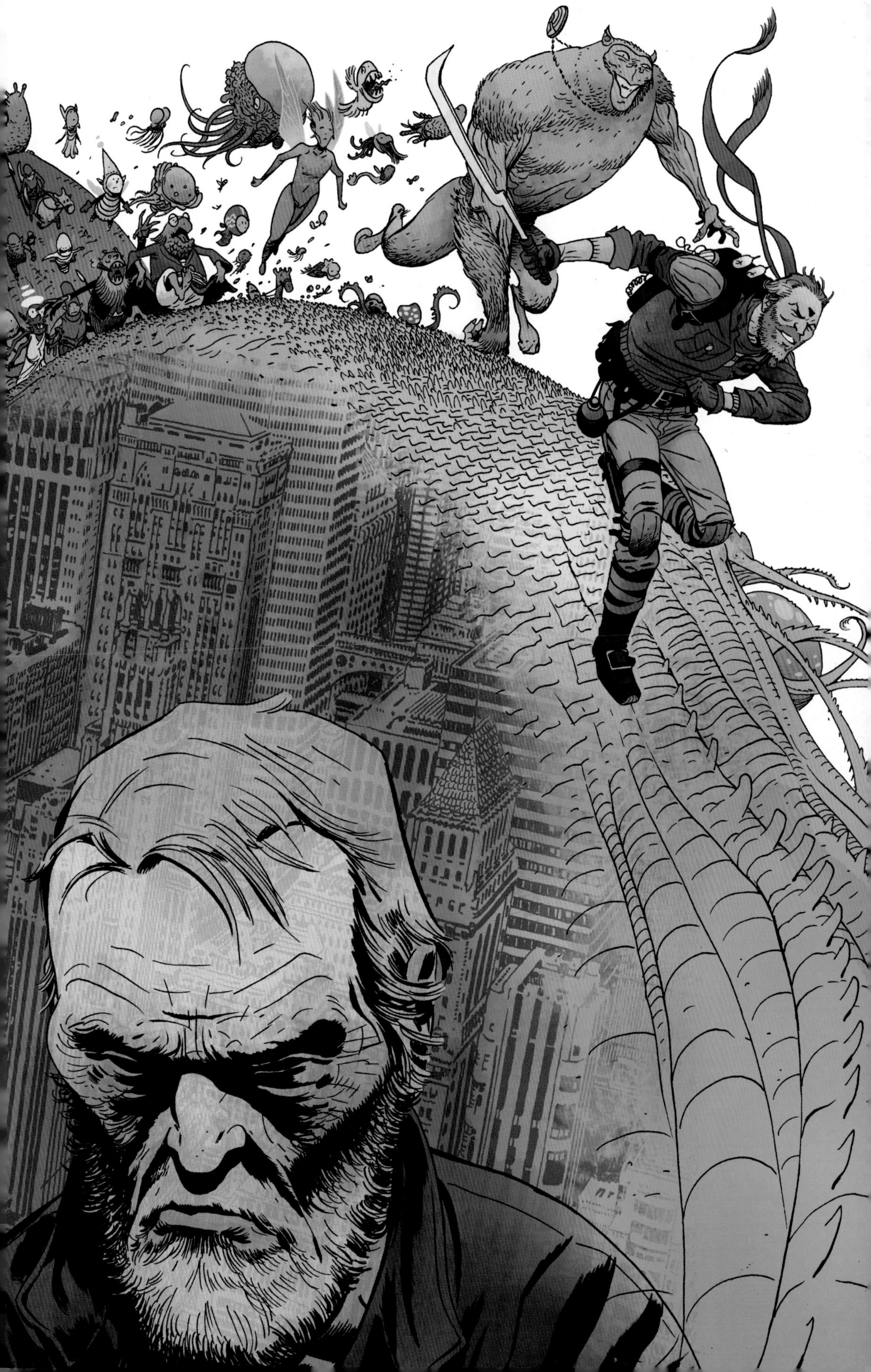

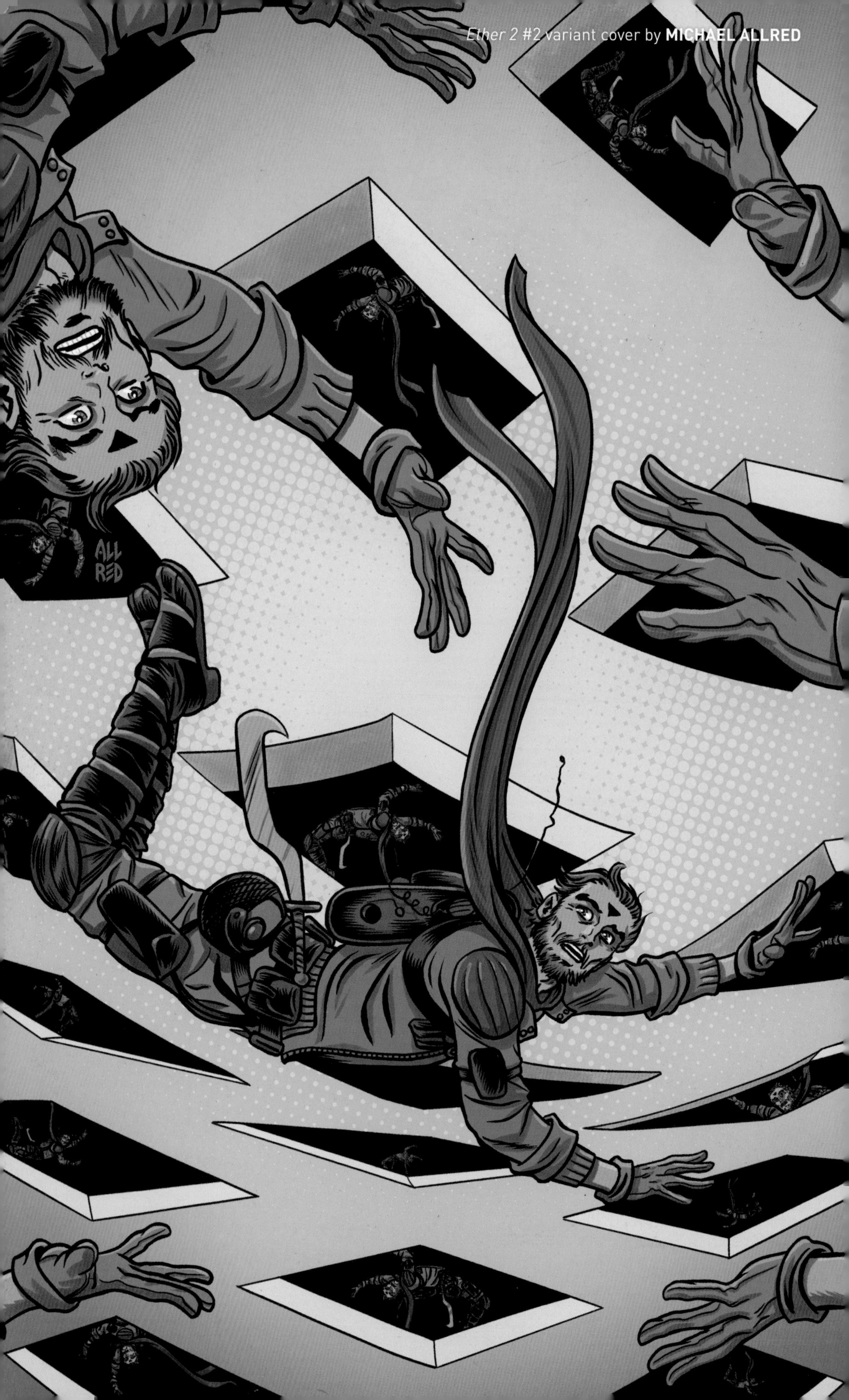
ALL RED

Ether 2 #2 variant cover by **MICHAEL ALLRED**

Ether 2 #5 variant cover by **JEN BARTEL**

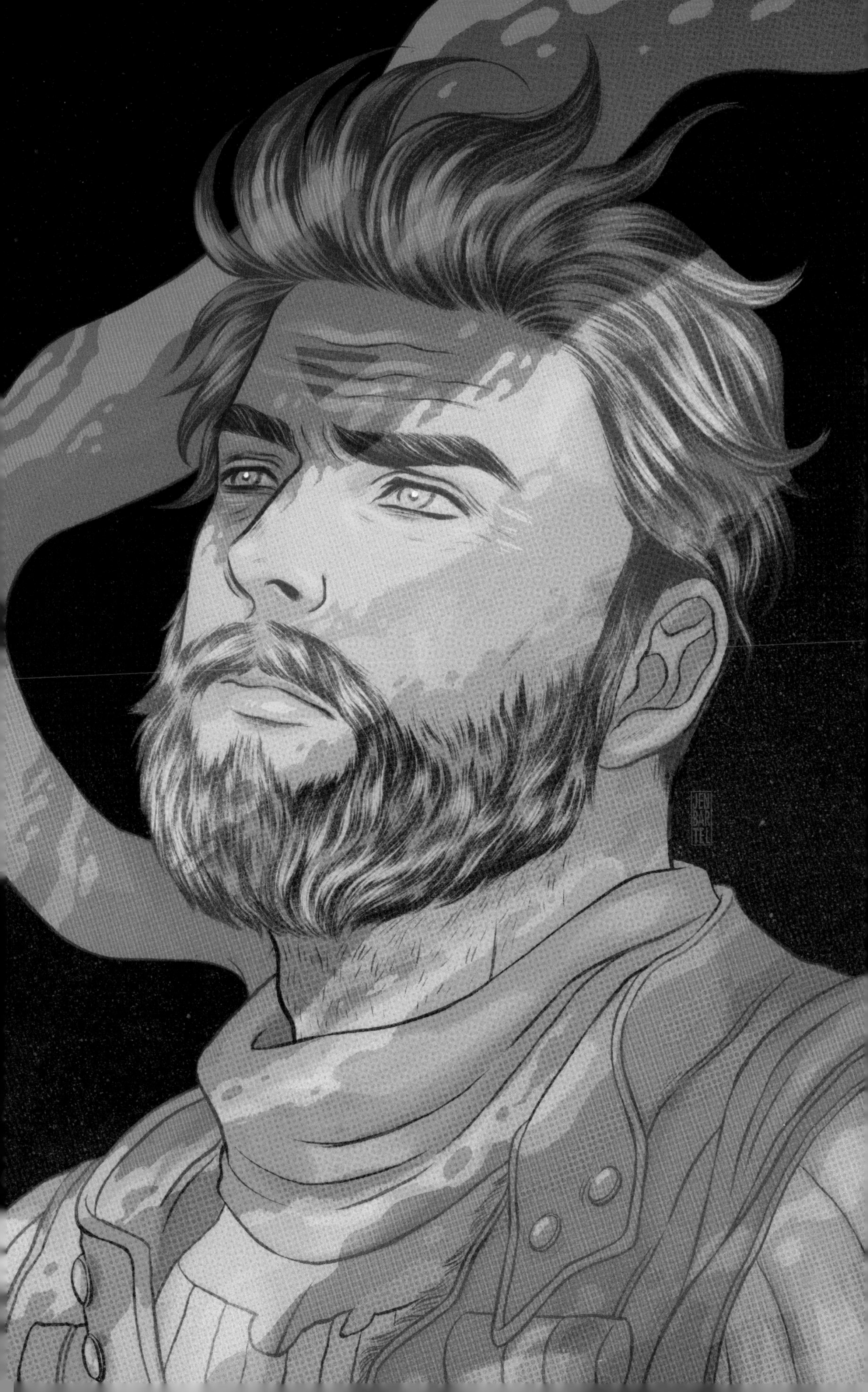
JEN
BAR
TEL

matt kindt

MIND MGMT

VOLUME 1: THE MANAGER
ISBN 978-1-59582-797-5
$19.99

VOLUME 2: THE FUTURIST
ISBN 978-1-61655-198-8
$19.99

VOLUME 3: THE HOME MAKER
ISBN 978-1-61655-390-6
$19.99

VOLUME 4: THE MAGICIAN
ISBN 978-1-61655-391-3
$19.99

VOLUME 5: THE ERASER
ISBN 978-1-61655-696-9
$19.99

VOLUME 6: THE IMMORTALS
ISBN 978-1-61655-798-0
$19.99

POPPY! AND THE LOST LAGOON
With Brian Hurtt
ISBN 978-1-61655-943-4
$14.99

PAST AWAYS
With Scott Kolins
ISBN 978-1-61655-792-8
$19.99

THE COMPLETE PISTOLWHIP
With Jason Hall
ISBN 978-1-61655-720-1
$27.99

3 STORY: THE SECRET HISTORY OF THE GIANT MAN NEW EXPANDED EDITION
ISBN 978-1-50670-622-1
$19.99

2 SISTERS
ISBN 978-1-61655-721-8
$27.99

DEPT. H
With Sharlene Kindt
VOLUME 1: PRESSURE
ISBN 978-1-61655-989-2
$19.99

VOLUME 2: AFTER THE FLOOD
ISBN 978-1-61655-990-8
$19.99

VOLUME 3: DECOMPRESSED
ISBN 978-1-61655-991-5
$19.99

VOLUME 4: LIFEBOAT
ISBN 978-1-61655-992-2
$19.99

ETHER
With David Rubín
VOLUME 1: DEATH OF THE LAST GOLDEN BLAZE
ISBN 978-1-50670-174-5
$14.99

VOLUME 2: COPPER GOLEMS
ISBN 978-1-61655-991-5
$19.99

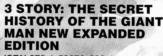